AN OLD-FASHIONED SOUTHERN CHRISTMAS

Southern comfort...Christmas cheer.

Four captivating stories of Christmas in the Old South by *Leisure's* leading historical romance authors at their heartwarming best!

LEIGH GREENWOOD
"A Fairy-Tale Christmas"

Leigh Greenwood's historical romances are "love stories that will warm your heart and soul."
—*Romantic Times*

CONNIE MASON
"A Child Is Born"

Connie Mason writes "the stuff fantasies are made of!"
—*Romantic Times*

NELLE McFATHER
"Susannah's Angel"

"Nelle McFather writes timeless tales of intrigue, mystery, and passion!" —*Romantic Times*

SUSAN TANNER
"A Warm Southern Christmas"

"Susan Tanner succeeds at creating memorable, emotional romance." —*Romantic Times*

Other Holiday Specials From *Leisure* and *Love Spell* Books:
THE NIGHT BEFORE CHRISTMAS
HOLIDAY INN
A WILDERNESS CHRISTMAS
A TIME-TRAVEL CHRISTMAS
A FRONTIER CHRISTMAS

AN OLD-FASHIONED SOUTHERN CHRISTMAS

LEIGH GREENWOOD, CONNIE MASON, NELLE McFATHER, SUSAN TANNER

LEISURE BOOKS   NEW YORK CITY

A LEISURE BOOK®

December 1996

Published by

Dorchester Publishing Co., Inc.
276 Fifth Avenue
New York, NY 10001

Printed in the United States of America.

AN OLD-FASHIONED SOUTHERN CHRISTMAS

A FAIRY-TALE CHRISTMAS
A CHILD IS BORN
SUSANNAH'S ANGEL
A WARM SOUTHERN CHRISTMAS

LEIGH GREENWOOD
A FAIRY-TALE CHRISTMAS

To my mother, for all those Christmases around the fire.

Chapter One

Shenandoah Valley, Virginia, 1880

"It's too much work, Gertie," Nan said to the thin, middle-aged woman at her side. "And with Gideon not coming home this year, it just doesn't seem worth it."

Nan Carson stood with her farm manager's wife in the wide hall of her family home. The dark oak floors gleamed with fresh wax. White wallpaper with tiny bunches of red poppies and blue cornflowers lightened the gloom created by the dark-stained oak doorways and the stairway which rose to a landing above. Disappearing doors opened to reveal on one side an enormous formal parlor furnished with elegant Victorian furniture upholstered in wine-colored velvet and on the other a less formal gathering room furnished with dark leather, cotton prints, and overstuffed cushions.

"But Jake and Eli have already put a pile of cedar and holly on the back porch," Gertie replied.

"I'll tell somebody at the church to come get it. They can always use some extra."

"It won't seem right not seeing this place decorated," Gertie said, persevering. "Folks come all the way out here from town to look at it. Won't seem like Christmas to half of them. Gideon liked it, too."

"Well, if he'd wanted the decorations put up, he should have come home," Nan said.

She still hadn't gotten over the disappointment of learning that Gideon was going to spend Christmas with his fiancée. It wasn't that Nan disliked Doris Morgan. She'd never met her. And Christmas was probably the best time for Gideon to visit his future in-laws, but this was the first year since their mother's death that Nan had been alone at Christmas, and she was finding it hard to keep her spirits up.

She was also finding it hard to accept the fact that her little brother was getting married while she seemed doomed to die an old maid. Not that thirty-one felt very old, but in Beaker's Bend she might as well be sixty. People got married by the time they were eighteen—or they moved away and never came back.

"Are you going to make cookies?" Gertie asked.

"Of course," Nan said, coming out of her abstraction. "Children get hungry every year."

"Then you'd better get started. Though how you

have the patience to decorate so many I'll never understand, especially after taking care of this huge old house."

"It's no trouble. All I have to do is dust and make my bed. There's nobody to mess anything up."

Framed black-and-white pictures covered the walls in the hall, pictures of her father and mother, pictures of Gideon and his many sports teams.

There were none of her.

Nan pushed the loneliness aside. She was fortunate to live in a nice home, own the best farm in the valley, and have so many wonderful friends. So what if she wasn't going to have a husband and children? She shouldn't complain when she had so many other blessings.

She wasn't complaining exactly. It was just that there was an emptiness inside her that seemed to get a little bit deeper and wider each day. She felt like a pumpkin dusted with November frost, the last in the field. The outside was still firm and brightly colored, but the inside was slowly drying up.

"Maybe I'll make gingerbread people this winter," Nan said, giving her shawl a twitch and settling a smile on her lips. "I made the Christmas village last year."

"The children love your gingerbread." Gertie chuckled. "Only you got to be careful they don't look like nobody. Last time they took to calling one the preacher's wife. She got so mad she nearly disgraced herself right there in the church social hall."

Nan's smile owed more to her sense of mischief

than to contrition. "Maybelle Hanks will be safe. I'll make certain there are no tall, spindly, sour-faced gingerbread women this year."

The butter hadn't had time to soften before the sharp, insistent ring of the doorbell brought Nan from the warm kitchen back into the chilly hall. "I'm coming," she muttered as she hurried along, her steps muffled by the runner.

The cut and beveled glass in the heavy front door distorted the world outside beyond recognition. Nan looked through the side lights that flanked the door. On the porch, Wilmer Crider huddled into a heavy coat and cap, ear flaps folded down. Nan picked up a wool shawl and wrapped it around her shoulders. A wintery blast whipped her skirts about her legs when she opened the door.

"What are you doing here?" Nan asked. "Who's at the inn?" She knew that Wilmer's wife, Lucy, had gone to stay with Ruby, her youngest daughter, through a difficult pregnancy. There wasn't anybody at the inn except Wilmer.

"L.P. and I got a sick fella out here." Wilmer pointed to the wagon just outside the front gate. "He walked through the door and fell down in a dead faint."

"What did Dr. Moore say?"

"Doc's with Ruby. She started having pains during the night."

Nan had a gift for healing, especially for making sick people feel comfortable and happy. Folks in the valley came to her when they needed help, some even when the doctor was available.

She heaved a sigh. "I'll take a look at him."

"You bundle up good," Gertie called from the back of the hall.

"I'm just going to the road."

"There's icicles hanging from the porch roof. You bundle up good."

Nan put on a heavy coat and wound a thick scarf around her neck.

"You can't go outside in those shoes," Gertie said, coming down the hall with a pair of sturdy shoes.

"I hope he's not very sick," Nan complained. "He could be dead before I get out the front door."

"I'll not have you down in the bed sick on Christmas," Gertie said.

The December air was frigid. The leaves of magnolias, hollies, and boxwood looked stiff, as if they would crack or break if they moved. Nan's breath billowed in white clouds before her, and the frozen ground crunched under her feet. The smell of a hickory and oak fire hung in the air. That would be Eli. He hated coal. Said it made the house smell bad. Nan pulled the rough wool of the scarf more securely around her neck.

The mountains that enclosed her valley rose in the distance, their tree-covered flanks dusted with a light covering of snow. Clouds heavy with snow filled the dull sky. Waiting. Threatening. The woolly worms had sported an especially thick coat this year.

The man lay almost buried in a pile of quilts in the back of Wilmer's wagon.

"I don't like the look of him," Wilmer said.

15

Nan didn't like the look of him either. He looked exhausted, glassy-eyed with fever. Chestnut-brown hair covered his head in waves. Several strands were matted to his damp forehead. His eyelids were only half open, almost obscuring the deep brown of his eyes. His face had lost all color, but it was clear and handsome and young. He was tall, so tall Wilmer had bent his legs to fit him in the wagon. His suit, starched shirt, and boiled collar announced that he was from a city. Probably somewhere up north. Nobody in the Shenandoah Valley dressed like that.

"Who is he?"

"Will Atkins. Comes from Boston."

"What's he doing down here?" She examined him carefully. "I'm sure he'll be all right once his fever breaks, but he'll need somebody to sit up with him tonight. Is there anybody with him?"

"His daughter."

"Good. I'll explain everything to her. Where is she?"

"There," Wilmer said, pointing to a person previously hidden by L.P.'s substantial bulk.

Nan's knees nearly went out from under her. A little girl of no more than four or five sat twisted around on the wagon seat. Her enormous, fear-widened brown eyes stared out from the most angelic face Nan had ever seen.

She was scared almost out of her wits.

Nan felt something clutch at her heart. This child was the image of the daughter she used to dream of having someday.

Nan wrenched her thoughts free of such fantasy.

She had no daughter, and this little girl was alone, frightened, tired, and probably hungry as well.

"Where's her mother?" Nan asked.

"There ain't no mother, just them two."

"She couldn't have come alone. Who looked after her?"

"Her father, I guess."

"Then she'll need someone to care for her until her father gets well."

"Don't look at me," Wilmer said. "I'm closing the inn. Got to go to Locust Hollow. Ruby's husband has come down with a fever too. There's nobody to do the chores 'til he gets back on his feet."

"What are you going to do with this man?"

"I was hoping you'd take him in."

"I'm a maiden lady."

"Nobody's going to talk, especially not with him passed out cold as a trout and Gertie and Jake here to look after you. Besides, who's going to take care of her?" He pointed to the child.

Nan walked around to the other side of the wagon. The little girl was bundled up in a coat and mittens, staring out from a fur-lined hood. Her leggings and shoes were city clothes, too thin to protect her from the ice and snow of this mountain valley. She had to be cold all the way through. Even if her father hadn't been sick, Nan couldn't have abandoned her.

"Hi. My name is Nan Carson. What's your name?"

The child didn't answer, just stared back at her. Nan saw fear in her clenched hands, her ramrod-stiff posture, her anxious stare.

17

"Where are you going?"

Again, nothing.

"Do you know anybody here in Beaker's Bend?"

"You know they don't," Wilmer said, "not with them dressed like that."

"I guess not," Nan agreed, "but they've got to be going somewhere. Somebody must be expecting them."

"Well, they'll not be getting there today."

"Not for several days," Nan said, coming to a decision. "Bring Mr. Atkins inside. I'll take care of him until his fever breaks, but you've got to take him again after that."

"Sure," Wilmer said.

"You're going to stay at my house," Nan said to the little girl. She held out her hand, but the child didn't move. Tears welled up in the child's eyes and rolled down her cheeks.

"Please don't let my daddy die."

A lump formed in Nan's throat. She reached out, unclasped the child's hands, and took them in her own. "Your father's going to get well, I promise. I'm going to take very good care of him. And I'm going to fix you something good to eat and tuck you up in a nice warm bed."

The little girl still looked fearful, but Nan felt her tiny hands relax and return her pressure. When Wilmer and L.P. lifted her father out of the wagon, the tears flowed faster and her hand squeezed tighter. Nan felt as if her heart would break. She put her arms around the child and drew her close. The tiny body felt frail, yet stiff with fear. Nan wanted desperately to comfort her, but she knew that only time would overcome her dread of being in a strange town surrounded by strangers, her father very ill. She must feel utterly alone. Abandoned.

Nan picked up the child. "I've never had a little girl of my own," she said. "For tonight, let's pretend I'm your mommy."

The child spoke unexpectedly. "My mommy's gone to heaven. Is Daddy going to heaven, too?"

Nan hugged the child a little closer. "No, your Daddy's going to get well, and you're going to have the best Christmas ever."

The child put her arms around Nan's neck and held tight. Unwilling to break her hold, Nan carried her to the house down a rock-lined path past a bed of dead roses, an empty flower bed, and a half-acre of brown, withered grass. She waited while Wilmer and L.P. struggled to carry Will Atkins up the steps. Gertie held the door open.

"Take him straight back," Nan told Wilmer.

"But that's your room," Gertie objected.

The big room, once Nan's parents', lay at the back of the house across the wide hall from the kitchen. Nan directed them to place Will on an oversized bed piled high with thick, soft mattresses. The room was filled with ornately carved dark cherrywood furniture, but Nan's touches could be seen in the gingham bed cover and sheers at the window to let in the light.

"I can't be running up and down the stairs all day and night," Nan said. "I'll sleep in my old room."

She put the little girl down. The child wouldn't let go of Nan's hand, so Nan knelt down beside her. "I'm going to take you to the kitchen while I see about your father." The child clutched tighter. "This is Gertie," Nan said, introducing her farm manager's wife. "She'll get you something to eat."

The child still clung to Nan. Nan choked up. How many times had she dreamed of holding her own child just like this? She didn't want to let go, but she knew she had to see to the father.

"You don't have to be afraid. I'll be right here."

Still she wouldn't let go. Nan didn't have the heart to force her to go with Gertie. Still kneeling, still holding the child's hand, she said to Gertie, "Bring some warm milk and bread and jam to the bedroom."

She turned to the child. "Would you like that?"

She didn't answer, but Nan thought she detected a brightness in her eyes. Nan led her into the bedroom, to a chair close to the bed. "Sit right here. You can watch everything that happens to your daddy. We're going to make him better. I'm going to light the fire. It'll soon be warm as toast." Nan lifted her into a chair. "I won't leave you, I promise. But I've got to make your father better. You want that, don't you?"

The child nodded.

"Then sit right here. I'll be back in a moment." The child looked scared, but determined to be brave.

Wilmer and L.P had undressed Mr. Atkins and put him into a nightshirt. Nan put her hand to his forehead. He was burning up with fever. His pulse was calm and steady, but she would have to keep him warm. She took an extra quilt out of a tall wardrobe and asked L.P. to bring in some more firewood for the woodbox. She went out and returned in a few minutes with a cool compress for her patient's forehead and a hot water bottle for his feet. She would give him some hot herbal tea as soon as it was ready, but right now she was more concerned about keeping him warm.

She put another log on the fire and turned her attention to the child. She was pleased to see her take a bite out of a thick slice of whole wheat bread covered with freshly churned butter and Concord grape jam.

Nan pulled up a chair next to her. "I wish you'd tell me your name."

The child wiggled a little, but she didn't look so scared. "Clara," she announced. She looked down at her shoes rather than at Nan.

"That's a lovely name. My name is Nan. I don't like it very much. I think Clara is much prettier."

Clara smiled rather nervously.

"When did your daddy get sick?"

"While he was sleeping. He wouldn't eat his breakfast."

Just as Nan thought. Two people in Beaker's Bend had already come down with similar symptoms. Their fever remained high for about twenty-four hours, then it broke, leaving them weak but none the worse otherwise.

"He should be just fine in the morning. Do you want anything else to eat?"

The child shook her head.

"You can have more." Nan thought she was probably too frightened to be hungry tonight.

"No, thank you."

"Then I'm going to tuck you into a nice warm bed," Nan said, wondering who had taught her such beautiful manners. She acted older than her age. She must be an only child surrounded by adults. Nan wondered how long ago her mother had died. "When you wake up, your daddy will be all better."

Nan stood. Clara seemed reluctant to leave the fire and the comfort of her father's presence, but she slid out of the chair.

"I'm going to put you in the room I had when I was a little girl," Nan said. "You can sleep in the bed I slept in when I was your age."

Her mother had insisted they keep it for the time Nan's daughters would need it.

Wilmer had brought the bags in, and Gertie had taken Clara's bag upstairs to a small room with bright, flowered wallpaper. All the handmade furniture was half size. Clara allowed herself to be undressed and put to bed. Nan marveled that a room that used to seem so friendly should seem so cold now.

"If you need anything, you just call," Nan told her. "I'm going to go downstairs to take care of your father, but I'll sleep in the room right next to you." She led her into the hall and showed her the right door. "I'll leave this open so I can hear you. All right?"

Clara nodded, but she seemed frightened again.

Nan hated to leave her, but Clara needed to go to sleep. She probably hadn't had any rest all day. After the trip and the scare of her father getting sick, she must be exhausted.

"Do you think it's okay to leave her up there by herself?" Nan asked Gertie when she came downstairs.

"I expect she'll sleep till morning. Poor thing looks worn to a frazzle. Now you come into the kitchen before your dinner gets cold."

"Bring it to the bedroom. I don't think I ought to leave Mr. Atkins that long."

"He'll be just fine."

"Nevertheless, I'll feel more comfortable if I sit with him."

Gertie went away grumbling under her breath, but Nan didn't pay her any mind. Gertie had never accepted the fact that Nan had grown up and was not the little girl she had been twenty-four years ago when Gertie married Jake Tanner and moved out from Beaker's Bend.

Will Atkins hadn't moved. Nan put her hand on his forehead, but she knew before she touched him that his temperature hadn't broken. His skin was hot and dry. It felt tight. Nan had cared for many people, but no one had ever made her as nervous as this man did.

It's because he's Clara's father.

But she knew that wasn't it. She was nervous because he was a good-looking man. She couldn't help but be aware of it. She had felt something happen inside her the moment she set eyes on him. Almost as if she was sixteen again.

Don't be foolish. This man will be up and on his way in a couple of days and you'll never see him again. He won't even remember your name by next Christmas.

Maybe, but she couldn't turn her eyes away from the handsome head that rested on her goosedown pillows. She couldn't help but wonder what had happened to his wife, and why he should be in the Shenandoah Valley at this time of year. She remembered his ready-to-wear wool suit and Clara's clothes that spoke of expensive shops in a big eastern city. He wouldn't stay in Beaker's Bend any longer than necessary.

She had brushed his chestnut hair back from his brow, but not even his disordered hair and pallid skin detracted from his handsome face. She brushed the back of her fingers against his cheek. The skin was hot and taut, the cheeks gaunt from fever, but the clean line of his jaw and the finely etched nose complemented the fullness of his lips.

Nan made herself stand away from the bed when Gertie came in to place her dinner on a table next to her chair.

"Jake's not easy in his mind about you having that man sleeping in your bed," Gertie said.

"I don't know why. I'm not sleeping in it, and Mr. Atkins is too sick to know where he is. If that's not enough, Jake can sleep at the foot of the bed."

Gertie looked affronted. Nan kissed the older woman's cheek. "You should be happy. Not an hour ago I was feeling down because Gideon

24

wasn't going to be home for Christmas. Now we have company."

"They'll only be here a day or two," Gertie said. "It'll just be that much lonelier when they're gone."

Gertie was right. Nan would miss them. Odd. She didn't know anything about Will Atkins, but she felt drawn to him. But then, a handsome, helpless man offered an irresistible appeal to any woman. She was less able to explain her feeling for Clara. Already she felt a strong attachment to the little girl, almost as if she belonged to her.

It had to be the season and that she felt lonely because Gideon wasn't coming home. Next year she'd make sure she had so much to do that she wouldn't have time to be lonely. Maybe she'd go visit Gideon and Doris. She knew he'd invite her.

But it was too late for this year, and she was thankful for Mr. Atkins and his daughter.

Nan twisted in her chair. She had forgotten how uncomfortable it was to sit up all night, even in a comfortable chair. She opened her eyes and glanced at the clock. Twenty-two minutes after midnight. She didn't get up. She had checked Will Atkins less than ten minutes ago.

Light from a single tongue of fire struggled to hold the darkness at bay. The pattern on the quilt, Will's shape in the bed, were criss-crossed with shadows cast by the posts at the end of the bed. The rest of the room lay in deep shadow.

Nan closed her eyes, but she remained restless. The floor creaked. Startled, she opened her eyes and sat up. Clara stood by her father's bedside.

Nan got up and knelt before the child. "You're supposed to be in bed."

"I couldn't sleep."

"You mean you've been lying up there all this time waiting for me to come to bed?"

Clara nodded.

"Didn't you sleep at all?"

The child shook her head.

"Then you can sleep down here," Nan said. She reached under the skirt of the bed and pulled out a trundle bed. "I'd almost forgotten this was here." It only took Nan a few minutes to make up the bed and retrieve the pillow and quilts from the bottom of the wardrobe. "Now, let's tuck you under."

Clara climbed between the sheets. "Are you going to stay here?"

Nan heard the fear in the child's voice.

"Yes," Nan replied.

Clara settled into the bed, but she didn't close her eyes.

"I'll be right back," Nan said.

She hurried upstairs, lifted the lid on a pine chest at the end of her old bed, and took out a large, hand-made doll fashioned of heavy linen with clothes of bright gingham faded with time. She carried the nearly shapeless doll downstairs.

"Here's somebody to keep you company," she said as she slipped the doll under the covers next to Clara. "Her name is Betty. She's a little prickly because my brother Gideon tried to cut all her hair off. I gave Gideon a black eye. Papa was real mad, but Mama understood."

Clara giggled and pulled the doll close. "She only has one eye."

"The other one must have fallen off in the chest. We'll look for it tomorrow and sew it back on. Now you go to sleep. Your father ought to be better in the morning, and you'll want to be awake to keep him company."

"Aren't you going to keep him company, too?"

"Of course, but he'll especially want you."

"You're sure Daddy's going to be all right?"

"Positive. Now close your eyes. The sooner you go to sleep, the sooner you can wake up and find him well."

Clara obediently closed her eyes, the doll clutched in her arms, but Nan could tell she wasn't asleep.

"What's wrong, honey?"

"I'm cold."

"I'll get you another quilt."

But that wasn't the answer either.

"Would you like to sit in my lap for a minute?"

Nan didn't know why she asked that, but she had obviously said the right thing. Clara was out of the trundle bed and in her lap before Nan could change her mind.

Nan felt awkward. She had never held a child like this, but Clara didn't feel the least bit unsure. She pulled her knees up under her chin, rested her head on Nan's bosom, clutched the doll in a tight grasp, and closed her eyes. In less than a minute she was sound asleep. She didn't wake when Nan leaned over to get the quilt to cover her.

Nan didn't know what to do. She knew she

Leigh Greenwood

should put Clara back in the trundle bed, but she was afraid she would waken her. The child might feel abandoned when she woke up.

It was some time before Nan drifted off to sleep again. She had a warm feeling inside that spread through her whole body. It made her feel good, contented. She felt almost like a married woman with a husband and a child to care for. She told herself not to be foolish, that only children indulged in make-believe, but she couldn't stop the feeling. Besides, she liked it. For the first time in a long while, she didn't feel as if the pageant of life had passed her by. It might be foolish, but it was only a small indulgence. It wouldn't matter. They'd be gone in a day or two.

Nan looked at the man in the bed and the little girl in her arms. She realized that she didn't want them to go.

Chapter Two

Will opened his eyes. As his vision slowly focused, he realized that he had no idea where he was. He felt terribly tired. He couldn't move. Then he remembered feeling sick. He must be at an inn. But where? He remembered a train conductor asking him how he felt, but he didn't recall anything after that.

Clara! What had happened to his daughter? He tried to sit up, but after barely lifting himself off the bed, he fell back. His vision went all blurry, and the ceiling dissolved into a pinwheel. But it soon cleared. With a great effort, he turned on his side. His gaze focused on the woman sleeping in a chair next to his bed; Clara lay asleep in her lap.

Where was he? Who was this woman? How had she gotten his shy daughter to trust her?

She had passed the first blush of youth, but

she was still a lovely woman, her complexion creamy-smooth, the only color the pale blush of her cheeks and the deep rose of her lips. And the black of her lashes and eyebrows. Her nearly black hair had been parted in the middle, pulled into a knot on top of her head. It made her look too elegant even for this comfortable, well-furnished room. She wasn't beautiful, but in sleep she wore an expression of such serenity he felt his anxiety ebb away. Whoever she was, she was kindness itself.

He was surprised that her husband had allowed her to sit with him. Even with his daughter to act as chaperon, men in the mountains were notoriously skittish about letting strangers near their women. He ought to know. He had grown up in the mountains.

Maybe it was because she'd been married for years. The way she held Clara—her arms holding her close, her chin resting on the child's head—showed she knew all about children. She must have several of her own.

He'd have to move to an inn as soon as possible. He didn't want to make any more work for her, or cause trouble between her and her husband.

But even as he told himself he ought to leave, his gaze was drawn back to the woman. Something about her appealed to him strongly. Maybe it was her kindness. He couldn't be imagining it. It must be terribly uncomfortable to have let Clara sleep in her lap all night, yet she looked perfectly content. No, she looked happy, as if she wanted to keep Clara close.

How could he not be drawn to a woman such as that? She had such a sweet, loving face.

He fell back, exhausted. He wondered how long he had been here. He hoped it hadn't been too long. Louise's parents were expecting him on the twentieth. They couldn't wait to get their hands on Clara. They'd been trying for years. Now they had succeeded, and they were impatient. After not forgiving him for taking their daughter away, they weren't likely to be pleased at his postponing their moment of triumph.

He thought of Louise's happiness when she learned she was pregnant, of how much she'd looked forward to having a half dozen children. She had died before Clara's first birthday. The loss had almost destroyed him. Now he was going to lose Clara as well.

He drifted off to sleep wondering for the thousandth time if there were any way to avoid it.

"Wake up, Nan. You had no business sleeping in this chair. Don't you know what it can do to your spine?"

Nan opened her eyes but didn't move. "Ssshhhh," she whispered. "You'll wake Clara and her father."

"Better I should wake them than you should be a cripple for life."

Nan glanced at the weak sunlight coming in the window. "I guess I'd better get up."

But Nan couldn't move. One arm and both legs had gone dead.

"Help me put her in the trundle bed." Nan

31

allowed Gertie to lift Clara from her lap. While Gertie tucked the sleeping child into the small bed, Nan rubbed her arm to restore the circulation. The pinpricks of returning feeling were unpleasant, but she didn't mind. Looking at Clara as she slept peacefully made it worthwhile. Nan had brought help and comfort to many people, but nothing had ever touched her so deeply as Clara asleep in her arms. For one night she had been able to experience what it would have been like to have a child of her own.

Nan got to her feet. She felt stiff, her muscles slow to respond, her movements awkward. She walked around the bed to get a closer look at Will Atkins. "He looks better." She felt his forehead. "His temperature has broken."

"I'll bet he's soaked the bed."

"Probably. Get some clean sheets. I'll get him a fresh nightshirt."

"You're not thinking of changing him, are you?" Gertie asked, scandalized.

Nan laughed softly. "Not that he would know the difference."

"You let Jake take care of him."

"Of course," Nan said. But she felt a tinge of regret. Being near this man infused her with an energy that made her more optimistic, more sensitive. She felt as though good news was on its way, as though something wonderful was about to happen.

Will Atkins sat on the edge of the bed, his legs sticking out from a nightshirt that was much too short for him. "I can't face anybody looking like this," he said, rubbing his chin over a two-day growth of beard.

"That's Mr. Carson's nightshirt."

"I don't want to take his clothes. What's he going to wear?"

"Mr. Carson's dead."

"She's awfully young to be a widow."

"Who are you talking about?"

"The young woman who sat up with me."

Jake chuckled, a big grin on his face. "That's Nan, Mr. Carson's daughter. She ain't never married."

Will felt a muscle in his throat tighten. "What's wrong with the men around here?"

"There ain't any, leastways not any that ain't already married," Jake said, as he poured the hot water into a basin and set it down on the stand next to the bed. "Old Mister Carson used to say she was too particular. Gertie says there weren't nobody good enough. I think she scared them off."

"What's wrong with her?"

"Nothing." Jake worked up a lather with the shaving brush. "It's just she's a real lady. A smart one, too. That's enough to put the fear of God into most men around here."

"In Boston, men would be standing in line to marry her," Will said, allowing Jake to lather his face. He would have preferred to shave himself—he'd never been able to afford the luxury of having someone do it for him—but he was too weak to hold the razor.

"Miss Nan don't hold with big cities," Jake said. "That's where Gideon went, and he ain't never come back."

"Gideon?" Will managed to mumble. He had to hold real still while Jake shaved his jaw.

"Her brother. He's marrying some city girl. That's why he ain't coming home for Christmas."

"But surely Miss Carson has more family." It was hard to talk when his upper lip was being shaved by a straight razor sharp enough to cut it off with a single slip of the hand.

"They're all dead."

"But this farm?"

"She owns it. Runs it herself, too. Well, actually Cliff Gilmer takes care of the cows and Bert Layne sees after the crops. Me and Gertie help with everything else, but Miss Nan makes all the decisions."

As Jake lifted Will's chin to shave his neck, Will couldn't deny a feeling of relief. He had been nervous about facing a husband less than delighted to have his home invaded just before Christmas. He was also curious to learn more about a woman who could not only run her own farm but was willing to take in a stranger who had fallen sick, who could win his daughter's trust enough for Clara to sleep in her lap, and whose kindness drew his thoughts back to her time and time again.

And not just her kindness. There was a sensuality about her, about the pucker of her full lips, the unblemished whiteness of her skin, the softness of her body's curves. He might be weak from fever, but he could feel a physical tug, the kind of pull he had felt very few times since his wife's death.

"Now you're to get back in bed," Jake said, as he wiped the last bits of lather from Will's face. "Your breakfast will be in shortly."

"I'd like to see my daughter."

"She's getting dressed, but she'll be having her breakfast in here with you."

"And Miss Carson?"

"Her, too. The room'll be full to busting with all of you and Gertie bustling about to make sure you don't do nothing improper."

"I wouldn't think—"

"You can think all you want," Jake said, "as long as you don't do nothing."

No, he wouldn't do anything, but his imagination wouldn't be nearly so obedient.

Will was so weak he could hardly hold his spoon steady. He found it hard to believe fever could drain so much of his strength in less than twenty-four hours, but he was determined that Nan wouldn't have to feed him. He didn't want to look helpless with Clara watching him.

"He's eating with a coming appetite," Gertie observed from the foot of the bed. "He'll be ready to go on his way by afternoon."

"Mr. Atkins is too weak to resume his journey for at least another day," Nan said. "Besides, Wilmer has closed the inn, so there's nothing for him to do but stay here until he regains his strength. You won't mind that, will you?" she asked Clara.

Clara nodded happily.

Will would have been amused at Gertie's effort to protect her mistress if he hadn't been the one she was protecting her from. He had already asked about alternatives to the inn, but Jake had told him nobody was taking in strangers during the Christmas season. "They have enough to do worrying over their relations who moved to the city but always come home for the holidays."

"Then if he's so weak, you ought to let him get his rest," Gertie said, her hands on her hips.

"Let Clara stay with me," Will said. "You must have a lot to do to get ready for Christmas." He was surprised that Clara was so happy to sit next to Nan.

"Not all that much. Would you like to help me?" Nan asked Clara.

"I don't know how," Clara replied.

"What do you mean *you don't know how?*" Nan asked.

"She's never had a proper Christmas," Will explained. "The woman who's been keeping her doesn't celebrate Christmas."

"What kind of heathen doesn't celebrate Christmas?" Gertie demanded.

"Lots of people, especially people like me who don't have anybody to share it with," Nan said, hoping to stem Gertie's embarrassing questions. "Now please ask Jake to bring all the greenery on the back porch into the front hall."

"You said you wanted to give it to the church."

"I changed my mind. Clara and I are going to decorate the front hall. Hurry up. We can't get started without it."

Gertie didn't seem pleased to leave Nan unprotected, but she went off to find Jake. Apparently she thought keeping Nan out of Will's bedroom for the morning was worth the risk of a few unprotected moments.

"I apologize for Gertie," Nan said.

"Don't. A lovely young woman like you can't be too well protected. I'm surprised you don't have bars at the gate to keep the men out."

"The only bars we need in Beaker's Bend would be to keep the men in. Now Clara and I are going to leave you to your rest. We'll wake you for lunch."

"I won't sleep that long. I feel much better."

"We'll see. Clara, give your father a kiss."

"You sure she's not too much trouble?"

"I'll enjoy having her. Christmas is a difficult time when you're alone. But having lost your wife, I expect you know that."

Will didn't reply. Once again he felt the overwhelming guilt of not being able to stay at Louise's side when she was so sick. He hadn't even been in town when she died. He wasn't sure he could ever forgive himself for that.

That was one of the reasons he was taking Clara to live with her grandparents. He didn't want her to grow up staying with strangers, seeing her father only on weekends and not always then. She needed the kind of love, support, and comfort that could only be provided by someone who could be with her every day, sit with her when she was sick, share her happy moments. He might not like Louise's parents, but he knew they would take good care of Clara.

"Any time is difficult when you're alone," Will answered.

Nan looked surprised. "I'm not alone. I've got Gertie and Jake, the people who work for me—the whole town."

"You're alone when you're without a family."

Will didn't know why he said that. Maybe because he'd felt so alone during the five years since Louise died. He loved Clara with all his heart, but she couldn't fill the emptiness left by his wife's death.

"Well I have a family today, don't I?"

Odd she should say that. He did almost feel like part of her family. Clara certainly seemed to. Just as inexplicably, the emptiness inside him didn't feel so overwhelming today. Maybe it was being in a real home with real people who cared. Even in the few hours he had been awake, he had felt more comfortable than he did in his apartment. It had been so long since he left the valley that he had forgotten how nice a real home could feel.

Louise had been just as anxious to leave the small town where they'd grown up as he was. Maybe more so. She probably worked harder to get ahead. Then she got sick and never recovered. It was as though giving life to Clara had completely used up her own.

He doubted that would happen to Nan Carson. He imagined she would glow with health. She was the kind of woman whose love and strength would never be exhausted. It would continually renew itself.

Will grew drowsy wondering why no one had claimed this woman. If he had been one of the village blades, he'd have camped on her doorstep. Just the thought of her lips, of the sweetness of her kiss, would have caused him to neglect any duties he might have.

He told himself he was too weak to get worked up over idle speculation, but he drifted off to sleep trying to imagine what it would be like to return each day to a home of Nan Carson's making.

"We won't be able to see out if we put anything else in that window," Nan said to Clara.

"But we've got all these branches left."

The room was littered with holly branches, pungent cedar, pyracantha heavy with clusters of dull red berries, pine boughs that filled the room with their fresh scent, magnolia branches with huge shiny green leaves and brown seed pods filled with plump red seeds, and tiny sprigs of mistletoe all on burlap sacks spread out to protect the carpets and floor. The broken pieces had been gathered up in a large wooden tub. Clara held a roll of red ribbon. Green and white lay just within reach.

They had decorated the parlor with spare good taste, but they had covered every corner of the gathering room. The deep brown of the walls and wood floor, the dark maroon of the leather chairs, the cheerful plaids and floral patterns, were overwhelmed by green and red.

Each window held a wreath fashioned out of cedar branches and fastened together with bits of wire. Holly, bright with red berries, lay in each window seat. Branches of pine topped with magnolia circled every table in the room. More than a dozen candles stood in the windows and on the tables ready to be lighted.

"We need to save some for the wreath to go on the front door."

"Let's make that now."

"How about waiting until tomorrow," Nan said, laughing. "I think we ought to begin making the decorations for the Christmas tree."

"Can we have a real tree?" Clara asked.

"Of course."

"We never had a real tree. Mrs. Bartholomew doesn't like Christmas."

"Who's Mrs. Bartholomew?"

"The lady I stay with when Daddy's gone." Clara paused. "He's gone nearly all the time."

"Well he's here this Christmas," a deep, masculine voice announced from the doorway. "Not in very good shape, but here nonetheless."

Nan looked up. She noticed how thin he was, as if he hadn't been eating well. But he was still very attractive. She wondered if Mrs. Bartholomew was a young woman.

Clara ran toward her father as he walked into the gathering room with careful steps.

"Easy, easy," he said when she seemed ready to throw herself into his arms. "You're liable to knock me over."

"He wouldn't eat the lunch I brought him,"

Gertie complained, entering the room on his heels. "He insisted on joining you."

"I'm punished for my disobedience," Will said, sinking into the only chair free of greenery. "I can't stand up long enough to hug my daughter."

"Of course not," Nan said, getting to her feet. "You ought to have eaten your lunch and gone straight back to sleep." She took a quilt from the sofa, unfolded it, and spread it over him.

"I seem to have slept away the better part of the day," he said. "Gertie tells me it's mid-afternoon. Have you eaten?"

"Hours ago," Clara said. "We had pork chops in gravy and lots of potatoes and—"

"Our lunch was too rich for your father. Bring his tray in here, Gertie. He can eat while we make the tree decorations."

"Eat in here?" Gertie asked, scandalized.

"Yes, in here," Nan repeated. "It's about time this room got used for something. Besides, it's no use decorating if nobody's going to look at it."

Gertie looked displeased, but she soon settled a tray in front of Will. "Don't spill anything," she said. "I don't have time for a lot of cleaning."

"Gertie!" Nan exclaimed.

"Well, I don't. Not with me doing all the cooking you haven't got time for now."

"Are we keeping you from—"

"You're not keeping me from a thing," Nan insisted, angry at Gertie. "There's more than enough time for the cooking I need to do."

Gertie sniffed in disagreement, but she left without saying anything more.

While Will ate his lunch of hot, clear soup, Nan showed Clara how to draw designs on colored paper and cut them out to make candy canes and other brightly colored ornaments. She showed her how to fold the colored paper to make boxes and pyramids. They glued narrow strips of gold and silver paper into shining garlands.

Nan couldn't remember when she had had more fun. The chance to show Clara a Christmas like none she'd ever experienced restored Nan's own excitement and anticipation. But one look at Will sitting in the chair watching his daughter with a rapt gaze made her realize that it wasn't just Clara. It was her father as well.

She had been acutely aware of his presence. His gaze followed her, his expression inscrutable. She felt as though he were trying to probe her mind and expose her thoughts. Nan had none except to make Clara happy. Well, she did wonder about him, his job, why he hadn't remarried.

She told herself it was silly to be curious about a man she had never seen before yesterday and wouldn't see again after tomorrow.

"Now it's time to string the popcorn," Nan said in a very businesslike manner when Gertie took away the lunch tray. She opened a box Gertie had brought in earlier, and immediately the smell of freshly roasted popcorn filled the air.

"That smells delicious," Will said.

Clara's eyes grew big.

Nan laughed as she handed Clara a needle threaded with a very long piece of string. "Don't eat too much. It takes a lot to decorate a big tree."

Gertie entered long enough to set a plate of golden yellow cookies on the table next to Will.

"Clara, show your father how I taught you to string the popcorn. While you do that, I'm going upstairs to bring down some very special decorations."

Nan returned several minutes later to find two chestnut heads together over a lengthening string of popcorn. Clara chose the kernels. Her father put them on the string. Then while Clara carefully pushed a fluffy white kernel to the end of the string, her father ate one of the golden cookies.

Nan couldn't help but notice how long and slender his fingers were. Her father's had been short and thick and powerful. Will's hands gave the impression of elegance. They didn't look as if they ever had a blister.

Forcing her mind back to her task, Nan cleared a broad hunt table, then covered it with cotton she unrolled in broad widths. "Let your father finish that," Nan said to Clara. "I want you to help me."

Clara came over to stare uncertainly at the cotton-covered table.

Nan knelt before the box and began to remove carved and painted wooden figures—men, women, children, dogs, a horse and sleigh, houses, trees, until she had an entire village.

"Ooooo, it's beautiful!" Clara cooed. "Where did you get it?"

"My father had it made for me when I was a little girl. Each year I got something else to add to it."

"Are you going to make a town?"

"No."

Clara's face fell.

"You're going to make it."

"Me?"

"Yes. All by yourself."

Clara regarded the figures with a rapt gaze.

"Are you sure?" her father asked.

"Positive," Nan replied as she came to sit in a chair next to him. "Setting up that village each year is one of my happiest childhood memories."

"Thank you for sharing it with Clara. She has so few happy memories of Christmas."

He'd never realized it before, but neither had he. Maybe that's why he had been anxious to leave his own home, why he hadn't thought it necessary to stay home with Clara. Nan, on the other hand, had experienced this happiness and was sharing this precious gift with two strangers.

He couldn't remember Clara ever being this happy, a happiness he had longed for without knowing it. Maybe that was why he felt so strongly drawn to Nan. Maybe it wasn't just her softness or her quiet allure.

"Forgive me if I'm prying, but don't you have any family?" Nan asked.

"Not really." Only Louise's parents, and they were about the last people he cared to see.

"You must have been going somewhere."

"To visit my wife's parents."

"Then you must resume your trip as quickly as possible. They must be anxiously awaiting—"

"My wife and I couldn't wait to leave home, especially Louise. We were so sure life would be better in the city. Any city."

"And was it?"

He reached for a cookie and ate slowly.

"Louise never regretted leaving, not even after she got sick."

He paused to watch Clara. She had made the first decision, where to place her church. She arranged several houses around it.

"I've had to work much harder since she died."

"So that's why you're never home."

Clara searched through the figures until she found what she wanted—a man, a woman, and a child. A family.

"Daddy," she called, "which is our house? The one we're going to live in when you get rich?"

"The big white one," Will said, pointing to the largest house in the set. "It's going to sit right across the street from the church."

"Where's your store going to be?"

"In the next block. Across from the bank."

They watched as Clara placed the two buildings, then chose the people to live in each one.

"So why did you come back?"

"I'm taking Clara to live with her grandparents."

Clara lifted a house out of the box that clearly belonged on a Southern plantation rather than in the Shenandoah Valley. "Daddy, who lives in this house?"

"Anybody you want, precious."

"I can't decide. You come help."

Will had difficulty getting up from the chair. He

had difficulty getting down next to his daughter, too, but he was thankful for the interruption. He didn't want to have to explain to Nan his reasons for taking Clara to her grandparents. Or defend them. He didn't owe her an explanation for anything—he was doing the best he could for his daughter while honoring his promises to Louise—but he couldn't bear for her to keep looking at him like that.

"That's a mighty fancy house," he said as he watched Clara trying to decide where to place the house. "A mighty fancy lady ought to live there."

Clara giggled. "No. This is Nan's house."

"I agree. Now, where can we find a Nan?"

Once again two chestnut heads came together as father and daughter set about the task of populating their village.

Nan watched, her mind prey to fruitless speculation. It would never have occurred to her to give up her child, not even for a short time. There must be some terrible pressure on Will to force him to take such a drastic step. It was plain that he adored Clara.

Looking at him over his daughter's head, she could swear there were tears in his eyes. At least he was misty-eyed. No man who looked like that wanted to give up his daughter.

She noticed Will glanced up at the plate of cookies, but they were too far away.

Nan got up and placed them on the floor next to him.

She hated to think of depriving grandparents

of their grandchild, but it was even more terrible
to think of separating a father from his daughter.
There must be some way to keep them together.
Right then Nan made up her mind to keep them
at Spruce Meadow until she found a way.

Chapter Three

"You have to bundle up real good," Nan told Clara. "It's very cold outside." Breakfast had been eaten and everything washed up. They were going to look for a Christmas tree.

"It's cold at home, too," Clara said. She was so excited that Nan had to help her into her coat.

"But not as cold as here," Jake said. "You'll have icicles on your nose by the time we get back."

Clara giggled. "Will I?" she asked Nan.

"Not if you bundle up." Nan pulled a gaily decorated woolen cap over Clara's head. "Keep your gloves on."

"Why are you always trying to do things without me?"

The three turned to find Will Atkins standing in the doorway to his room. He was dressed in a suit with an overcoat and hat. Only his boots seemed sturdy enough to endure the hunt for a Christmas tree.

Clara giggled. "Daddy's not bundled up. He'll have icicles on his nose."

"This is all I have," Will said.

"You can't possibly go," Nan protested. "You're not strong enough to make it up the hills."

"I was hoping for a place in your wagon."

Nan looked undecided, but Clara took her father by the hand. "You can sit next to me."

"Okay," Nan said, giving in, "but you've got to let Jake lend you some clothes, and you've got to stay in the wagon. I won't have Jake trying to drag you out of the woods."

"You don't have a very good impression of me, do you?"

Nan didn't dare let him guess the impression she did have. She had lain awake half the night trying to think of ways to help him keep his daughter. But instead of thinking about his job and housekeepers to stay with Clara, she found herself wondering what he liked to eat, what made him laugh, what he liked to do for fun, where he had taken his wife when they were spooning.

"You've been very sick. You won't do Clara any good if you get sick again."

"Is that all you care about?"

His look made Nan uneasy. He was looking too deep, demanding an answer she didn't want to give. "What else should I care about?"

"Me."

Nan felt herself grow warm. Words stuck in her throat. Her thoughts came in hesitant fragments.

She felt foolish and utterly helpless to do anything about it. She was attracted to this man, more than to any other she had ever known, but that was no reason to be rendered brainless.

"I care about you, Daddy," Clara said.

"I'm concerned about your father, too," Nan managed to say. "But what kind of nurse would I be if I let him get sick again?"

"Let's go," Clara said, tired of standing about talking. "I want a big Christmas tree that goes all the way to the ceiling."

"We'll see," Nan said, using the diversion of bundling Clara up and putting on her own clothes to ease the tension with Will. "Jake has picked out one he's sure you'll like."

"Where is it?" Clara asked.

"You'll see," Nan said, scooting the child outside and into the wagon.

Soon they were on their way, Jake driving the team, Will and Nan seated on either side of Clara.

"We got the biggest tree in the woods," Clara announced as she bounded up the steps and raced through the door Gertie held open. "It'll fill the whole room."

"Not quite that large," Nan said, "but it's the biggest Christmas tree we've ever had."

Will and Jake struggled up the steps and through the door with a holly tree heavy with berries.

"Take it into the gathering room," Nan said. "In front of the big window."

A fire popped noisily in the fireplace, providing

cheer as well as warmth to the frost-bitten quartet.

"I never thought a fire could feel so good," Will said. He dropped his end of the tree and backed up to the fireplace.

"You're taking all the room, Daddy," Clara complained, angling for her share of warmth.

Gertie came in, carrying a tray with three mugs and a heavy clay pitcher.

"Who wants hot cider?" Nan said, rubbing her hands together.

The three warmed themselves in front of the fire, drank hot cider, and ate thick ham sandwiches while Jake attached the tree to a stand. Will helped him stand it up in front of the window.

"It doesn't touch the ceiling," Clara said, disappointment in her voice.

"It's all right," Nan said. "I've got something special to go on top."

"What is it?"

"I'll show you when we've finished decorating the tree."

Clara ran for the popcorn strings.

"Save them for later," Nan said. She opened another one of the many boxes Jake had brought down the day before. She reached inside and pulled a beautiful hand-painted glass ball from the depths of cotton. "Ask your father to help you tie this on the tree."

Clara stared at the ornament. "I might break it."

"I broke lots of them, but every year I got more."

With her father's help, Clara managed to tie the ball on the tree.

"How many more?" Will asked when Nan opened a third box. "My fingers are full of pricks already."

"Not many," Nan answered.

After they had tied on the last painted ball, Nan and Will helped Clara put the gold and silver chains on the tree. The six popcorn chains went on last.

"And now for the top," Nan said. She opened another box and pulled out a beautiful angel with long, flowing hair and a long white dress. "It takes a ladder. Can you do it?" she asked Will.

"Sure," Will said. He was a little unsteady, but Nan made herself concentrate on holding the ladder rather than on Will.

"There," he said, when he had settled the angel on the top of the tree.

He climbed down and all three stepped back to admire their handiwork.

"You deserve a treat after all that work," Gertie said.

She set a plate of cookies on a small table. Will reached for one immediately.

"I only gave you five," Gertie told him. "Any more would spoil your dinner."

Will blushed slightly. "I didn't realize I had made such a pig of myself."

"Don't worry your head about it. Everybody in Beaker's Bend is crazy about Nan's shortbreads. They're the first thing to disappear every year." Gertie gave him a closer inspection. "You could use a little fattening up. Don't you eat regular?"

"It's hard, traveling all the time."

"Leave Mr. Atkins alone, Gertie," Nan said. "His eating habits are really none of our concern."

"Well, somebody ought to look after him. Everybody knows God never did make a man with sense enough to look after himself." Gertie turned to Clara. "I've got some hot chocolate in the kitchen. It's a lot better than that old cider."

"Go on," Nan said, when Clara cast her an inquiring look. "Gertie makes the best hot chocolate in the whole valley."

As she left the room, Gertie gave Nan such a pointed look that Nan felt herself blush. Gertie's change of attitude puzzled her. Just that morning she had acted as if she wanted Will out of the house at the earliest moment. Now, if her sly hints, head noddings, and glances out of the corners of her eyes were any indication, she had decided Nan ought to marry him and take him in hand.

Nan suddenly felt weak. Marry him! That was what Gertie meant, but that wasn't what bothered her. She, too, had been thinking about marrying him. That bothered her a lot.

She didn't know anything about Will Atkins except that he traveled so much, he couldn't take proper care of his own daughter. That was the difference between men and women. If she had a child, she would never give it up, not even for the most successful business in the whole world. It was a choice only a man would make.

But she couldn't think Will was the kind of man to do that either, even though he had said he was going to. He loved his daughter too much. Nan didn't believe he could live without her.

"Gertie doesn't think much of men, does she?"

"Don't let her fool you. She spoils Jake something awful. She'd take his boots off if he'd let her. Have some more cider. Jake says it's the best we've had in years."

Will looked as if he was going to say something else, but instead he reached for the cider, then another cookie.

"I have to eat my allotment before Gertie decides to take them back," he explained when Nan smiled at him.

"Eat all you want. They're very easy to make."

"And very rich."

"You keep eating like that, and you'll look like Santa Claus."

"Why isn't your brother coming home this Christmas?"

"He's spending it with his fiancée's family."

"Why don't you have a fiancé, or a family? How did a lovely woman like you escape being snapped up?"

Nan was tempted to tell him it was none of his business. "The time never seemed right. When the boys came courting, I was busy nursing my parents. After they died, nobody came anymore."

"You're content to remain here?"

"What do you expect me to do? Put an ad in the paper telling everybody the door's on the latch?"

"No, but you could move out of this valley. There are thousands of men who would move heaven and earth for a woman like you."

"They don't have to move anything but themselves."

"No one can find you here."

"My brother thinks I ought to leave. He says I'll never find a husband."

"Then why are you still here?"

"This is my home," Nan replied, angrily. "These are my people. Besides, people who move out of the valley become changed so much they don't have time for their own daughters. I don't want anything like that to happen to me."

"You don't know anything about my situation," Will said. "I'm doing it because it's best for Clara."

Nan refused to apologize for her anger. She hadn't meant to hurt him, but he had hurt her, and she had struck back. He had no right to judge her, to tell her what to do, not when his own life was in such a tangle.

"You think sending Clara to live with her grand-parents is so terrible?" Will asked.

"I think it's the most awful thing you could do."

"I agree with you."

"Then why are you doing it?" Nan asked, so surprised she didn't think to control her curiosity.

"Because there's nothing else I can do. Gertie's right. A man can't take care of himself. He's even worse at taking care of a child."

Clara came back into the room. She picked up her doll and climbed into the sofa. She leaned against one of the over-stuffed cushions and stared at the Christmas tree. Will chose a cookie and moved back to the fire, but his gaze never left his daughter.

Nan got up to light the candles. She had been right. Will didn't want to lose his daughter. Her heart overflowed with compassion for a man forced by circumstances to give up the one person he loved most in the whole world.

"Are you sure you have to give her up?" Nan whispered as she came to stand next to him before the fire. The light from the candles played on the windows and the gleaming glass balls on the Christmas tree.

"I have no choice," Will replied. "I've tried, but I don't have time for both Clara and my business."

"Then why . . ."

"Why don't I do something else?"

Yes, she had been going to ask that.

"I'm a salesman. It's what I know, what I do best. It's really the only way I know to make a living. The business was Louise's dream. She wanted it for our children. She made me promise to do it for Clara."

Clara lay down on the cushion, eyes only half open.

"Do you think she cares?" Nan asked in a harsh undervoice.

"Not now, but when she's older she'll—"

"She'll what? Want a lot of money she'll end up leaving to her children? She'd rather have you."

"Not everybody can make the choices they want."

"They can if they have the courage."

"What about you?"

"I haven't been offered any choices."

"You could leave."

"And go where? Do what? All I know how to do is run this farm."

"You could go with your brother."

"And be the old maid sister, hanging on his sleeve, taking care of his children? No, thank you. I'd rather stay here and live my own life. If I'm going to take care of other people's children, I'd rather it be the people of Beaker's Bend. I've known them since I was born. We're all part of the same family. I'll never be truly alone as long as I'm here."

"But you'll never have a family of your own."

"There's always a chance."

"It looks like each of us is afraid to take a chance," Will said.

Will looked down at his daughter, who had fallen asleep. "I never understand how children can fall asleep in the middle of a lighted room with people talking."

"Gertie would say it's because they have a clear conscience."

"I say it's because she hasn't stopped running all day. You shouldn't encourage her to be so much trouble."

"I don't mind. It's nice to have a child in the house. I'm going to miss her when she's gone."

"Speaking of that, we'll be leaving tomorrow."

Nan was shocked that he had made plans to leave without talking to her; she was hurt that he wanted to leave so soon. "You can't. You're still not strong enough to travel."

"We'll stay at the inn for a day or so, then continue to Lexington."

"If it's only one day, you might as well stay here."

"We've caused you a lot of work. Besides, the neighbors will begin to talk soon. I lived in a small town long enough to know what gossip can be like."

"It won't make any difference. Everybody knows you're here by now."

"Thanks, but I think we'd better go."

Nan had expected to be a little dispirited when Will and Clara left, but she wasn't prepared for the feeling of desolation that weighed her down. Now, Christmas was going to seem more gloomy than ever. The decorations, the tree, all the preparations would be a silent accusation that she didn't have the courage to leave Beaker's Bend and search for a new life.

Maybe Will and Gideon were right. Maybe she was foolish to stay here, waiting year after year for the man she feared would never come. It would be even more difficult now. Will Atkins and his daughter had filled her heart, and it would be hard for anyone to oust them. Not that anyone was looking to claim her hand.

No one had since Harve Adams.

Will felt so tired that he barely had the energy to drop his clothes on the floor and crawl into bed. He had done his best to make Nan believe he had recovered his strength, but now that he was alone he could admit that he was about to drop in his tracks. His clothes would be wrinkled in the morning, but he was too tired to care.

His body tightened into a ball in the cold bed. As he lay there, waiting for the bed to warm and his body to relax, he thought again that he didn't want to leave. It would be so easy to stay. And stay. But he needed to go before he became any more attracted to Nan. There was no future in becoming interested in a woman who would never be happy outside this remote valley.

Of course he couldn't consider coming back to live in the valley. He had made too many sacrifices for the life he and Louise had wanted, the life they had worked so hard to build, that he had clung to for five years.

Besides, there was nothing to come back to. These last days were unreal, a fairy tale. Christmas would pass and the magic would fade, leaving only the memory of yet another dream.

Jake entered the front hall to take Will and Clara's luggage to the wagon. "I saw L.P. yesterday," he told Nan. "He hasn't heard from Wilmer since he left for Locust Hollow. The inn's still closed."

"Maybe you should leave your luggage here," Nan said to Will. "Just in case Wilmer's not back."

"I think we should take it along," Will said.

"Do we have to go?" Clara asked. Her spirits had not recovered since her father told her they were leaving. She looked at Nan through teary eyes.

"I'm sure they'll have a Christmas tree in the inn," Will said.

"I want my tree. Not another one." She threw

herself down on the sofa in tears.

Will sat down next to his daughter. "We'll be at your grandparents' house on Christmas. They'll have a Christmas tree, too."

They rode to town in strained silence. When they reached the inn, they found it still shut up.

"Mr. Crider ain't come back," L.P. said. He looked at the leaden sky. "If he don't come back soon, he'll be snowed in up at that hollow." He paused. "Maybe he don't want to come back. He said he means to get shut of this place."

"You mean sell it?" Nan asked, incredulous. "He's run the inn for as long as I can remember."

"Ruby's been after him to move to the Hollow. Besides, Wilmer's been wanting to take it easy. Says running an inn ain't no business for no old man."

"Can we go back to Nan's?" Clara asked. "Please, Daddy, say we can."

"Of course you can," Nan said, not waiting for Will to answer. "My feelings would be hurt if you stayed with anybody else."

Clara looked straight at Nan. "We don't know anybody else."

"Only for one more night," Will said. "Then we must be on our way. In fact, I ought to go to the train station to reserve our seats."

Nan took Clara into the general store while her father went to the train station. Rows of shelves bowed with the weight of their contents were barely illuminated by the light from two small kerosene lamps suspended from the ceiling.

Nan doubted that the potbellied stove turned out enough heat to keep molasses from freezing. She wasn't surprised the store was empty. It was too cold to linger. Even the floorboards creaked in protest as she moved about. Hurrying to make her purchases, she found Clara staring at the brightly colored sticks of candy Mr. Whitehall kept behind a glass cover.

"Would you like one?" Nan asked.

"Yes, please," Clara said.

"Is this the poor child of that man who's been staying with you?" Mrs. Whitehall asked.

"Yes," Nan answered, a little surprised at the way Paralee Whitehall had phrased her question and even more surprised by her judgmental attitude.

"When are they leaving?"

"They had planned to move to the inn today, but Wilmer's still away. They'll resume their journey tomorrow."

"I saw him heading toward the train station just now. He looked plenty recovered to me."

"I suppose that's why people ask me about doctoring and you about pork bellies," Nan said, a sting in her voice. "He's still weak from the fever. Let's go, Clara. We've got several other stops to make."

Miserable old busybody, Nan mumbled under her breath. *She'll have to sing a different tune if she wants any cookies from me this Christmas.*

"Why are you mad at that lady?" Clara asked.

Nan chastised herself for being so careless. She was so used to being alone that she had fallen into the habit of talking out loud to herself. That would never do around a curious child.

"Just annoyed. Now let's hurry. I want to see if they managed to decorate the church."

For the last seven years, Nan had been in charge of the Christmas decorations, but she had given it up this year. She just didn't have the heart. But now she was anxious to make certain it was done right. The lessons and carols service on Christmas Eve was an important evening for the whole town. Everybody would be there, from tots to grandparents.

Will found them just as they came out of the church.

"What took you so long?" Nan asked.

"I was looking around town. I hadn't seen anything of Beaker's Bend. I didn't realize it was this large."

"We have nearly a thousand people," Nan told him proudly. "We're the biggest town in the whole valley."

"I don't understand why you put up with Whitehall's mercantile," Will said. "You can't possibly find half the things you want in there."

Nan opened her mouth to contradict him, but realized that she had made the very same complaint not twenty minutes earlier. Grady and Paralee Whitehall didn't make much attempt to cater to their customers. They stocked what Grady's father used to stock, and the people of Beaker's Bend were expected to make do with it.

"It is something of an irritation, but we can get anything we want sent in on the train."

"But you ought to be able to get it right here," Will insisted. "There's no reason why . . ." He stopped, looking a little apologetic. "I didn't mean to get wound up. That's one of the difficulties of liking your work. You can't stop thinking about it all the time."

"I don't suppose there's anything wrong with that as long as you don't ignore the really important things."

But he had already admitted he was unable to attend to the most important duty a man could have.

"I'm taking you to lunch," Will announced. "Don't worry, I already told Gertie. Where can we eat in this town?"

Nan laughed. She didn't know why, but she did. "Do you always invite people to eat without knowing where to go?"

"Sure. They always know the best places."

"The best place in Beaker's Bend is the drug store. It's also the only place."

"Lead the way," Will said.

But they got sidetracked when Nan led him into the park in the center of town. A dozen trees, each more than a hundred years old, towered over numerous saplings of much more tender years. Through the center of this woodland glen a stream gurgled and splashed over a bed strewn with large stones. The creek took a sharp turn in the middle of the square and headed north toward the Shenandoah River.

"I'd been wondering how this town got its name," Will said, as they traversed the wooden bridge across the icy water. "I assume this is Beaker's Creek."

Nan nodded.

"I used to go fishing in a stream very much like this. I never considered it a successful day if I didn't come home with at least a half-dozen fish."

"The creek passes through the farm," Nan said. "Gideon used to go fishing all the time."

"Your own mountains, your own valley, your own town, and now your own fishing stream. I can see why you don't want to leave. I can't say I blame you."

They came out on the other side of the park to find another row of buildings facing them across a wide area which served as a road. It was sprinkled with enough trees to provide places for people to sit in the shade in summer.

"It gives the impression of the town being built in the middle of a forest," Will said.

"Every few years, when the leaves are deep and the snow stays under the trees for weeks, we have people wanting to cut them down. But then we remember how cool and delightful this is during the summer, and we decide we can put up with the snow and leaves a little longer."

They entered the drugstore and walked to one of the four wooden tables worn smooth with age and use. Six kerosene lamps make the interior bright and cheerful. A potbellied stove, glowing red, made it warm and cozy. On each side, rows of neatly shelved patent medicines rose to the ceiling. Pilfer-proof glass showcases contained jewelry, perfume, and enticing nicknacks.

"We're lucky it's Christmas and everybody has a house full of food to eat up. You can't find a seat here the rest of the year."

They sat down. A young girl in a starched white apron set three bowls of steaming potato soup down before them. Pots of hot coffee and tea followed.

"Where's the menu?" Will asked.

"There is no menu," Nan told him. "Whatever Etta Mae cooks is what you get."

"What a darling little girl."

The booming voice caused Will to swallow his steaming soup too fast. He looked up through watering eyes to see a tall blond woman towering over them. "Is this your daughter?" she asked Will. "But of course she is," Etta Mae answered herself. "Nan keeps refusing all the fine young men so she doesn't have one of her own. I have something special for you, sugar, when you're done with your dinner. This could be your little girl if you weren't so picky," Etta Mae said, turning to Nan. "You tell her, Mister. It's not good for a woman to hide herself away on that farm."

Nan nearly choked. "Etta Mae! Mr. Atkins doesn't want to hear your opinions on what's good for me. And I've heard them too often already."

"Everybody agrees with me."

"I'm sure they do, but it would be more to the point if you would tell us what we're going to eat."

Leigh Greenwood

But Etta Mae hadn't said anything Will hadn't already been thinking. Nan would make a perfect mother for Clara. Already the child adored her, followed her around, quoted everything she said. She seemed to have a natural feeling for what to do and say to make Clara feel happy and secure. More than he did.

He knew Clara loved him, but sometimes he didn't know what to do for her. He became impatient.

But he couldn't think of Nan as Clara's mother without also thinking of Nan as his wife. That thought shocked him. She wouldn't fit into his life. Besides, he had never considered marrying again. He never expected to find a woman he could love after Louise. But Nan had shaken that assumption right down to the foundation.

Sitting across from her right now, nothing seemed more natural.

"Why are you taking so long over your prayers?" Will asked his daughter. The fires had been allowed to go out for the night, and the house was getting cold.

"Jake said it was going to snow," Clara told him as she climbed in bed and let him pull the covers over her. "I wanted to remind God so he wouldn't forget."

"Why do you want snow so much?"

"Then we won't have to leave Nan."

It was some time before Will could get to sleep. He was haunted by the suspicion that in holding on to his attachment to Louise and his commitment to the future they had wanted, he had built a living tomb for himself, had locked himself in a past that was dry and empty.

He couldn't shake the conviction that life and love was here, now, in the valley, with Nan.

Chapter Four

As he got dressed, Will watched the snow come down so thick outside his bedroom window that he could hardly see the well less than thirty feet away. He couldn't see the barn or the smokehouse at all. He hadn't seen it snow like this since he was a boy. If it kept up, he wouldn't be able to leave today. If it snowed like this all night, the train wouldn't make it to Beaker's Bend inside a week.

He wasn't certain whether he was glad or frustrated. If he had left a day ago, he would have had regrets but no confusion. Now he didn't know what he felt, and he didn't know what he wanted to do about it. The snowstorm was going to force him to come up with some answers.

"Jake has already been to town this morning," Nan told Will when he entered the kitchen. "The passes to the north are closed. No trains in or out." She finished setting the table and turned to check the coffee.

"Does that mean we can stay here?" Clara asked. She had fallen into the habit of getting up with Nan. She was seated at the table, politely waiting for Gertie to finish cooking breakfast.

"Yes," Will said, giving his daughter a smile.

"Yippee!" Clara squealed. "Can we stay until Christmas?"

"I think you'll have to," Nan said.

Clara jumped up, ran over to Nan, grabbed her around the waist, and hugged her so hard that Nan grunted. Then she hugged her father. After that she hugged Gertie, which startled Gertie so much, she nearly spilled grits from the pot she was stirring.

"Sit down before you overturn something," her father said.

"Let's all sit down," Nan said. She didn't feel capable of standing much longer. The genuine warmth of Clara's hug had been a delightful surprise. But it was the look in her father's eye that made her feel weak in the knees.

She had been aware that since their lunch yesterday, he looked at her in a different manner. There was a new energy about him. Nan could almost feel it, as though something connected the two of them so that everything he felt touched her in some way.

Her skin burned. Her nerves seemed to be on end. The tension in the house had begun to escalate; she expected him to do or say something soul-shattering at any minute.

She was in love with Will Atkins, a man she knew virtually nothing about. Further, she didn't approve of what she did know.

How could she be in love with a man who would give away his child? She must be losing her mind. But it wasn't her alone. She could see something new in his eyes, hear it in his voice, feel it in his presence.

He felt it too.

Gertie broke in on her thoughts. "I guess you'll have time to do your baking after all. With all this snow on the ground, you wouldn't be able to do much else."

"Yes," Nan said, reining in her galloping imagination. "Set out the butter so it can get soft."

"May I help?" Clara asked.

"Certainly."

"Are you trying to leave me out again?" Will asked.

"Can Daddy help make cookies?"

"Sure," Nan said, smiling, "if he thinks he can stand woman's work."

"It's got to be better than chopping wood, which is what I suspect Jake will have me doing if I don't luck into something easier."

But there wasn't enough to do for two extra people.

"The work would go twice as fast for half as many hands," Gertie muttered when she stumbled over Will for the dozenth time.

"But it wouldn't be half as much fun," Nan said.

"I got my own work to do," Gertie replied,

wiping her hands. "I'll be back later." With that, she put on her coat and went out the back door.

"She does the Christmas cooking for her sister," Nan explained to Will. "She's never been very well, and she has seven children."

"That might be why she's never been very well," Will replied.

They soon forgot about Gertie and her family. Clara broke the eggs into a bowl, and Will beat them. Nan blended the sugar and butter together, then let Will beat in the eggs as Clara spooned them into the bowl. Will added the flour; Nan mixed it in.

Nan laughed. "You've got flour all over you."

Will looked down at the white dusting on his navy blue vest. "So I have."

"Here, let me put an apron on you." Nan took a fresh apron out of a drawer. When Will bent down so she could loop it over his head, Nan almost froze. He was so close. His eyes. His lips. Her gaze locked on his mouth. She had never looked at him so closely before. His lips were full and firm, his chin slightly cleft, his nose chiseled and slightly rounded. Her gaze rose to his eyes. Deep brown. Wide and questioning.

Forcing herself to break eye contact, Nan looped the apron over his head and stepped behind him to tie the strings. When she reached around to take hold of the strings, Clara started to giggle.

"You're hugging Daddy."

Nan was glad Will couldn't see the heat color her cheeks. She didn't know whether she imagined it, but he seemed to stiffen. Nan tied the apron quickly, picked up her spoon, and gripped the bowl.

She felt safe now, from herself and from Will.

"I'd hate for you to ruin your clothes," she said, choosing to ignore Clara's remark and to avoid looking into Will's eyes.

But the easy atmosphere was gone. As Will stood next to her, adding the flour a little at a time, she was intensely aware of his presence. She was relieved when he moved back to help Clara with the next batch of eggs. Nan took her time rolling out the dough. By the time she had finished, she felt more in control of her voice and body.

"Will, you can cut out the cookies. Clara, you decorate them. You can put a pecan half on each one, or a piece of red candy."

"I want more colors."

Nan set out everything she had. "There, do it any way you like."

Quiet settled over the kitchen. Will cut out the cookies and arranged them on cookie sheets, and Clara decorated them in a manner all her own. Nan added her own flour this time.

"Nobody will believe you made these," Will said, shaking his head over his daughter's fanciful decorations.

"It doesn't matter. If nobody wants them, I'll give them to Clara to take with her."

The thought of Clara and her father leaving was becoming more and more painful. In four days they had become a necessary part of Nan's life. She couldn't imagine having to face a day without them. Her mind told her that their presence was only temporary, that Will had to return to his business, that she would fall back into her old routine in just a few days.

But her heart would have none of it. The empty space deep inside her had been filled by this pair. She felt as close to them as to her brother.

Nan mixed the new batch of dough with more than her usual vigor. She had fallen in love with a man she expected to walk out of her life just as suddenly as he had walked into it. He might look at her as if she were his favorite cookie, but he had said nothing to indicate that his feelings were stronger than friendship.

She placed the dough on a marble-topped table and began to roll it out with a rolling pin.

This was silly. If Will's work was so important that he didn't have time for his daughter, he certainly wouldn't have time for a wife. Nan wasn't willing to give up one kind of loneliness for another. A life spent waiting for the man she loved to come home, knowing he could stay only a short time, would be worse than loneliness. It would be torture.

What if he had a normal job? Would she go with him wherever he went?

She didn't know. She had lived her whole life in Beaker's Bend. She knew the people. She had a place in the community. She wouldn't know what to do in a city. Any city. Even the thought of moving to Charlottesville or Richmond scared her.

Besides, she didn't know anything about being a mother to a five-year-old girl, and she wanted more children. She didn't think Will would want more, not when he didn't have time for the one he had.

"If you roll that dough any thinner, you'll be able to see through it," Will said.

His closeness shocked her. She had been so lost in thought that she hadn't seen him move to her side. Close enough for their elbows to brush. Close enough for her to smell his shaving lotion. Close enough for her hands to shake. She gripped the rolling pin to steady them.

"I guess I was daydreaming," Nan said. She rolled up the dough and started again. "Making cookies isn't very taxing," she said, petrified that he would ask what she'd been daydreaming about. "I've fallen into the habit of thinking over all sorts of plans."

With quick, practiced moves, she rolled the dough to the proper thickness, handed it to Will, and quickly started on another batch. She concentrated fiercely on the dough. She could feel Will looking at her. She didn't look up.

Suddenly Nan realized that the smells of baked cookies and vanilla flavoring were filling the kitchen. Smothering an exclamation of disgust, she dropped her rolling pin and grabbed a cloth. A blast of heat hit her in the face when she opened the oven.

"Watch out, they're hot!" she warned as she took the first tray of cookies from the oven. They were brown around the edges, but they hadn't burned. She felt like an idiot.

"They're all ruined," Clara exclaimed when she saw that the tiny pieces of candy she had used for decorations had melted and run together.

"They taste just as good," Nan reassured her, relieved to have something to divert attention from her lapse.

"Can I have one now?"

"In a minute. They're still too hot."

Clara went back to decorating more cookies, but Nan noticed that the child watched longingly each time she took out a tray. Her father watched with equal intensity.

"Now can I have one?" Clara asked when she finished her tray of cookies.

"Why don't you wait until we finish decorating all of them," Will said. "Then we can all have some together."

Clara looked a little disappointed, but Nan could tell she liked the idea of everyone eating cookies together. Poor child, she probably had to enjoy most of her treats alone. Nan knew from long experience that food tasted better when you had someone to share it with.

"Okay, these are the last cookies," Nan said as she closed the oven. Gertie came in the back door just as Nan handed Clara a plate of shortbreads. "Here, take these into the gathering room. Your father can put some more wood on the fire. Gertie will fix our lunch. I'll bring in the cups and hot chocolate."

"We're going to have hot chocolate?" Clara exclaimed.

"Yes, and I'm going to put a big piece of marsh-mallow in each one."

Clara slipped off her chair, grabbed the plate of

cookies, and hurried to the gathering room.

"I don't know how you always manage to think of just the right thing," Will said.

"It's not hard. I just remember what I liked when I was a little girl."

"You must have been a very happy child."

"I was. Now you'd better go fix the fire. It's bound to be down to embers by now."

When Nan entered the gathering room, Will met her at the doorway and gave her a kiss.

"W-what—" Nan stammered, shocked. She could feel the heat rush to her face. All her thoughts from the kitchen came flooding back.

Clara giggled. "Daddy moved the mistletoe," she said, pointing to a sprig tacked over the doorway. "He said he could kiss a lady if she stood under the mistletoe."

"That's true," Nan said, too surprised to move.

"That was for letting Clara help with the cookies," Will said.

Nan hardly knew what demon prompted her to add, "I let you help as well."

"So you did." Will took her by the arms and kissed her again, rather more enthusiastically than before.

"Daddy's kissing Nan," Clara informed Gertie when she walked into the room.

"So I see," Gertie said. She eyed the pair critically. Nan had stepped back, confused at being caught. Will looked as though the results were surprising, pleasant but surprising.

"Does your father kiss a lot of females?"

"Gertie!" Nan exclaimed, scandalized.

"Daddy only kisses me," Clara declared.

Gertie regarded the pair once more. "Good." With that she turned and left the room.

Nan gasped, then stared at Will. Her mind was a blizzard of sensations; her body was too weak to take responsible action. She was petrified that he might take offense at Gertie's remark, but she thought she saw imps of amusement in his eyes. When his lips curved in a smile, she knew it.

They burst out laughing simultaneously.

"I apologize for Gertie. I don't know what's gotten into her."

"She's just protecting you. I would, too, if I were in her place."

Nan decided she'd better put the cups down before she dropped them. She had spent the better part of the last twenty-four hours convincing herself Will had no serious interest in her. His kisses had shattered that conviction. She had never been kissed like that by any man. More importantly, no kisses had ever had such an earth-shattering effect on her.

"Let's eat," Clara said.

"I'll pour the hot chocolate," Nan said, pulling herself together.

"I'll pass the cookies," Clara said. "Daddy might eat too many."

"He does like shortbreads," Nan said. "Maybe I'd better give you the recipe so you can make them when you go back home."

"I don't want to go back home," Clara announced. "I want to stay here with you."

"You have to go with your father."

"I want Daddy to stay too."

"I have to work," Will said. "I need to make money to buy clothes and food and a house to live in."

"Nan has a house and lots of food. I don't need any more clothes. Let me stay with her. I don't want to stay with Grandmama and Grandpa."

Nan felt sorry for Will. It was difficult enough to have to give up his daughter, even if it wouldn't be for very long. But it must be even harder when Clara couldn't understand the reasons why he felt he had no other choice.

"It's very sweet of you to want to stay with me," Nan said, "but I'm sure you'll love your grandparents."

"Maybe they won't like me. They don't like Daddy."

Clara was threatening to work herself up to a real cry.

Nan took her in her arms and held her close. "You don't have to go anywhere right now. If the snow keeps coming down, you'll be here for days and days. Now why don't you go see if Gertie has lunch ready. It'll soon be time for your nap. You've had a very busy morning, and I have lots of things planned for later."

"Thank you," Will said to Nan when Clara went into the kitchen. "I don't know what to do when she gets upset."

"She's just frightened. It's hard for a child to face something new, especially when she has to face it alone."

"I know, but it's better that she be left with her

grandparents than somebody who has no reason to love her."

"Are you sure her grandparents will?"

"Yes. They don't like me, but they'll love Clara because she's Louise's child."

"Why didn't you give her up when your wife died?"

"I kept hoping I'd figure out something else, that I wouldn't have to do it."

"Why did you give up?"

"Mrs. Bartholomew died. She was the second woman to keep Clara. I could see the list getting longer and longer. As Clara gets older, she's going to need somebody she can count on. If it can't be me, it ought to be her grandparents."

For a moment Nan could see depths of pain she had only suspected. Her heart went out to him.

"Isn't there anything else you can do?"

"Not unless you're willing to take her. I've racked my brain for two years, and there's no other way."

Nan had never considered taking Clara. The idea was unexpected, but she knew right away that was exactly what she wanted to do. "I'll be happy to take her."

Will stared at Nan. "I was just joking. I never meant to—"

A crash riveted their attention to the doorway. Clara threw herself at her father, a plate of sandwiches broken on the floor.

"Please, Daddy, can I stay with Nan? I don't want to go to grandmama. I want to stay here. Please, can I?"

79

Will looked harassed. Nan knew men never liked to have their plans questioned or overset.

"We can't impose on Nan like that."

"But she wants me to stay. I heard her say it."

"It's wonderful you like Nan so much, but your grandparents are expecting you," Will said. "Now you have to clean up the mess you made and apologize to Nan for throwing away your lunch."

"I didn't mean to," Clara said, barely managing to keep from bursting into tears.

"Don't worry about it," Nan said. "I'll clean up while your father takes you up for your nap. If it's stopped snowing when you get up, we'll go outside and build a snowman."

Will didn't go back downstairs after he put Clara to bed. For a long while he simply sat on the bed watching his daughter sleep. He was struck by her innocence and how much he loved her. He had never been gifted with words, but he had always taken his obligations to her very seriously. He didn't know how to show it except by working hard to provide for her future. That had been Louise's dream as well. But now he wasn't sure it was the best thing for Clara after all.

Nan had upset all his calculations.

Maybe Clara wouldn't care about money as long as she could go to sleep holding his hand every night. Maybe it was more important to her that he be around to sit in front of a fire and eat cookies. He thought of the lonely hotel rooms, the long trips, the weeks he didn't see her. He wondered if it was worth it. Right now it didn't feel as if it was. In all the times he had put her to bed, he'd never just sat, holding her hand, thinking back on all the little things they had done together during the day. It wasn't until he was marooned on a farm in the middle of the Shenandoah Valley that he found out what he was missing.

And all because of Nan Carson, a woman who represented everything he had walked away from.

She would be perfect for Clara. They already loved each other as mother and daughter. He doubted Louise's parents could love her as much. Besides, they were too old to have the care of a five-year-old. They had other grandchildren with prior claims on their affections, and they still cherished a lingering anger against him for taking Louise away.

If they had only known. Louise had been adamant about leaving the mountains. She had been insistent that they build a business to insulate them against the poverty of her childhood. She had loved her daughter, but she had also resented the time the child took away from her work.

Nan found a way to include Clara in everything she did. She included both of them. They had gotten a lot done in the last three days. Clara had helped dust and straighten the house. They had helped clean up after meals. He had even filled up the woodboxes and helped Jake with the milking. It hadn't been a chore. It had been something they had done together.

Will realized that it was something he had done because he wanted to be with Nan, to be a part of whatever she did. He wanted to be a part of it so much, he wouldn't mind staying here for the rest of his life.

The thought quite literally caused Will to turn stiff with shock. He couldn't have fallen in love with Nan! Not in just three days!

No, he was in love with a dream, with this fairy-tale Christmas, with the seductive quality of a woman at once kind and generous, a woman who attracted him both physically and spiritually. The attraction was nearly irresistible—desire deepened by liking and caring—but it wasn't the kind of feeling to build a marriage on. Nan wasn't like Louise. She wouldn't fit into his world.

What a tangle.

He got up and walked over to the window. The snow was still coming down so heavily that it was hard to see the road to town. The farm looked beautiful, all white and silent. The house was warm and comforting. His new life in the city was wonderfully exciting, but how could he have failed to see the charm of the life he and Louise had left without a backward glance?

It had taken Nan to show him he had thrown away something very precious. He valued his new life, but now he knew it had come at a great price.

Nan wasn't in the gathering room when he came down, but Gertie was. "I want to speak to you a minute," she said to Will.

"Do you think you should?" Jake asked.

Will thought he looked uncomfortable.

"With her parents dead and her brother more concerned with his own affairs than his sister, somebody's got to look after Nan."

"Is something wrong?" Will asked.

"That's what I'm about to ask you," Gertie countered.

Will looked blank.

"Nan just told me you might let Clara stay here."

"I mentioned it without thinking."

"Well, you'd better think about it right now. Nan has her heart set on keeping that child. She's upstairs right now going through the attic looking for something she can give her for Christmas."

"We haven't even talked about it," Will protested.

"It's too late for talking. You take that child away now and you'll break her heart."

"You'll break both their hearts," Jake added.

"She can't know what it's like to have a child around all the time. It's not the same as for a few days."

"I know that, and you know that, but Nan can only see the family she never had. She wouldn't care if that child were a little demon instead of the little angel she is." Gertie squared her shoulders and planted her hands on her hips. "Now I'd like to know what you mean to do."

"What do you mean?"

Gertie snorted in contempt. "She's in love with you, you daft man, and I want to know what you mean to do about it."

Chapter Five

Will was speechless, but whether more at Gertie's news or his reaction, he couldn't say. He felt as if the pins had been knocked out from under him. He couldn't believe Nan was in love with him. He hadn't tried to make her fall in love with him, and he didn't want the responsibility for her unhappiness when she discovered that he didn't love her.

He couldn't let Clara stay now. It would mean they would have to be in constant communication with each other. He liked Nan far too much to endure that.

"I don't mean to do anything about it," Will answered finally. "I don't see that I can."

"You made her fall in love with you," Gertie said, incensed. "You can't have yourself carried in here when you need help and then waltz out again when you don't."

"I had no hand in my being brought here. I would have left that first morning if I had even suspected my being here would hurt Miss Carson."

"You can stop calling her *Miss Carson*," Gertie snapped. "It's not like you haven't been calling her Nan for days, coiling yourself around her like some weasel-eyed varmint. And it's too late to run away. The damage has already been done."

"What do you suggest I do?"

"Marry her."

"Marry her!" Will exclaimed. Gertie had to be crazy. Grown men didn't go around marrying women they'd known less than a week.

"You don't have to look like the idea is such a shock."

"I haven't thought of marrying anyone since my wife died."

"That was nearly five years ago. It's about time you thought about giving that precious little girl a mother, and you won't find a better one than Nan."

"Nan won't thank you for pushing her off on him like this," Jake said.

"She won't know if you don't tell her," Gertie shot back. "Besides, if I don't speak for her, who will? She won't say anything for herself. After Harve Adams left for Richmond, she gave up thinking any man would want her."

"That's crazy," Will said. "There ought to be dozens of men lining up to ask for her hand."

"There would be if she was to pay heed to every Tom, Dick, or Joe who hankered after her farm. But Nan wants a husband who will love her and give her lots of children. She doesn't deserve anything less."

"I agree with you," Will said. "But I can't marry her just because she thinks she's in love with me."

"She doesn't know it yet," Gertie stated, "but I do."

"It's impossible. I have to go back to Boston. She would never leave this valley."

"She would for the right man."

"But the right man wouldn't take her away from it."

"Maybe so."

"I'm sorry. I've never met a woman I admire more than Nan, but I don't love her."

"She wouldn't have to know."

"She'd know from the beginning. Besides, I like her too much to do that." Will looked out the window, but nothing had changed. If anything, it was snowing more heavily now than before.

"I doubt you could get to town in this blizzard," Jake said.

"Maybe Mr. Crider will reopen the inn."

"If he got caught in that hollow, he won't be back for a couple of weeks. Maybe more."

Will felt concerned. He also felt guilty. The best thing for Nan would be for him to take his daughter and leave immediately. The best thing for Clara would be to let Nan keep Clara.

And what about himself? What was best for him?

He didn't know. As late as yesterday, he would

have answered a quick return to Boston. But Nan and the life here in her mountain valley had cast its spell over him. Maybe he had never lost his love for the mountains; maybe he had just needed a chance to do something else for a while, a chance to see what else he could become.

Now he knew. He had proved himself. He could afford the luxury of asking himself what he really wanted.

Nan.

The single word exploded on his mind. Maybe he didn't fully love her, but he wanted her as much as he had ever wanted any woman.

But not the same way she wanted him.

"Well?" Gertie prompted.

"I don't know," Will said, talking more to himself than to Gertie. "I just don't know."

He turned and left the kitchen.

"He don't seem to know his own mind," Jake said.

"Good," Gertie said, a slow smile beginning to spread over her lined face. "That's the best sign I've seen so far."

Will found Nan in the attic surrounded by piles of wrapping paper.

"What on earth are you doing?"

"Looking for a Christmas present for Clara. It was foolish of me not to have bought something when I was in town."

It was even more foolish of him not to have bought something. True, he hadn't known a blizzard was going to snow him in, but he did know he was heading toward his in-laws empty-handed. He had been counting on being able to complete his shopping in Lexington.

Even worse, he should have thought to buy Nan something. He would never be able to repay her for what she had done for him and Clara, but it was important that he try. Now she was worried about giving his daughter a present, with no thought for herself.

"You don't have to give her anything. You've given both of us far too much already."

"None of that will count on Christmas morning. You ought to know that."

He should, but he hadn't. Had he forgotten what it was like to be a child?

"I'll give her the dollhouse," Nan said, half to herself, not listening to him. "That and my princess doll."

"But those are your things."

"I know," Nan said, smiling as she turned toward him, "but I don't play with them anymore."

"I know that," Will said with an answering smile, "but you can't be giving away parts of your past."

"By the time you've finished building your business and Clara goes back to live with you, she'll be too big to want to take any of this with her." Nan turned back to her trunks. "I know I had more furniture than this."

Will took Nan by the arms and pulled her to her feet. "Listen to me. Maybe having Clara stay with you isn't a good idea after all. Maybe I ought to see if I can hire somebody's wagon to take us out of the valley."

"You couldn't get anywhere with a wagon. Why would you want to try?"

"I think you and Clara are becoming too attached to each other. Maybe it's better if—"

"Surely you're not afraid she'll come to love me more than you? She adores you. Besides, I'd make sure she never forgot you for so much as a minute."

Her gaze was open, genuine.

"I know you would. You'd be wonderful for her, but I'm not sure she'd be so wonderful for you."

"Of course she would. I haven't had so much fun in years. I never thought I'd look into these trunks again, but I've been up here for hours. I can hardly wait to go through the rest. I can't believe I've forgotten so much."

Nan tried to turn back to her trunks, but Will wouldn't release her.

"I can't let you do this. It's not right. It's too much."

"But I want to."

"You've got to stop baking cookies and decorating trees and racking your brain for things to give her."

"We couldn't sit here for days doing nothing."

"Don't you see you're making it hard for me to take her away?"

Nan hadn't realized until now just how much she had come to depend on Clara's staying with her. The fear of losing Clara was as sharp as physical pain.

"I don't want you to go," she said.

"I've got to. We've both got to."

"Why?"

"Because if we stay much longer, we may not want to leave."

He knew. Somehow, he knew she loved him. She was glad. She would never have been able to tell him.

Nan lowered her eyes. "Would that be so terrible?"

"It would for you."

"Why?"

"Because you deserve so many things a man like me can never give you. You deserve a husband who loves your valley as much as you do, who wants a house full of children, who dreams of Christmas by the fireplace with candles in the windows and cookies and hot chocolate."

She looked straight at him, her gaze penetrating to his heart.

"Maybe I could learn to dream of something else."

"You would try, but it would take the heart out of you."

Her eyes clouded with hurt. "How do you know?"

"I know." Will leaned over and kissed her lightly. Then he took her in his arms and kissed her.

"There's no mistletoe up here," Nan said when she managed to catch her breath.

"I don't need mistletoe to want to kiss you. I'm terribly thankful for all you've done for Clara and me, and for all you want to do."

"Is that all?" She was looking at him in that way again.

"It's all there can be for us."

Nan had known that. She had told herself over and over again, but she had stubbornly continued to hope. Now he had told her, and she still didn't believe it.

I suppose you won't believe it until he walks out the door and takes his daughter with him.

Maybe not even then. A kind of magic entwined them. Will felt it too. His kiss told her so. Oh, he didn't know it, not consciously, but it was stirring deep inside him. Otherwise he wouldn't be worried about her. He wouldn't have thought about the kind of husband she deserved. He wouldn't have thought about her marrying at all.

"I still think you should leave Clara here," Nan said. She had herself in hand now, her protective barriers in place once more. "I'll take her to visit her grandparents. I think she ought to get to know them. You go back to your work. Make all the money you want. When you're through, I'll bring Clara to you. I'll send her with Gertie if you'd rather."

"That woman would cut my throat."

Nan smiled. "No, she likes you. She didn't at first, but she does now. She said you'd make some woman a fine husband if you could just stand still long enough."

"I thought I'd been doing little else since I got here."

"You've been restless ever since you found you couldn't move into the inn. You can't go anywhere

91

until after the storm is over, so go back downstairs while I finish looking through the rest of these boxes. Christmas Eve will be here before you know it."

She needed time to go through the boxes before Clara got up from her nap, but she also needed time to think. She had to decide what she was willing to give up for Will. She wanted to be ready when he asked.

Will stared at the snowy landscape. It represented everything he had worked so hard to avoid, everything he and Louise had fled. Yet now it called to him with an urgency he would not have believed possible as little as two days ago. He knew the strength of the call lay not in the land, the people, or the life. It was Nan. He had known that the moment he kissed her.

But had he gotten over Louise's death?

He turned away from the frosted window and paced the room. He didn't know. He hadn't wanted to see other women. He hadn't even thought of remarrying. Yet the idea planted in his mind by Gertie would not go away. Its hold seemed to grow stronger as the minutes passed, but he couldn't blame it on Gertie. She might have been the first to put the thought into words, but the fertile ground was of his providing. His attraction to Nan was more than thankfulness for her kindness or simple appreciation of an attractive woman. He was strongly attracted to her as a woman whose company he enjoyed, whom he admired, whose nearness aroused feelings in him that had lain dormant for years.

He had begun to think of her as a part of his day, as part of the pattern of his existence. It didn't matter whether he left Clara with Nan or with her grandparents. He couldn't just go back to Boston and forget Nan.

Louise is dead. Nan is alive.

He stopped and stared out the window again. The scene was more beautiful than a painting. Limbs of spruce, pine, and magnolia trees bent low under the weight of snow piled high on their branches. A white ribbon of snow topped miles of split rail fences, limbs of oaks and maples, like icing on a cake. It covered the entire earth, the blacks, browns, and greens, with a pristine mantel of white. The scene was softened by the heavy fall of snow as it floated to earth in large, fluffy flakes.

He wished he could leave now. Every moment spent with Nan in this comfortable house, in this idyllic setting, sapped his strength and reduced his resolution.

Only clinging to a dead past will make you go back to Boston. Nan loves Clara. Clara loves Nan.

You love Nan.

He turned away. Everything about these last few days was so unreal, so dreamlike, it distorted his sense of reality. It made him think that somehow he could find a way to have Nan, this idyllic valley, his business, *and* his daughter. His mind told him it wasn't possible. His heart convinced him not to give up hope.

*   *   *

The rest of the day was somewhat awkward. Jake and Gertie didn't come up to the house for dinner, so the three of them ate in the kitchen.

"Let's have snow cream for dessert," Nan suggested.

"What's that?" Clara asked.

"You live in Boston and you don't know what snow cream is?"

"No."

"Shame on you," Nan said to Will as she folded her napkin and got to her feet. "You get the snow. I'll prepare the mix."

Nan beat two eggs into some heavy cream. Then she added a dash of vanilla flavoring. "Do you like apples?" she asked Clara. The child nodded. "Then we shall have apple ice cream. We'll add cider. Don't tell your father, but I'm going to add a good bit of apple brandy, too."

The back door opened. A blast of biting cold air invaded the warm kitchen, followed by Will. Clara burst out laughing.

"Daddy, you look like a snowman."

"A few more minutes out there and I'd have been an ice man," Will said, shaking the snow from his clothes.

"Take him into the gathering room and make sure he gets warm," Nan said to Clara. "I'll be in with the ice cream in just a minute."

When Nan entered the room, Clara and her father were seated on the rug before the fire. Clara leaned against her father, his arm around her, both of them staring into the flames.

Nan's heart filled to overflowing. She almost hated to interrupt them. She wondered how many times they had been able to enjoy such a moment together. If Will could only realize that moments such as this, days such as they had enjoyed, were far more important to Clara than a large inheritance.

But maybe it was important to Will. Maybe his feeling of self-worth depended on his success.

She remembered that her father had never been so happy as when he had a good year with the farm or when one of his business ventures turned out particularly well. The same had been true of her mother. She seemed to equate her self-worth with her success with the house or the community.

They were all guilty of using senseless measures of self-evaluation. Probably the whole world worked that way, but she wasn't going to do it any longer. She was worthy of love because she had so much love to give, and Nan was going to start acting like it.

"Have you ever considered living somewhere other than this valley?" Will asked.

Clara had been put to bed, and they were seated in chairs drawn up to the fire. Nan had blown out all the lights except a night lamp on a table across the room. The firelight cast dancing shadows along the walls and caused Will's expression to change constantly.

"Yes."

"Where?"

"The question of a particular place never came up."

Nan knew what he was asking, but she didn't know how to answer. She had always wanted to stay in the valley, but she had also assumed she would go with her husband.

Only now she wasn't sure she could ever be completely happy away from the people and the places she had grown to love. She knew that no matter where they lived, she couldn't be happy with Will if he remained so deeply absorbed in his business.

"Would you still consider it?"

"I couldn't say until I was asked."

"Well suppose some man like me wanted you to marry him and move to Boston."

She wasn't going to let him hide behind anonymous pronouns. If he wanted to find out how she felt, he was going to have to ask her point-blank.

"I'm not likely to meet a man like you in the valley. The farthest anyone here would be likely to move would be Richmond."

"Well suppose someone did."

"I can't answer about *someone*."

Will stared into the fire. The shadows cast by the firelight danced across his face like so many devils.

"Suppose *I* asked you to marry me and move to Boston. Would you consider it?"

"Yes."

"Well?"

"Well what?"

"What would you decide?"

"It would depend on whether you loved me."

"Of course I would love you."

She noticed the tense. She wondered if he had. "You haven't said it."

"I didn't mean that... I wasn't talking about... This is insane!" he muttered as he got to his feet. He paced before the fire, his fingers digging in his hair. Suddenly he turned to face Nan. "I'm not acting like myself. Maybe it's the snow or the season. Maybe I'm still delirious. Maybe I've been seduced by three of the most wonderful days in my life. But I'm in love with you, and I want to marry you."

Nan had only received one proposal, and though it had come with conditions, it hadn't been anything like this. She wasn't about to marry a man who thought he had to be delirious to love her.

Nan stood up. "Then I suggest you go to bed. Maybe the fever or delusion will pass."

Will virtually jumped in front of her.

"I didn't mean it like that. It's just that I don't know how I could have fallen in love with you so fast. I hardly know you."

"Sorry, but I don't feel like providing you with a character study."

"I'm doing this all wrong."

"Yes, you are."

"You're a lovely, kind, wonderful woman and I'm making you feel like I don't like being in love with you."

"Do you?"

"I hardly know. I hadn't even thought about it until Gertie said I ought—"

"Gertie! What did she say?"

He looked like a man who had stepped into a trap and only realized it the split second he put his foot down.

"She said it was going to be mighty quiet around here after Clara left."

Nan knew Gertie hadn't said any such thing, but there'd be plenty of time later to find out exactly what she had said.

"That has nothing to do with marrying you."

"I wouldn't leave her here if you didn't want to marry me. Knowing she would be with you all the time and I couldn't be would drive me crazy."

He seemed to have a particularly strong association between loving her and insanity. Nan decided that didn't bode well for a stable marriage.

"If I were to consider marrying you, I'd have to know I was going to be more important than your business. You can't send me to my grandparents when you don't have time for me."

"That's a cruel thing to say."

"Sending Clara away is cruel."

"I don't have any choice."

"Yes, you do. Sending Clara away is a consequence of other choices."

"You wouldn't marry a man who could do that?"

"No."

"Even if you loved him?"

"Not even then."

"But you do love him, don't you?"

"I . . . Don't you think . . ."

"Answer me. It's all I have left."

Without warning, Will took her in his arms and kissed her passionately. "Tell me, please."

"I love you," Nan whispered. "I think I always will."

Chapter Six

Nan slept late the next morning. She was shocked to find when she looked at the clock that it was close to eleven.

She threw back the bedcovers, and her bare feet hit the ice-cold floor. Stifling a strong desire to climb back into the warmth of her bed, Nan dressed quickly. She didn't understand how she could have slept so late, not even after lying awake half the night thinking about what Will had said.

Yes, she loved him, enough to follow him anywhere. She'd probably never love anyone else. But as long as his business or his success—she didn't know which—was more important than anything else, she couldn't marry him. She had thought about it until dawn, but the answer always came out the same.

She wanted a husband and children and a home

of her own. She would work with her husband, she would support him in every way she could, but she and their family had to be the most important thing in his life. On that there could be no compromise.

But reaching that decision made Nan feel even more miserable than before. She looked around. She had spent her girlhood in this room. She had hoped and dreamed and built her castles in the air here. Now it seemed they were all going to fall down in the same place.

Well there was no use getting maudlin over it. She'd had two chances. She had chosen not to take either of them. She couldn't blame anybody but herself. It was foolish to pine over decisions she wouldn't change if she had the opportunity.

Harve hadn't been the right man for her, and she had known that. She wouldn't have married him even if her mother hadn't been too sick for her to leave.

Will wasn't the right man, either, not even though she loved him so much she thought her heart would break.

Nan washed her face with cold water, then hurried downstairs. Clara sat in the gathering room rearranging her village for at least the sixth time.

"Where's Will?" Nan asked Gertie as she accepted a cup of coffee.

"He saddled a horse and rode off to the village the minute the snow slacked off," Jake said.

The snow had stopped completely, and the sun glistened with blinding intensity on the pure white of the virgin snow.

101

"Did he say why?"

"No, just that he had business to attend to."

The faint hope that remained splintered and shattered. If his business was important enough to draw him out in all this snow, he'd never change. It would be better for her if he left as soon as possible.

Nan put down her coffee and marched into the gathering room. "Have you ever built a snowman?" she asked Clara.

"What's a snowman?"

"Get your coat. I'll show you."

"I can hardly see," Clara complained after she had been bundled into a heavy coat, gloves, a scarf, and boots.

"It's very cold outside," said Nan, who was just as thoroughly covered. "And it takes a long time to build a good snowman. Now let me see, we need a hat and scarf and coal for the buttons and eyes. I wonder if Gertie has any carrots. Of course we could use a parsnip."

"What do you need all that for?"

"I'll show you," Nan said, infusing her voice with a gaiety she didn't feel. "We're going to build the biggest snowman in Beaker's Bend."

Clara didn't seem to be having much fun at first. The snow was so deep, she had trouble walking even when she followed in Nan's footsteps. It was also bitterly cold. But by the time Nan had rolled the first ball about a foot thick, Clara caught the spirit. She rolled the ball all over the yard while Nan started on the second. They laughed and shrieked and had so much fun, they got the balls too big. They had to get Jake to lift one on top of the other.

"It's a good thing you didn't make them any bigger," Jake said. "I wouldn't be able to put the hat on his head."

Clara rolled the third ball all by herself. Her nose was bright red and her gloves were covered with snow, but she didn't utter a word of complaint.

"Now we have to make his face," Nan said when Jake balanced the third ball of snow on top. "That's why I brought the coal." Nan chose two big pieces for his eyes and several little pieces for his mouth. "Now you do his nose." Nan handed Clara the parsnip.

"I can't reach it," she said.

Nan lifted her up. Clara jammed the parsnip into the snowman's face with such vigor that his head fell off.

Jake put it back on and shoved a long, narrow stick through the middle to hold it in place.

This time Clara put the nose in place with great care.

"Now," Nan said, "we have to do his buttons. I'll do the top ones and you do those on the bottom."

"People don't have buttons on their bottom," Clara said.

"Snowmen do," Nan insisted.

That was good enough for Clara. She happily placed six pieces of coal on the bottom ball of snow. Nan only had two left for the middle. Nan wrapped the scarf around his neck.

"Now for the hat. Do you think you can reach that high?"

"I can if you hold me."

"It'll have to be Jake. I'm not that tall."

But Will was. Why wasn't he here? What could he be doing in town that was taking so long? He should have helped his daughter roll the balls of snow. He should be holding her up so she could put the hat on the snowman. It was a hunting hat with flaps that folded down. It wasn't an elegant hat, but it was the only kind of hat Nan's father ever wore.

"There, it's all finished," Nan said as she stepped back to admire their work.

Clara looked around. "We messed up the yard."

Nan decided that Mrs. Bartholomew must never have let Clara make a mess when she played. The snowy perfection of the large yard had been seriously marred by the numerous tracks they made rolling the balls, but Nan didn't mind. They had a wonderful snowman, and the trees were still gorgeous.

"I'll race you to the house," Nan said. "I'll bet Gertie has lunch ready."

Clara didn't move. "I wish Daddy was here," she said. "I want to show him our snowman."

Nan wished he were here, too, but she was also angry that he should deny Clara the pleasure of sharing her first snowman with him. She was even more angry that he had never taken the time to build a snowman with his daughter. If she married him, she was going to make some major changes in his life.

But she had already decided she wouldn't marry him. There was no use thinking of it. It would only take the hurt longer to go away.

"He'll be back before long. You can show him then."

"It might melt."

"Not today."

"Are you sure?"

"Positive. Now let's get inside before we turn into snowmen as well."

"I can't be a snowman," Clara said as she struggled through a snowdrift piled up against a buried bush. "I'll be a snow girl."

"And I'll be a snow woman," Nan said. She picked Clara up and carried her to the steps.

"Can we build a snow horse and a snow cow?"

"You'll have to talk to your father about that. I'm not good enough. Anyway, it's too cold to stay out here anymore today."

They warmed their feet and hands in front of the fire, but Will didn't return. They ate hot beef and gravy on thick slices of toasted bread and had hot baked apples spiced with cinnamon and cloves for dessert. Still Will didn't return. Clara went to bed for her nap, and Nan baked six loaves of Christmas bread to take to church that night. No Will. He stayed away so long that the wild thought occurred to Nan that he might have gone back to Boston without telling her. She dismissed it immediately, but she was completely out of patience when he returned barely in time for dinner.

"Where have you been?" she demanded. "Clara's been worried sick about you." Nan didn't let the fact that Clara had only asked once trouble her conscience. The child had probably become so used to her father's absence that she accepted it without thinking.

"I had some business to take care of."

No apology, no nothing. In fact, he looked very pleased with himself. She guessed he looked so happy because he'd been able to get in touch with his office in Boston. He'd probably tied up the telegraph all day.

Nan tried to tell herself that what Will Atkins did didn't concern her in the least, but she failed miserably. She saw him slipping further and further away. No matter what her mind said, her heart had not given up all hope. She might know she was being foolish, but she couldn't help it.

"You'll have to hurry if you're to get dressed before dinner."

"Dressed? What for?"

"We're going to church for the Christmas Eve service."

"Did I know that?"

"You would have if you'd been home today."

Good God! She sounded like a nagging wife, and she wasn't even married to the man. She wouldn't be surprised if he tried to sneak away in the middle of the night.

"I was going to tell you, but I slept too late."

"No problem. I'll be down in a jiffy."

Nan would have held dinner back if it had been possible, but it didn't matter. Will was back in five minutes. At least, living out of a suitcase had taught him to concentrate on the essentials.

* * *

"We have to hurry," Nan said as she got up from the table. "We'll have dessert when we get back."

"How are we going?" Will asked. "I doubt a wagon can get through all those drifts."

"You'll see. Just make sure you bundle up."

When they stepped outside, Jake was waiting with a long-legged white horse harnessed to a sleigh. The harness bells jingled as the horse pranced expectantly.

"A sleigh!" Clara squealed and dashed down the steps. She stumbled in the deep snow, but she got to her feet and climbed into the sleigh before either Nan or her father could reach her.

"Sit between us," Nan advised as she covered Clara with a fur robe. "It's going to be awfully cold."

But Clara was too excited to feel the cold. The bells jingled merrily as the sleigh moved smoothly over the snow. Moonlight reflected off the pristine surface, making the night almost as light as day. They hadn't gone far before Clara bounced up in her seat, pointed, and shouted, "There's another one."

In front of them, a sleigh pulled onto the road from a farm lane.

"You may see more before we reach town."

Clara saw three more, and she waved and called out to each one. They all waved back, laughed, and called to each other. At the church, however, everyone hurried inside out of the cold with no more than a few hurried greetings.

107

Will felt as though he had stepped into a different world.

A small pipe organ played Bach softly in the distance. Candles seated in beds of greenery illuminated each stained glass window. Running cedar had been wound around the end of each pew. Two enormous white candles on the altar and two branches of smaller candles on each side caused the brass and silver to glisten and gleam. Above the altar was a scene of Christ surrounded by children.

As Will followed Nan into the Carson family pew and knelt to offer his prayer, he felt at peace with himself for the first time in a long while.

The service of lessons and carols lasted less than an hour. Will had heard better choirs and seen bigger organs, but this service moved him as others never had. He felt chill bumps all up and down his spine when the children's choir came down the aisle, their youthful voices—some sweet, some hopelessly out of tune—raised in song. Their white smocks and freshly scrubbed faces made them seem like angels.

The young people and the adults followed. Will guessed each family in the community must be represented by at least one member in the choir. He wasn't much of a singer. His deep bass voice always seemed to be an octave below where it should be. But Nan sang with a light, clear voice. Much to his surprise, Clara did as well.

He had never heard his daughter sing. He didn't know until now that her voice was as pure and sweet as any in the choir. His vision became misty, and he reached over to put his arm around her shoulder. They would sing together again. Soon.

Everyone repaired to the social hall for hot drinks and the bounty of the Christmas season. Will had forgotten how much food could appear at a country gathering. He could have eaten dinner all over again. He contented himself with hot, spicy punch and about a half dozen of Nan's shortbreads. Clara did her best to sample every kind of cake and cookie in the room.

By the time they headed for their sleigh, Will was certain he'd been introduced to every person within ten miles of Beaker's Bend. Clara exchanged shouted good-byes with several new friends she met in the social hall.

"Can I go to Peggy's house tomorrow?" she asked her father even before she snuggled under the fur robe.

"Tomorrow's Christmas," Will said. "I doubt that's a very good time."

"Peggy asked me most especially to come."

"I think you'd better discuss it with Nan, but we'll talk about it tomorrow," Will added when Clara turned to Nan ready to ask her right then. "It's a beautiful night," Will said, changing the subject. "It's a shame it's so cold."

It was also a shame Clara wasn't home in bed. He would have liked the opportunity to ride home alone with Nan. He slid his arm along the back of the seat until his fingers reached Nan's shoulder. He felt her stiffen, but she didn't pull away. He gently rubbed her shoulders. Her muscles tightened, then gradually relaxed. He let his hand rest

109

on her shoulder, his thumb moving gently against the nape of her neck.

Will didn't think he'd ever seen a more beautiful night. As the other sleighs turned off into their lanes, the silence deepened until they had the night to themselves. Even the forest animals had fallen silent. A full moon bathed the world in a bluish light. It seemed almost as bright as day but was much more intimate. Snow-covered trees and endless fences cast inky black shadows across their path, causing the horse to shy now and then. Only the steady jingle of the harness bells broke the silence.

With sudden and unmistakable clarity, Will realized that he had become a different person from the man who left Boston a week earlier. These last days had removed a kind of crust, an artificial overlay, gradually developed during the last fourteen years. Something inside him had now reached back to a time he had lost, or forgotten. In doing so, it had pulled the present into focus. He saw himself clearly now—no cloudy spots, no shadowy corners.

The life he and Louise had built in Boston had become his past. He had to let go of it in order to live in the present, in order to build a future for those he held most dear.

He understood all this because of Nan, this quiet miracle of a woman who had invaded his life and transformed it in a twinkling. He wanted to tell her how much that meant to him, how much she meant to him. How much he loved her.

He would. He would never stop telling her.

The drive ended much too soon. Clara had fallen asleep against him. He carried her upstairs. Nan undressed her while he turned back the bed and took her wet clothes downstairs. When he came back into the room, she called, "Daddy," in a sleepy voice and held out her arms to him.

Nan slipped out, leaving Will alone with his daughter.

He sat down on the bed and put his arms around Clara. She hugged his neck.

"I want you to stay with me always. Nan, too," she added sleepily.

"I will, darling. Maybe Nan will, too."

"Talk to her, Daddy. Make her stay."

"I will, sweetheart. Now it's time to go to sleep. It'll be Christmas when you wake up."

Nan was struggling with the dollhouse when he closed the door to Clara's room.

"Since you seem determined to give away your childhood, let me carry that for you." The dollhouse was sturdy and quite heavy.

"Set it here on this table." Nan had set up a table clearly made to hold the dollhouse. "Now we get to put everything inside."

"*You* get to put it inside," Will said. "I wouldn't know where to begin."

"Then you can bring down the rest of the things on my bed."

Nan had apparently emptied her attic. There were two dolls, a baby crib, a stroller, a sturdy winter coat, mittens, and an assortment of candy. There were also two dresses, a pair of shiny black

111

shoes, and enough ribbons and bows for Clara to wear a different one every day for weeks. Will was embarrassed by the bounty.

"Clara is never going to want to leave after this."

Nan paused. "I hadn't thought about that. If you think—"

"I didn't mean it like that. It's just that I never know what to get her. I keep putting it off until half the time I end up not getting anything."

"Which is all the more reason you should leave her with me," Nan said, getting to her feet. She turned around to find herself face to face with Will. His arms closed around her.

"Do you really want a daughter badly enough to take Clara?"

"I wouldn't be *taking* Clara, just taking care of her for a while."

"Don't you want children of your own?"

"Yes, but—"

"Wouldn't you need a husband for all of that?"

"Of course, but what—"

"Do you still love me?"

"Will Atkins, I answered that question last night. I'm not so fickle as to change my mind today."

Will kissed her soundly.

"And you're certain you couldn't marry a man callous enough to give up his daughter."

"That's not exactly what I said, but the answer is still the same."

Nan tried to wriggle out of his embrace, but Will grinned and held her tighter. "I was just making sure."

"Are you certain you didn't take a nip from that bottle Homer Knight had hidden under his jacket?"

Will laughed. "No, I didn't sample Homer's white lightning, or whatever it was. But I'm feeling tipsy just the same."

Nan didn't understand. He seemed to be delighted that she wasn't going to marry him. Yet he held her in his arms and had kissed her several times. That didn't make sense. She would have been hurt that he was so happy if she hadn't been convinced he was talking about something else all the while.

"Maybe you'd better go to bed until you get over it. You're not making any sense."

"I'm not ever going to get over you." He kissed her again. "Now I'm going to go to bed because I can't wait for Christmas morning."

He waltzed her over to the mistletoe. "Ever since I was a little boy, I've wanted to kiss the woman I loved under the mistletoe on Christmas Eve."

"It's time to stop this nonsense," Nan said. She was finding it difficult to keep her spirits up. Will seemed to be having a good time, but she just wanted to go to her room and cry. "I don't know what kind of silly game you're playing, but—"

"I'm not playing a game. I'm deadly earnest. The only thing silly is that I didn't have enough sense to know what to do earlier."

"I don't understand—"

"Don't try to understand. Just believe."

"Believe what?"

"That I love you."

Then he kissed her. Nan started to draw back; she felt certain she ought to, but she couldn't. She didn't want to. She had been allowed a small window of time to taste some of the joy life could have given her. She didn't know why she should be restricted to just a taste, but she decided to take every bit she could get. It would come to an end soon enough.

Nan wound her arms around Will's neck and leaned into the kiss. Quite suddenly, she wanted to be as close to him as possible. She wanted to feel the warmth of his body against her own, the pressure of his chest against her breast, the security of his arms around her. For one brief moment she wanted to forget leaving home, motherless daughters, the pressure of business. Just once she wanted to feel prized above all worldly possessions.

She wanted to feel that Will loved her for herself alone.

Only two other men had kissed Nan. The memory of their chaste kisses was obliterated by Will's passionate embrace. He stunned her when he forced his tongue between her lips. She went weak in the knees. She thought she would faint when she felt the heat of his desire pressed against her abdomen.

Nan had never been so close to unchecked emotion, to raw need. It both frightened and excited her.

Will broke their kiss. He looked visibly shaken. "I think it's time I went to bed," he said.

"That was more than a stolen kiss under the mistletoe," Nan said.

"Too much, and not nearly enough."

"I don't understand."

"You will," Will said, and kissed her on the nose. "I promise you will."

Chapter Seven

Nan was surprised to find she wasn't the first one in the kitchen on Christmas morning.

"What are you doing here?" she asked Gertie. "Why aren't you enjoying your own Christmas?" Eggs, biscuits, sausage, grits, ham and gravy, jellies, butter—everything was ready for an enormous breakfast.

"Christmas is no fun for two old people. Jake and I wanted to watch Clara. He's lighting the fire right now. You go tell Clara and her father they've got fifteen minutes. After that, we start without them."

But it didn't take Clara that long. In exactly twenty-one seconds she was out of bed, into her robe and slippers, and downstairs wanting to know why the door to the gathering room was closed. Will wasn't far behind. He had taken time to comb his hair and brush his teeth, but everything else was left for later.

"When do we get to open our presents?" Clara asked for the fifth time.

"After you finish your breakfast," Nan said.

"But I'm not hungry."

"You have to eat something," Will said. "Gertie has worked very hard to fix a nice breakfast."

It was apparent to all four adults that while Clara might appreciate Gertie's effort, she wished she had saved it for some other time. She toyed with her food, barely tasting what was put on her plate. She ate only half of a hot biscuit covered with butter and grape jelly.

"I think it's time to open the presents," Nan announced.

Clara was out of her chair and at the door like a flash.

"Close your eyes," Nan said.

Clara slammed her eyes shut and put her hands over them.

"Don't open them until I say so," Nan said. She guided Clara out of the kitchen, down the hall, and into the gathering room. "Now open your eyes."

Clara dropped her hands. She looked around at the many gifts. "Which one is mine?"

"All of them," Nan said.

Clara's eyes grew wider and wider. "Everything?"

Nan smiled and nodded.

"Can I, Daddy?"

Will nodded.

There were two dolls, one a beautiful, blond

117

princess doll dressed in a lovely white gown, the second a country doll with pink cheeks and freckles on the end of her nose. She wore a calico dress with an apron, a sunbonnet on her unruly red hair, and black boots on her feet. Clara walked straight to the second doll, picked her up, and hugged her close.

"You have to give both your dolls names," Gertie said.

"This is Peggy," Clara said.

"The little girl she met at church last night," Nan whispered to Will when he looked totally at sea.

"And the other?" Gertie prompted.

"That's Nan," Clara said.

"I don't look a thing like—"

"I think that's a perfect name," Will said. "Now before you get busy with your other presents, Daddy has something for you."

Will produced a package from behind one of the chairs. Clara tore the paper off to reveal a pretty white Sunday dress and a new pair of shiny black patent leather shoes. Clara couldn't wait to try them on. She kicked off her slippers, shrugged off her robe, and pulled her nightgown over her head.

"Where did you get that?" Nan asked in an undervoice.

"I told him about it," Gertie said. "I saw it at the mercantile."

"It was the only thing in the place I'd buy," Will said.

Clara put her shoes on bare feet and stood up and adjusted her dress.

118

"You look beautiful," Nan said. "I think you ought to give your father a great big kiss."

Clara ran over and gave her father a big hug. "Now I'll look at the rest of my presents."

Nan picked up a package wrapped in plain paper and handed it to Will. "It's not much, but I thought you might like it."

"Shortbreads!" Will crowed with laughter. "I'm never going to live this down, am I?"

"I'm afraid not. If I forget, Gertie's bound to remember."

Gertie and Jake were exchanging presents. They weren't aware of anybody else just then.

"I've got a present for you," Will said. "It's a little strange, but I hope you'll like it. Actually, I've got more than one, but open this one first."

Puzzled, Nan accepted the envelope Will handed her. Inside she found a folded piece of paper. When she opened it up she found a crude picture of a store with Atkins Mercantile written across the front.

"Now this one," Will said, handing her a second envelope.

Inside Nan found a second piece of paper, this time Atkins Hotel was written across the front of a building that looked more like a country inn than a hotel.

"I don't understand," Nan said.

"You'll never make an artist," Gertie said, looking at the pictures with a critical eye. "Not if you can't draw Wilmer's inn or Grady's mercantile any better than that."

Nan grabbed the pictures and looked at them

119

again. Then she looked up at Will and back at the pictures.

"You didn't . . . You couldn't . . . I didn't know . . ."

"For goodness sake," Gertie said, "they aren't that bad."

"It isn't that," Nan said. "Don't you see? His name is on them."

"I'm not blind," Gertie replied. "Though why he'd want to put his name on those buildings is more than I can understand."

"You bought them, didn't you?" Nan said, turning to Will.

He nodded.

"You're not going to take Clara to her grandparents?"

He shook his head.

"You're not going back to Boston?"

"No."

"Will someone tell me what's going on?" Gertie demanded.

"Where am I going to live?" Clara asked.

"Right here, darling," Nan said. She gave the child a hug, but her eyes never left Will.

"Where's Daddy going to live?"

"That depends on whether Nan likes my last gift," Will said.

He took a small box out of his pocket and opened it. A diamond ring nestled in a bed of deep blue velvet. Nan looked at the ring, then at Will.

"I would have gone with you. You know that, don't you?"

"Yes, but I discovered I didn't want to go. It's ironic, but I discovered my new life was hollow, an illusion. Everything that's real and lasting is right here."

Will took the ring out of the box. His eyes never left Nan's face, but somehow he managed to slip it on her finger. They stood there, holding hands, staring into each other's eyes.

"Where's Daddy going to live?" Clara asked again.

"Right here," Gertie answered. "Now why don't we go into the kitchen? Nan and your father have a lot to talk about."

"But they're not saying anything."

"Yes, they are. You just can't hear it."

"Are they going to do that a lot?"

"Probably."

"So that's what you did yesterday." They were seated on the sofa, Nan nestled in Will's arms. "I knew Wilmer wanted to sell, but what about Grady? His family has owned the mercantile for a hundred years."

"Maybe, but Paralee wants to join her son and daughter in Charlottesville. And when a woman wants something—"

"I know. Daddy used to say, *when a stubborn woman wants something, a wise man lets her have it.* Is that how you felt about me?"

"You helped me to see what I wanted most. Once I knew that, the rest was easy."

"Truly? You won't regret it in a few years?"

"I haven't changed what I want to do, just where

121

I want to do it. I plan to build a business empire from one end of the valley to the other."

"But you'll come home every night?"

"Every night."

"And you won't be away at Christmas."

"Never again."

"And Clara can have some brothers and sisters?"

"As many as she wants. When can we get started?"

"What's that funny sound?" Clara asked Gertie.

"I think it's Nan saying yes."

"It doesn't sound like yes to me."

"It will when you're old enough to understand the question."

SCOTTISH SHORTBREAD

This recipe came down in the family of an English nurse whose family came from Scotland. It's just about my favorite cookie in the whole world. It's also terribly rich, practically pure calories. They get made as early as November and put in the freezer. Despite being frozen solid, they disappear well before Christmas. It takes at least two bakings to get us through the season.

1 ½ cup flour
⅓ cup sugar
¾ cup butter (*must* be real butter)

Blend all ingredients well. The dough will be stiff. Mash into a 9 × 9 lightly buttered dish. Press evenly and firmly into entire baking dish. Prick top with a fork. Bake at 350 degrees until pale golden brown. Cool and cut into squares.

I sometimes dust the top with granulated sugar or dot it with cinnamon hearts before baking. Anyone from Scotland would be horrified.

CONNIE MASON

A CHILD IS BORN

To Alex, my Christmas Eve grandchild.
And to my wonderful readers, who
make writing for them a pleasure.

Prologue

A light breeze rustled the leaves of the ancient chestnut tree, providing an enchanting serenade. The moon was high and full, bathing the couple below in dappled white light as they met beneath the shadow of the spreading branches.

"Don't go, Kent, please don't go."

Angel's heartrending plea nearly unmanned him. "You know how important becoming a doctor is to me, Angel. I'm only going to school. I'll be back one day."

Angel shook her mass of blond curls in vigorous denial. "No, you won't. I feel it in my heart. If you leave, nothing will ever be the same again. Why must you go all the way to England for your education?"

127

"The best medical schools are there, Angel. That's why my parents are selling out and moving to England. They want to be with me. I'm all they have."

Angela Keller's lush red lips trembled as she brushed the tears from her green eyes. "What about me? What about us?"

Kent Turner's dark eyes turned bleak with sadness. "You're young, Angel, too young to know what you want." He gave her a shaky smile. "When I return in four or five years, you'll probably be married with a child or two at your knee."

"I'm sixteen," Angel reminded him. "Many girls are married at sixteen."

"And I'm nearly twenty. If you were older . . ."

His expression turned wistful and his voice fell off, thinking how wonderful it would be to have Angela with him in England. But he knew her parents would never allow it. His parents were well-to-do but not in the same class as the Kellers. His parents were shop owners whose business had prospered, but they were definitely middle class. Angel's parents were prominent plantation owners, who used slave labor to work their land. His parents would never own slaves. He and Angel had met by chance when she came into his father's store with her brother. With time their friendship had progressed to the point that they were forced to meet in secret without her family's knowledge or approval.

For one thing, Angel was young—far too young to know her mind or heart, and Kent realized that. As much as he cared for Angel, he'd let nothing interfere with his dream of becoming a doctor. If she was still unmarried when he returned from England, then he wouldn't hesitate to court her. Angel was everything he wanted in a woman and he truly loved her, but she needed time to grow up.

"I'm old enough, Kent. I love you. I'll run away with you. I'll go to England with you. Please, Kent, don't leave me like this."

"Oh, God, Angel, I love you, too, but we can't be together right now. Don't make this any harder for us. I'll write you every week, I promise. If you still feel the same about me when I return, I'll speak to your parents."

Angela stared at him, memorizing his handsome face, fearing it would be the last time they would be together like this. She knew she was young, but not too young to know love. Why couldn't Kent understand that? Somehow she had to show him how much she loved him.

"Kiss me, Kent," she whispered, twining her arms around his neck. "Hold me. I need to feel your arms around me."

Kent groaned in painful yearning. "I don't think that's a good idea, Angel." They had kissed before, but he had been careful to keep his passion tightly leashed. This time it was different; it would be years before he saw Angel again.

"You would deny me even one last kiss?"

It was more than he could endure. His arms came around her, hard yet tender, trying desperately to keep their parting within the bounds of decency. He nearly succeeded—until Angel

129

Connie Mason

whispered something in his ear that set his body aflame.

"Make love to me, Kent. If I never see you again, give me something to remember you by. I want you to be the first, no matter what happens in the future."

Kent drew back in honest surprise. "You don't know what you're saying, Angel. You know I can't do that to you."

"Don't make me beg, Kent."

Though it cost him dearly, Kent stepped away, holding her at arm's length. "No, Angel, it isn't right, though Lord knows it's killing me to deny us this. One day you'll thank me."

"Thank you? I think not. How can you deny us when it's what we both want?" She flung herself at him, her firm young body pressing urgently against his.

Kent groaned, his healthy, virile body reacting violently to Angel's ill-conceived invitation.

"Please, Kent, make love to me," she repeated, aware that Kent was close to relenting. She was convinced that if she could get him to commit himself now, he wouldn't be able to leave her. She had it all worked out in her mind how their making love would bind him to her with an invisible cord.

Trembling, unable to resist the lure of her lush lips and ripe body, Kent could not find it in his heart to deny her, though he knew he was acting unwisely.

With mutual consent, they sank to the ground. Kent proved to be a tender lover, all Angel could

130

ask for and more. He made her first time memo-rable and she'd never forget it. She savored the knowledge that Kent wouldn't be able to leave her now, not after what they had just shared together.

"It was wonderful, Kent," she said dreamily. "You won't regret staying in Georgia. Half the plantation will be yours after we marry."

Kent paused in his dressing to stare at her. "Angel, this changes nothing except to prove that we were meant for one another. We'll marry as soon as I graduate from medical school. I'm serious about wanting to become a doctor."

Angel's eyes widened in shock. "How can you leave me after . . . after what we just did? I gave you my heart, my soul, my body."

"And I'll cherish them forever, but if you recall, I tried to dissuade you."

Humiliated beyond endurance, Angel's face turned red and her hands clenched angrily at her sides as rage consumed her.

"Papa and my brother are right! You're not good enough for me. Go to England. Be a doctor, but don't expect me to be waiting for you when or if you return. I hope I never see you again, Kent Turner."

Kent knew Angel meant none of those hurtful words, but he did nothing to contradict or chal-lenge her. Her anger was easier to deal with than her tears. He should never have made love to her—he knew it—but it had seemed so right at the time. It was a moving experience, one he would store away and savor when he was away at school.

"Good-bye, Angel," he said softly as she turned and walked away. "I'll always love you, no matter what happens, no matter where our lives take us."

If Angel heard him, she gave no indication. She didn't dare turn around for fear he'd see her tears. She'd never forget Kent Turner or the way he had made her feel. He had introduced her to love in a way that bound her to him forever. She'd never forgive him for leaving her like this, but she doubted she'd ever love again in the same way she loved Kent Turner.

Chapter One

Rome, Georgia—December, 1864

The stench of blood and gore filled the operating tent. A violent skirmish with elements of Hood's army had filled the makeshift hospital to overflowing. Doctor Kent Turner flexed the fingers of his right hand, grasped the saw with a firm grip, and bent to the task of removing a man's leg which was too badly mangled to save. It was a method he wouldn't have chosen had an alternative existed. He had seen the empty hopelessness in the eyes of men whose limbs had been severed and he felt compassion for their loss.

The mangled limb fell free, and Kent began the grim job of sewing the flap of skin over the stump. He thanked God that they still had ether and the soldier was aware of nothing that was taking place.

Once Kent's job was finished a corpsman took over, removing the man to the recovery tent, where scores of other wounded awaited evacuation to a hospital.

"That's it for the night, Captain," one of the orderlies said as he helped Kent remove his blood-splattered apron and wash up. "It's eight o'clock. You've been performing surgery nearly the entire day without stopping to eat. You must be famished."

Kent was too bone-weary to answer. He merely nodded as he massaged the back of his neck and shoulders.

"Go on to your quarters, Captain, I'll see that someone brings you something to eat."

"Thank you, Private Dobbs, though I might be asleep before the food arrives."

"Things won't be so hectic when we join Sherman's army at Atlanta," Dobbs opined. "There will be a real hospital there, and more doctors available to treat the wounded. Operating conditions in battle zones are primitive at best."

Kent agreed wholeheartedly as he recalled the pale face of the young soldier whose limb he had just removed, praying the man would last the night. Then he stepped from the tent into the brisk December night, somewhat revived by the pungent scent of pine smoke rising from campfires scattered throughout the encampment. He breathed deeply, realizing that he had spent too many hours with the cloying, sickening odor of blood and death.

Turning in the direction of his tent, Kent's steps

dragged on the hard-packed, frozen earth. He hoped tomorrow would be better, that this terrible war would end, that the senseless sacrifice of life would never be repeated. He had seen too many deaths as a result of hand-to-hand combat. When he completed medical school, he had remained in England to practice his profession, until rumors of war had lured him back home. He had returned just as war began, and he had joined the fray early in 1861. Despite his Southern roots, he violently opposed slavery and had offered his services to the Federal army. He wanted to save lives, but far too often he had patched up wounded men only to see them die of mortal wounds during another battle. He shook his head wearily. Senseless. So utterly senseless.

Suddenly a small body darted out from the nearby mess tent, colliding into Kent and sending them both sprawling. Momentarily stunned, Kent almost didn't react quickly enough as the small form righted itself and started to sprint away. Coming to his senses, Kent reached out and caught a handful of material, abruptly halting the refugee's flight.

Kent realized immediately that his captive was a child, a young one at that, for the slight weight of the child's body offered little resistance against his considerable strength.

"What are you doing here?" Kent asked, surprised to find a child roaming about the compound at this time of night.

The child's eyes were glazed with terror, and Kent took note of the fact that the child was a girl, a very young girl, with golden hair, huge green eyes and a thin, pale face. She looked petrified and his expression softened, his heart filled with compassion.

"I'm not going to hurt you, little one. What are you doing here this time of night? Do your parents know where you are?"

Suddenly the girl started coughing, her thin body wracked by fierce spasms.

"My God, you're ill! I'm a doctor—I can help you."

Lifting the little girl in his arms, he carried her to his tent and set her down on the narrow cot. He was grateful that an orderly had been there earlier to light a candle and start a fire in the campstove. As he set the child down, Kent noticed that she hugged a sack to her chest. He didn't try to pry it from her hands, sensing that it was important to her. Instead, he opened a medicine chest, took out a bottle and spoon, and proceeded to measure out a dose.

"Open your mouth, honey, this will help your cough."

The child shook her head, keeping her mouth tightly shut.

"You want to get well, don't you? I won't hurt you."

She stared at him, her throat working noiselessly. When she finally spoke, her voice was hoarse and raspy. "You're a Yankee. Yankees killed my papa."

Kent flinched. "I don't kill men, honey, I save their lives. I made a vow when I became a doctor to hold all human life in high regard. What is your name?" Looking at the child, a long-forgotten memory stirred in the hidden recesses of Kent's mind. The blond hair, the green eyes, made him think of someone he had known long ago and had never quite forgotten.

The child gave Kent's words considerable thought before replying. "My name is Amanda Bogart. Mama and Aunt Bessie call me Mandy."

"How old are you, Mandy?"

Mandy straightened. "I'm seven. Mama says I'm big for my age." Kent thought her rather small and undernourished.

"Will you take this medicine, Mandy? It will make your throat feel better."

Mandy thought about that for a moment, then opened her mouth. Kent carefully spooned the liquid down her throat and watched her swallow. Then he set down the spoon and perched beside her on the cot.

"It's warm in here," Mandy said, turning her body toward the stove to soak up the heat. "Feels good. I hate the cold."

"What are you doing here, Mandy? What's in that sack you're holding?"

Mandy hugged the sack against her thin chest as if her life depended on it. "You can't have it."

"I don't want it. Whatever is in it is yours to keep."

"Really?"

"Really."

"Captain Turner, I've brought you something to eat."

Mandy looked on the verge of flight as Kent strode to the front of the tent, opened the flap, and accepted a tray of food from an orderly. He carried it to a small folding table and set it down. His appetite left him when he saw Mandy staring hollow-eyed at the meager repast.

"Are you hungry, honey?" Mandy nodded, her eyes never leaving the feast of bread, cheese, cold meat, and a juicy apple. "I'm not hungry at all, and I hate to see food go to waste. Help yourself."

Mandy's large green eyes shot upward to meet his. When she saw that he meant what he'd said, she slid from the cot and picked up the bread, stuffing it into her mouth until Kent feared she'd choke. While she ate, he noted that she had laid the sack down on the cot and he moved cautiously to inspect the contents. He wasn't too surprised to find it held leftovers from the mess tent. A few stale biscuits, three apples, four potatoes, two onions, and a small portion of salted beef.

When Kent turned to question the child, he saw her stuff half the food from the tray into the pockets of her threadbare coat.

"Who is the food for, Mandy?"

Mandy froze, her little face so solemn that Kent wanted to reach out and hug her. If his infant daughter had lived, she'd be about the same age as this little girl.

"Mama is . . . sick. Aunt Bessie says she needs nourishing food. She said Yankees always had enough to eat, so I sneaked out to get Mama some food."

"That was very foolish of you. You could have gotten into trouble."

"I wouldn't have gotten into trouble," Mandy insisted. "Aunt Bessie says I'm smart for my age even though there is no longer a school for me to attend."

"Your Aunt Bessie is right, honey—you're a very smart little girl. Also a brave one. But don't you know how dangerous it is for you to be out and about by yourself this time of night?"

Mandy nodded gravely. "I know, but Aunt Bessie is too old to work even if there was work, and Mama is . . . sick."

"Finish your food and I'll take you home. Do you live far?"

"Not far. After the Yankees burned our house and took all our food and livestock, we moved in with Aunt Bessie." She walked back to the cot, picked up the sack of food, and faced Kent squarely. "You don't have to take me home, Mr. . . ."

"Turner. Doctor Kent Turner, and I'm not about to let you wander off by yourself. Besides, if your mama is sick, perhaps I can help her."

Mandy looked doubtful. "I don't think she'll be very happy to see you. She hates Yankees."

"I'll take my chances." He picked up his doctor's kit and ushered the child out the door. "I'll saddle my horse and have you home in no time at all."

Kent stared in consternation at the collection of ramshackle slave shacks Mandy had directed him to. Beyond the huts he could see the gutted

139

outline of a large building, probably a plantation house burned to the ground. Many such grand plantations had been destroyed and crops decimated recently during Sherman's march to the sea. Thinking back to his youth, Kent recalled a Bogart family who once lived in the vicinity. Could it be their home that had burned? He wondered what had happened to the family.

"Are you sure this is where your mama and Aunt Bessie live?" Kent asked uncertainly.

"Yes, see," she said, pointing to a shack halfway down a rutted lane. "That's our house."

There was a light in the window but no smoke coming from the chimney. On a cold night like this, that in itself told a story about the abject poverty of the occupants of the hut. Kent set his horse into motion, its hooves echoing hollowly against the frozen earth.

Kent's doubts were put to rest when he heard someone call out to Mandy. He halted his mount and carefully set Mandy on the ground. Immediately she flew into the arms of a woman standing in the doorway of one of the cabins. He dismounted and followed.

"Oh, Mandy, where have you been? Aunt Bessie and I have been frantic with worry."

It had grown so dark that Kent couldn't see the woman's face, but her words effectively conveyed her anguish over Mandy's disappearance. Glancing into the house, he saw no fire in the hearth. A meager light came from a candle sitting on a scarred table. Suddenly the woman looked up and saw him standing in the shadows. She drew back in alarm, her arms tightening around her daughter.

"Who are you? What do you want? There is nothing here to steal. You Yanks have already robbed us of everything we own and hold dear." She hugged Mandy fiercely. "Has he hurt you, Mandy?"

Kent halted so as not to frighten the woman. He was close enough to see that she had wrapped a ragged blanket around herself for warmth. He thought it a wonder she and her daughter hadn't frozen to death with no fire to warm the hut.

"I pose no danger to you, ma'am," Kent said politely. "I've brought your daughter home. I found her in our camp and feared she would come to harm if I didn't escort her back."

The woman's brows raised in honest shock. "You were in the Yankee camp, Mandy? Whatever were you thinking of?"

"Nothing happened to me, Mama," Mandy assured her. "Doctor Turner gave me something to eat. And I've brought food for you and Aunt Bessie. I know you've been sick and Aunt Bessie said you needed to eat more."

"Your daughter is a thoughtful child, Mrs. . . ."

"Bogart. Angela Bogart." She eyed the insignia adorning the captain's blue uniform with loathing. "Thank you for bringing Mandy home. Good-bye, Captain." She started to close the door in his face.

Kent stared at Angela Bogart in consternation. Her soft Southern drawl failed to conceal her consuming hatred for Yankees. Something deep

141

and penetrating stirred within him. She said her name was Angela. No, it couldn't be. There must be hundreds of Angelas living in the area. A long suppressed but vivid memory demanded he find out if this Angela was the same one he had known briefly yet passionately as a young man. A responsive chord he hadn't felt since he'd laid his own wife and child to rest prevented him from turning and walking away from the young widow and her child.

Placing a restraining hand on the door, he held it open and walked inside uninvited. "I'd like to help if I may. I'm a doctor. If someone here is ill, perhaps I can be of service. Mandy has a nasty cough, and I have medicine in my bag that will help her." He closed the door behind him to keep out the bitter wind, though in truth it was nearly as cold inside the cabin as it was outside.

Angela Bogart appeared to be a woman without hope. Kent recognized the hopelessness in the dull green depths of her eyes, in the paleness of her face, and in the slump of her narrow shoulders. As Angela moved more deeply into the small room, her face was dimly outlined in the soft candlelight; seeing it, Kent drew his breath in sharply. The woman was indeed the Angela he had known and loved ten years ago, before he left for medical school. As young as he had been, she was the grand passion of his life, next to medicine.

He had recalled their one night of splendid love many times during the past ten years. He had written to her every week as he had promised, but she had never replied. Then, three years after he left he heard from a mutual friend that she had married.

She was still beautiful, he thought, but undernourished and gaunt. The sunken hollows of her cheeks emphasized the sharp angles of her cheekbones and made her green eyes appear huge in her thin face, which was wreathed by a mass of golden hair. She moved awkwardly, and he was stunned when the blanket around her shoulders slipped, revealing her distended belly.

My God, she's pregnant! Kent thought with growing dismay. And from the looks of her, in the last stages of pregnancy.

Angela Bogart stiffened, peering at the Yankee doctor through the murky darkness. Could it be? Had she heard right? She supposed there were a hundred doctors with the last name of Turner; it was common enough.

"We don't need your kind of help, Captain," Angela hissed angrily. "If not for you and your kind, my husband, father, and brother would still be alive, and my child and I wouldn't be forced to seek shelter in a slave cabin."

She moved closer to confront him, and her knees nearly buckled beneath her. If Kent thought she was pale before, now her face was suddenly devoid of all color. "Kent Turner." She released his name on a shuddering sigh. "I heard you had joined the Yankee army. How does it feel to turn traitor? Do you enjoy killing your friends and former neighbors?"

Kent winced. "I'm a doctor. I don't take lives, I save them, Angel."

143

Connie Mason

"What do you want?" Angela said with more passion than she'd exhibited or felt in months. "We have nothing left to steal."

"I want to help you. I won't go into the mechanics of war, Angel, except to say that it's not the Federal army's intention to starve innocent women and children."

Angela gave a bitter laugh. "Isn't it? I no longer have a home, Captain Turner. Nothing remains but a burnt shell. Your army mercifully left these cabins because they were of no value to anyone."

"Have you no relatives to go to? This is no place to raise a daughter and bring another child into the world."

Angela walked laboriously to the only chair in the cabin and lowered herself carefully onto it. "There is no one. Mama and Papa are both dead, and Ashley's parents perished long before I married him. He was an only child. I haven't heard from my brother in months. For all I know he's dead, too. He has a fiancée living in Savannah, but her circumstances are probably no better than mine."

While Angela and Kent conversed, Mandy opened the sack and proudly spread food on the table before her mother. "Look, Mama, look what I brought you." She handed Angel a stale biscuit and an apple, her little face wreathed in a smile. "I want you to get well. Aunt Bessie said nourishing food would do you a world of good."

"Where did you get this, Mandy? Bogarts don't beg."

"I didn't beg, honest, Mama."

Angela sent Kent a scathing glance. "Yankees aren't known for their charitable acts. You were very naughty, Mandy."

Mandy hung her head. "I wanted to help."

"Promise you won't do anything like that again."

"I promise."

"Very well. Since you've already been fed, go over to Mose's house and ask him to please go find Aunt Bessie and tell her you're home. She's out looking for you."

Mandy scampered from the cabin, turning once to look at Kent. "Thank you, Doctor Turner." She was gone before Kent could reply.

With the child gone, Kent focused his attention upon Angela Bogart, recalling with fondness her enchanting smile and wishing he could see it again. "Why haven't you built a fire in the hearth? It's no wonder Mandy has a lung infection."

"If you were more observant, you'd note there is no wood with which to build a fire. Mose's oldest son went out this morning to gather wood but hasn't returned. More than likely he just ran off."

"How many people live in these huts?"

"Just one other family. But they're leaving soon for the city. Since your president freed the slaves, there is no reason for them to remain here and starve."

"You'd be wise to do the same."

Angela pulled the blanket closer around her. "As you can see, I'm in no condition to travel anywhere right now."

Never had Kent felt so angry, so damn bitter. This senseless war was harder on women and children than it was on the men who fought the battles. He had never raised a gun to take another life and hoped he'd never have to. He had joined the war to save lives, not take them, be they Yankee or Rebel.

"It's going to be bitter cold tonight. I'll gather wood for you." He turned to leave. Angela's sharp retort stopped him.

"I didn't ask for your help, Captain Turner, and I don't want it."

A nerve in Kent's jaw jerked spasmodically. Obviously she had never forgiven him for leaving Georgia. If she knew how difficult it had been for him to make that decision, she might feel differently. "Nevertheless, you're getting it." Without another word, he slammed out the door.

Angela stared at the door, trying to decide if Kent Turner was an angel of mercy or a devil in disguise. Hatred for all Yankees, particularly Kent Turner, and the need to survive for the sake of her children warred within her. Absently she nibbled on one of the biscuits that Mandy had so proudly placed before her as if it were the finest banquet. It tasted so good that she finished it and started on another. Before she realized it, she had eaten three. Ashamed of herself for being so greedy, she set aside the others for Aunt Bessie and bit into an apple. As she savored the sweet fruit, she thought about the Yankee doctor.

Years ago Kent Turner had used, then discarded her. That was how she saw it, anyway. Then he had added insult to injury by turning traitor and joining the Yankees. She couldn't forget that

Yankees had killed Ashley, Papa, and probably Blake. Fiercely loyal to the South, Ashley had been among the first to volunteer despite his lack of training and experience. He had been wounded eight months ago, came home briefly to recuperate, then returned to rejoin his unit. The house had been standing then, and during that brief idyll from the war she had become pregnant. Not two weeks after he returned to his unit, she was notified that Ashley had been killed during a fierce battle in which many lives had been lost. He had died without knowing she was expecting another child.

Her thoughts turned abruptly from Ashley to Kent Turner. He had changed little in ten years. He had matured, certainly, grown more brawn and muscle. His looks were deceiving, she reflected. He wasn't what one would expect a doctor to look like. His size and bulk were those of a seasoned infantryman. He was still incredibly handsome, still rugged; his black hair and dark eyes were just as riveting as she remembered. She recalled many things about Kent, but none of them more damning than the fact that he was a Yankee.

Hugging the threadbare blanket tightly around her narrow shoulders, Angela could hardly recall what life had been like before the Yankees invaded her land. At sixteen, she had loved Kent passionately and proven it by giving him her body. She had never found it in her heart to forgive him for relieving her of her virginity, then callously leaving. When his letters started coming, she had ignored them, and in time the letters stopped and her heart had mended. Unfortunately, she had never forgotten him and that one magical night he had given her. Seeing him now was like meeting a ghost from her past, one that brought back painful memories.

Although she still cared for Kent, Angel had married Ashley. Married him because she knew he could provide a comfortable home for her and their children, and he would have, had the Yankees not disrupted their happy existence. Her years with Ashley had been pleasant and rewarding, if not completely fulfilling, and his death had been devastating to both her and Mandy.

Suddenly the door burst open and Mandy rushed inside, followed closely by a dark-skinned old woman with kinky gray hair and dark eyes that spoke eloquently of her weariness. Loose folds of skin hung on a thin frame that showed signs of having once been robust. "Are you all right, chile? Mandy done tole me there was a Yankee in the house. Is he gone? He didn't hurt you none, did he?"

"I'm fine, Aunt Bessie," Angela said, grateful to her old nurse, who had stayed with her despite the bad times they had gone through. "I've saved you something to eat. I know you're as hungry as I am."

Aunt Bessie shook her woolly head. "I ain't hungry at all, Angel. Save it for tomorrow. You're eatin' for two. Or give it to Mandy. I swear dat chile is always hungry."

"Eat the food, Aunt Bessie. There will be more tomorrow."

All three occupants of the room turned as one toward the door. Kent stood in the opening, carrying an armload of kindling. He walked calmly to the hearth and dumped the wood on the grate.

"What's dat Yankee doin' here, Angel?" Aunt Bessie asked as she took a protective stance in front of Angela and Mandy. If the situation wasn't so damn pitiful, Kent would have laughed at Aunt Bessie's meager effort to protect her charges.

"I'm not going to hurt anyone, Aunt Bessie," Kent assured her as he took a match from his pouch and struck a spark to the dry kindling. It blazed immediately into life, filling the cramped room with heat and light.

"I told Doctor Turner we don't want his help," Angela contended. "Yankees aren't welcome here."

"I think Doctor Turner is very nice," Mandy piped up. "He gave me medicine for my cough and something to eat."

Kent smiled at the child, so innocent, so utterly honest, so totally without guile—too young to be corrupted by war but old enough to be hurt by it. Why must the innocent be the ones to suffer? Couldn't Angela Bogart see she was hurting her child by refusing the help she so desperately needed? It was as if he had never known her all those years ago. Had she been so embittered by war and deprivation that she was now blind to the suffering of her family?

"You can protest all you want, Angel, but as long as I'm able, I'll see that your family neither starves nor freezes."

"You're a Yankee. Why should you care?"

Connie Mason

Kent searched her face, sensing her pain, her confusion, her utter hopelessness.

"I'm a human being, Angel, and it's nearly Christmas, a time of good will toward men. I was also once a friend. Or have you forgotten? Ten years is a long time."

Chapter Two

"You know dis man, Angel? He don' look like no friend to me." Aunt Bessie said, glaring at Kent. "He's a damn Yankee."

"He wasn't always a Yankee," Angel replied, recalling that night many years ago when she'd begged Kent to make love to her and she had become a woman in his arms.

"I knew Angel when we were both very young," Kent said. "I was born and raised near here until I went away to medical school in England."

"But you're a Yankee," Mandy reminded him, thoroughly confused. How could someone born in the South be a Yankee?

"Why ain't you wearin' a gray uniform?" Aunt Bessie challenged in an accusatory tone.

"It's a long story. I'm a doctor, I wanted to help

151

the wounded, and I don't believe in slavery. I did what my conscience demanded. I treat Yankees and Rebels alike. My job is to save lives."

"Noble of you," Angel said with a hint of sarcasm.

Kent ignored her barb. "Why didn't you answer my letters, Angel? What happened?"

Aware that Mandy and Aunt Bessie were listening with more than a little curiosity, Angel saw no reason to share her past with them. "Why don't you and Mandy take some of this food over to Mose and Delia, Aunt Bessie?"

"And leave you alone with dis here Yankee?" The old woman sounded indignant.

"You can trust me, Aunt Bessie, I won't hurt Angel."

Despite everything, Angel believed him. "It's all right, Aunt Bessie."

Reluctantly, the old woman gathered up the leftover biscuits and meat, took Mandy by the hand, and left.

"You haven't answered my question, Angel," Kent said once they were alone. "Why didn't you answer my letters?"

"That was a long time ago, Kent. I don't even remember anymore. I was only sixteen, for heaven's sake."

"I heard you got married three years later. Did you love your husband?"

"Ashley was a good man. He loved me, and I cared deeply for him."

"Were you happy?"

Angel stared at her hands. *Not as happy as I*

would have been with you, she thought but did not say. "We had Mandy. That made me very happy." She looked up. "What about you? I heard you'd married in England. Did you bring your wife back with you?"

"Jennifer is dead. She died birthing our daughter. The babe lived but a day."

"I'm sorry."

His dark, expressive eyes revealed the grief and pain of his loss. "We can't relive the past. We have to look to the future."

Angel laughed harshly. "Future? What future is there for me? I have nothing left. Nothing . . . Nothing . . ."

He grasped her shoulders, giving her a little shake. "How can you say that? You have Mandy. She's an adorable child. And soon you'll have a new babe. That's more than I've got."

She shrugged from his grasp, glaring up at him. "Am I expected to feel sorry for you? You're a traitor. Just go away and leave me alone."

"I can't do that, Angel. Fate has brought us together for a reason. I'm going to help you whether you want it or not. First and foremost, I'm a doctor. Mandy said you've been ill. Will you let me examine you?"

Angel recoiled in alarm. "Don't touch me. There is nothing wrong with me." She couldn't bear to have him touch her for fear of reviving those long-ago memories. She recalled his touch as pure magic.

"When is your child due? Have you felt movement?"

153

She stared at him in mute defiance, refusing to answer.

Sighing wearily, Kent hoisted himself to his feet and walked out the door. He returned a few minutes later with his doctor's bag. Removing an elongated instrument with a horn at one end, he turned to Angel. "I want to listen to the child's heartbeat."

"No."

"Angel, be reasonable. I'm concerned about you."

"I can't imagine why."

"For old time's sake, if nothing else. Now will you let me examine you?"

"No."

"Then answer my questions. When are you due?"

"Two, maybe three weeks. I'm not certain."

"Are you having any problems?"

"None to be concerned about."

"Very well, Angel, have it your way. But I'm leaving a tonic for you. It will build up your strength. I'm also leaving something for Mandy's cough. Supplies should be coming through in a day or two, and I'll bring more medicine and food the next time I come."

"There won't be a next time, Yankee. I don't want you coming back here. The sight of you sickens me. You remind me of all I've lost, of how much my family has suffered because of Yankees."

Too weary to argue, Kent placed the bottles of medicine on the rickety table. "I've been gone too long from my duties, Angel. If I don't return to camp soon, someone will come looking for me despite the lateness of the hour."

"Far be it from me to keep you from your duties, Captain Turner."

"I'll be back. Maybe not tomorrow, but soon. Is there any food in the house other than what Mandy took from the mess tent tonight?"

"A few potatoes and carrots still remain in the ground to be dug up. And rutabagas and turnips. Sometimes Mose traps a rabbit or squirrel. We won't starve, not that it's any business of yours."

"I wish you didn't hate me so, Angel. Ten years is a long time to hold a grudge. Leaving you that night was the hardest thing I've ever done, especially after we . . . I didn't want to, Angel, but it happened so fast. We were both so young and impetuous. When I felt you in my arms, my blood ran hot."

Angel rose slowly, placing a hand in the small of her back to ease the pain. "Is that what you think, Kent? That I'm holding a grudge? You're wrong. I forgot you quickly enough," she lied. "You humiliated me, made me feel like a fool after I literally threw myself at you. I met Ashley soon afterward and learned what it was to really love someone." Lies, all lies. "Now that I know you joined the Yankee army, I realize how lucky I was to be rid of you. I never thought you'd turn traitor."

"I was true to my conscience."

"As I am true to mine. You should leave, Captain Turner. I'm tired."

She did indeed look weary, Kent thought as he closed his bag and prepared to leave. She lacked that healthy glow pregnant women often exhibited, looking pale and drawn instead. He wished there was more he could do for her. After all these years, there was still a place in his heart that had never released the memory of a radiant Angela, her face glowing with delight as he made love to her.

"Very well, Angel, I'll leave, but I'll be back to check on you and Mandy. Meanwhile, take the tonic and rest as much as possible."

After Kent left, Angela stared at the door, her mind in a turmoil. Why now? she wondered dully. She'd thought she had gotten over Kent Turner years ago. Why had fate thrust him back into her life at a time when she was most vulnerable? At one time she had been considered beautiful. She smoothed her blond hair back from her pale face, aware that her former beauty had all but vanished during these hard times. The child she carried had sapped her strength as well as her youth and beauty, but she didn't regret the child she carried inside her. She feared for its life.

Without proper medical attention, care, or food, how could her child survive? How could she survive the rigors of childbirth in the primitive conditions under which she lived? Furthermore, she was responsible for two other lives. Aunt Bessie was too old to fend for herself and Mandy needed her.

Angel sighed heavily. If only Blake were alive. It had been so long since she had heard from her brother that she feared he was dead.

* * *

Kent returned to camp and retired immediately. It was very late and he was exhausted, but sleep eluded him. Angel—the woman he'd tried to forget but couldn't—had suddenly entered his life again. And after all this time, she still hated him. Obviously, knowing he served in the Union army had fanned the flames of her hatred into a blazing inferno. He knew how she felt, but could not in all conscience turn his back on Angel and her desperate need.

She had changed in ten years, but so had he. In his eyes she was still lovely. Her pale, fragile beauty made him all the more protective of her. And little Mandy was a treasure he'd give his life to safeguard.

The next morning, Kent awoke to chaos. A wagonload of wounded Rebels arrived at dawn, and he was called upon to patch them up so they could be shipped north to a prison camp. They were escorted by a half-dozen hardened Federal soldiers.

Kent was examining a man with a bayonet wound in the side when the sergeant in charge of the prisoners approached. "Patch that one up good, Doc. He's a valuable prisoner. We have reason to believe he has information on where the enemy will concentrate their troops next. We're taking him to headquarters."

Kent's dark eyes filled with compassion as he worked on the young lieutenant, whose wound was grave and possibly life-threatening. The man's eyes were closed. Kent thought he looked vaguely familiar, but if he had met the man before he couldn't recall where or when.

"I'll do my best, Sergeant, but I suggest you not move him for several days if you expect him to survive long enough to provide the information you need."

"What about the others?"

"I've examined them all; only this man's wound is serious enough to prevent travel."

The sergeant cursed beneath his breath. "How long before he can be moved?"

"Like I said, a few days."

"Since the others are well enough to be transported, I'll take them on to Atlanta. Eventually they'll be shipped North to prison."

"And the wounded man, Sergeant . . . ?"

"Norton, sir. I'll leave him behind with a guard and return for him in three days." He sent Kent a meaningful glare. "There will be hell to pay if he escapes."

"That's your department, Sergeant Norton. Mine is to save lives. Now if you'll excuse me, I have wounded men to care for."

Kent watched Norton walk away before turning back to the wounded Reb. The man's eyes were closed and he was bleeding profusely from the wound in his side. Kent went to work immediately, stanching the blood and sprinkling on antiseptic to prevent infection. He had just finished applying a bandage when the Reb opened his eyes. They were green, vaguely familiar, and strangely moving.

"Where am I?" the lieutenant asked in a voice made hoarse by pain.

"In a field hospital. You'll be just fine."

The Reb eyed Kent's blue uniform with loathing. "You're a Yankee."

"I'm a doctor. Barring infection, you can be moved in a few days."

The man closed his eyes and groaned. "To a prison camp, no doubt. Excuse me for not being enthusiastic about that. You should have let me die."

Kent allowed himself a brief moment of pity before moving on to the next patient.

"Wait, Doctor," the Rebel said, clutching at Kent's sleeve. "Where are the Yanks who brought me here?"

"They left one man behind as guard and the rest continued on their way with the walking wounded. They're returning for you in a few days."

The Rebel closed his eyes. "I see." He did see, only too clearly. Obviously the Yankees knew who he was and intended to extract information from him, hence the guard to make sure he didn't escape. He was carrying a verbal message from President Davis to General Hood, and since he was passing so close to his sister's plantation he had decided to make a small detour in order to check on her. Unfortunately, he had no idea Yankees were in the area and had run smack dab into a fierce battle, suffering a serious wound in the bargain. He knew he had to escape and give his message to General Hood before he was taken to Sherman.

Suddenly his eyes flew open. "Where am I?"

Kent saw no harm in divulging that bit of harmless information. "This is the 218th field hospital, located just outside of Rome, Georgia."

Kent moved on to another patient, unaware of the slow smile that curved the Rebel's lips.

"Captain Turner, wake up. Bad news, sir."

Kent turned over on the cot as the orderly burst into the tent. "What is it, Dobbs? Have more wounded arrived?"

"No, sir, nothing like that. It's the Reb prisoner, Captain. He's escaped."

Kent reared out of bed. "What! What about his guard? How in the hell could he have escaped? The man was as weak as a kitten."

"Not as weak as we thought," Dobbs opined. "Sometime during the night while Private Pitts dozed, the prisoner found the strength to hit him over the head with a bedpan and escape."

"He can't have gone far," Kent said, amazed at the Reb's fortitude. The last thing he needed was an inquiry into the man's escape. "Gather a few men together and conduct a search of the area. The man was severely wounded, for God's sake; his escape has probably led to his death. How is Private Pitts?"

"He has a lump on his head the size of an egg, but otherwise he's uninjured. He's worried about Sergeant Norton and what he will do. Rumor has it the Reb was a liaison between President Davis and his generals. They believe he carried an important message to General Hood. General Sherman is anxious to question the man."

"We'll find him," Kent returned, "although I pity the poor bastard."

A Child is Born

*   *   *

Angela awoke from a fitful sleep. She could find no comfortable position on the hard straw mattress, and the babe had been unusually active during the night. She breakfasted on cornbread made from corn the Yankees had missed when they raided the plantation. Fortunately, Aunt Bessie had found a few eggs in the woods yesterday, laid by chickens who had scattered when the coop burned. There was also a cow and her calf hidden in the woods. Mose had had the foresight to conceal the animals when he heard that Yankees were in the area.

Mandy stirred awake shortly afterward and then Aunt Bessie arrived. The old woman took one look at Angel and shook her head. "Yo shore yo feelin' all right, chile? Yo looks right poorly."

"I didn't sleep well last night, Aunt Bessie," Angel said wearily.

Aunt Bessie sent her a sharp glance. "Is it yore time?"

Angel shook her head. "No, it's not that. Not yet, anyway."

"Did dat Yankee doctor upset yo?"

"Perhaps a little," Angel admitted.

"I thought he was nice," Mandy chimed in. "Are you sure he's a Yankee, Mama? He didn't act like one."

At loss for an answer, Angel said, "Eat your breakfast, honey. Lord knows where our next meal is coming from."

"Mama."

161

"Yes, Mandy."

"Are you still mad at me for going to the Yankee camp?"

"No, honey, but it was very naughty of you. I would have been devastated had something happened to you."

"Do you think Doctor Turner will come back?"

Angel stared at her daughter in consternation. "I hope not."

"I wish this old war was over. Do you think Saint Nicholas will find us here? Did you know it's almost Christmas, Mama, and we don't even have a Christmas tree?"

"I think we'll have to forgo gifts and a tree this year, Mandy. Saint Nicholas has more important things on his mind."

"More important than little children?"

Sadness dimmed the vivid green of Angel's eyes. "I'm afraid so."

Suddenly Mandy's face brightened. "I know something Saint Nicholas can bring me! And it won't put him out at all. He can bring me a new baby brother on Christmas Eve."

Angel gave her a misty smile. What would she ever do without her precious daughter? Mandy never thought about herself, only of others. "I wouldn't count on the baby arriving precisely on Christmas Eve, nor can I guarantee it will be a boy."

Mandy gave her mother a long, thoughtful look. "Christmas Eve, Mama, I know it. And it *is* going to be a boy."

Angel didn't have the heart to contradict her

determined daughter. Or to tell her she and the child might not survive the birth. Whatever answer she was about to give was lost when she heard what sounded like someone scratching on the door.

"You think it's dat Yankee?" Aunt Bessie asked, looking at Angel for direction.

Angel shook her head, knowing in her heart that it wasn't Kent at the door. "Open the door, Aunt Bessie." A thrill of anticipation shot through Angel and she began shaking. Either her intuition was working overtime or something extraordinary was about to happen. She felt it in every fiber of her being, in every beat of her heart.

Aunt Bessie approached the door cautiously, cracked it open enough to peer through, then flung it wide with a shriek. "Lawdy, lawdy, look who's here, Angel!"

Angel felt the blood drain from her face as a man pushed through the opening and fell to his knees, obviously spent. She saw at a glance that he was wounded, and when he gave her a weak smile she nearly fainted with joy.

"Blake! My God, it's Blake!"

Chapter Three

Blake looked at Angela, opened his mouth as if he wanted to say something, then collapsed, beyond speech or communication as he passed out at their feet.

"Oh my God," Angela wailed as she dropped to her knees beside him. "Help me get him into bed."

Between Aunt Bessie and Angela, they settled Blake on the only bed in the room. Immediately Angela located Blake's wound and breathed a sigh of relief when she saw a neat bandage. "Looks like he's been treated by a doctor recently. He's bleeding again but not seriously. Tear strips from my spare petticoat, Aunt Bessie, and I'll replace the bandage."

They worked over Blake for a time while

Amanda watched quietly. She hadn't seen her uncle in a very long time and barely remembered him.

"Maybe Doctor Turner can help him," she suggested with childlike innocence.

Angela sent her daughter a quelling look. "No, Kent Turner must never know Blake is here. Is that clear, Mandy?"

"Why, Mama? He'd help Uncle Blake, I know he would."

Angela tucked the loose end of the clean bandage in place around Blake's waist, then turned to Mandy. "Doctor Turner is a Yankee. He'd see that Blake was sent to a northern prison. From what I've heard, Blake wouldn't survive a Yankee prison."

Mandy shook her head in vigorous denial. "No, I'm sure he wouldn't—"

"That's enough, Mandy. Go see if Mose caught anything in the trap today. Blake needs something substantial in his stomach."

Dutifully, Mandy left the cabin. A few minutes later, Blake opened his eyes and smiled weakly at Angela. "God, Angel, it's good to see you." His eyes drifted down to her protruding stomach. "I see I'm going to be an uncle again. Ashley must be damn proud of his family."

Angela's green eyes dulled with pain. "He would be if he were alive to see it. I never even got to tell him about the baby. He came home to recover from a wound about eight months ago and was killed shortly after he returned to his regiment. How did you know where to find me?"

she asked, abruptly changing the subject. "The big house is gone."

"I know. I went there first. Then I saw smoke coming from the chimney of one of the slave cabins and came down in hopes of finding some of your people. It never occurred to me that you'd be living here. In any event, I knew I could go no further."

"Where did you come from? Who treated your wound?"

"I was on my way to see you when I ran into a battle and suffered a wound. I was taken to a field hospital not far from here and managed to escape. No one thought I had the strength to overpower my guard, let alone leave my bed. But I fooled them all."

"A field hospital," Angel repeated slowly. "Did Kent treat you?"

Blake's brow furrowed. "Kent? Are you referring to a Yankee doctor?"

"Yes, Kent Turner. Surely you remember him. His parents owned a business in town. He went away to medical school in England and joined the Federal army when he returned."

Blake paled visibly. "You've seen him, spoken with him? He's a Yankee, for God's sake!"

Angel stared down at her hands, recalling how shocked she'd been to encounter Kent again after all these years.

"If I recall, you used to be sweet on him."

"You were mistaken," Angel said coolly.

Blake grew thoughtful. "Now that you mention it, the doctor who treated me did look vaguely familiar. Quite possibly it was Kent Turner."

"Oh, God, he can't find you here," Angel said, her voice rising in alarm.

"Why would he?"

"'Cause he's gonna come back, dat's why," Aunt Bessie interjected. "He done tole us he's gonna come back."

"When?" Blake asked, his voice quivering with exhaustion.

"A few days," Angel said. "He's bringing food and medicine."

"Why? Why should he do that? Do you trust him?"

"No more than I trust any other Yankee," Angel replied bitterly. "Look what they did to our family, to my home, to all those I love. I hate Yankees."

Blake closed his eyes, too weary to reply.

"Get some rest, Blake. We'll talk more later."

He lifted his head fractionally, his voice hard with determination. "I have to get to General Hardee as soon as possible. I have an important message from President Davis."

"You're too weak to go anywhere right now. Go to sleep. Aunt Bessie will stay with you while I go see what's keeping Mandy." She turned to leave.

"Angel, wait—have you heard from Mary Ellen?"

"Not for weeks. But I think she's safe enough in Savannah."

"Not if Sherman has anything to say about it. If we don't stop his march to the sea, no one in Savannah will be safe." His head dropped back down on the pillow and in despair he turned toward the wall. Angel tiptoed out the door, feeling his anguish as keenly as if it were her own.

*   *   *

Kent knew there would be hell to pay when Sergeant Norton returned and learned the prisoner had escaped. He had sent men out to search two days in a row, but they had returned empty-handed. Kent was amazed that the wounded man had escaped at all, let alone traveled any distance in his condition. At first, Kent had felt certain they'd find the prisoner somewhere in the immediate vicinity, but evidently he had miscalculated the seriousness of the man's wounds. Or else the prisoner possessed superhuman strength and even greater determination.

Since there was a lull in the number of wounded being brought to the hospital, Kent decided to visit Angela and Mandy. He hadn't been able to banish Angel from his mind since encountering her again two days ago. Despite her protests to the contrary, Angel needed him, and abandoning her in her need was out of the question. He had been unable to preserve the life of his own wife and child and was determined to do all in his power to save Angel and her baby.

If Angel hadn't married Ashley Bogart all those years ago, or refused to answer his letters, she would most likely be his wife now. The love he'd once felt for her had never died, and seeing her again brought back all those feelings he'd thought he'd suppressed, along with a few more, like protective instincts and fatherly feelings for her daughter and unborn child. Lord, was he getting maudlin in his old age? Not that thirty was so old, but he had seen so much of death and dying that he felt ancient.

His mind made up, Kent filled a sack with food from the supply wagon that had just arrived, adding several blankets, soft cotton material, needle, thread, and medicine for both Mandy and Angel. After informing Dobbs that he'd be back shortly, he took off at a fast gallop.

Mandy saw the horseman approach and ran into the cabin to tell her mother.

"Who is it?" Blake asked anxiously.

"I don't know," Angel replied as she peered out the door. When she saw the blue uniform, she drew back in alarm.

"Yankee comin'," Aunt Bessie said from her vantage point behind Angel.

Wiggling past both women, Mandy shaded her eyes against the glare of the wintry sun and cried, "It's Doctor Turner!"

"Hide under the bed," Angel hissed to Blake as she grabbed a tattered shawl from a hook and stepped outside to greet her unwelcome visitor. "Don't either of you say a word about Blake," she said to Aunt Bessie and Mandy as she closed the door firmly behind her.

Kent was inordinately pleased to see Angel waiting outside for him. He dismounted and smiled, but received no welcoming smile in return.

"What do you want?"

Kent frowned. She seemed nervous. "I told you I'd be back. How have you been feeling?"

"Well enough."

"And Mandy? Did the medicine help?"

"Yes," Angel admitted grudgingly. She saw his gaze slide past her to the cabin and grew frantic. Did he suspect anything? Did he even realize that the Rebel he'd treated had been Blake?

"I have some things for you and Mandy. May I come in?"

Angel started violently. "That's not a good idea."

"Angel, what is it? Is something wrong? How can I help?"

"You can leave," Angel said in a pleading tone. "Thank you for everything you've done for us."

Kent searched her face, noting the dark circles marring the delicate skin beneath her eyes, the anxious, almost fearful expression on her face. He wasn't about to leave until he found out what was troubling her. Without asking permission, he strode boldly past her and flung open the door. He saw Mandy and Aunt Bessie, both looking oddly frightened, but nothing else out of the ordinary. He carried the sack of food into the cabin and placed it on the table. Angel followed him inside, visibly relieved when she saw that Blake had hidden under the bed as she'd directed.

"Hello, Mandy," Kent said, sending the child a friendly smile. "If you look inside the sack, you'll find something for your sweet tooth."

Mandy didn't wait for her mother's permission as she tore into the sack. She squealed in delight when she found a small packet of hard candy. Kent had been saving it for a special Christmas treat but could think of nothing more special than giving it to Angel's child.

"Thank you, Kent," Angel said, wishing he would go, yet touched by his thoughtfulness. "Hadn't you better leave now? I know it must be difficult to find time from your busy schedule to visit us. We'll be fine."

Kent's expression grew thoughtful. "What are you frightened of, Angel?" His keen gaze swept past her to the rumpled bed, noting immediately the dark red stain on the sheet that hadn't been completely covered by the blanket. Blood. His eyes came back to rest on Angel. "Where is he, Angel?"

Angel paled. "I—I don't know what you're talking about."

"I think you do." He took a step in Angel's direction, unaware that his action might appear menacing. To Blake Keller, peering from beneath the bed, it looked and sounded threatening. And he'd rather die than let harm come to his sister and niece.

"Don't touch her, you bastard!"

Crawling from beneath the bed, Blake wobbled to his feet, prepared to defend his sister no matter what it cost him.

Kent recognized the wounded man instantly. It was the Reb lieutenant who had escaped from the field hospital two days ago. Angela flew to her brother's side, shielding him with her own fragile body. It was the identical green eyes that gave Kent his first clue as to the identity of the Reb. It had been a long time since he last saw Blake Keller, but there was no mistaking him now.

"Don't hurt him. He's wounded," Angela pleaded desperately.

"I'm not going to hurt your brother."

"You know?"

"I didn't at first, but I do now." He turned to Blake. "How in the hell did you make it this far in the condition you were in?"

Blake managed a weak smile. "Pure grit and determination, for all the good it did me. I suppose you're going to take me into custody."

"I'm going to have a look at that wound before I do anything," Kent said. "My doctor's bag is outside with my mount, Aunt Bessie. Would you please get it for me? As for you, Lieutenant Keller, perhaps you'd better sit down before you fall."

Blake eased down on the bed, eyeing Kent warily. "My sister had no idea I was in the area. Showing up at her door like this is all my doing."

Kent paid little heed to Blake's words as he began unwinding the bandage from around the wounded man's middle. "It's healing," Kent announced to no one in particular.

"What are you going to do?" Angel asked in a hushed voice. "He'll die in prison. You know yourself the horrible conditions in which prisoners are forced to live."

"I'll leave something in case infection sets in," Kent continued calmly. "And I'll be back tomorrow or the next day to check on him."

Angel allowed herself to breathe again when she heard Kent's words. "You're not taking him away?"

172

"Did I say I was?"

"You're not going to report him to the Yankees?"

"I told you he wouldn't," Mandy said, skipping up to Kent and taking his hand.

Kent grinned at Mandy, ruffling her bright hair with his free hand. "I'm in this war to patch up the wounded and save lives. I don't want to see Blake in a prison any more than you do. I won't tell where he is, but neither will I betray my uniform. With any luck, no one will ask me if I know where to find Blake. If they do, I don't truthfully know how I will answer. But rest assured, I won't knowingly lead anyone to this cabin."

Blake stared at Kent, wanting to trust him but fearing to. "I'll leave. I won't put my sister and niece in danger."

"No! You're not well enough yet," Angel exclaimed in alarm.

"Stay," Kent said. "I'll try to warn you if danger exists. That's all I can promise. Sergeant Norton won't return for a day or two. Meanwhile, rest and get your strength back. When you do leave, I don't want to know where you're going. I have to go now, but I'll be back."

He closed his bag and stood up to leave. "If something unforeseen should happen, send Aunt Bessie." Without waiting for an answer, he strode out the door. Angel followed.

"Kent, why are you doing this?"

Kent sent her a searing glance. "Let's just say for old time's sake. Did you really think I'd turn in your brother?" He took her hands, drawing her

173

close. "I haven't forgotten how much I cared for you once."

Angel flushed. "I was a spoiled child then. I've grown up in ten years."

"And become even more fascinating with maturity."

Angel laughed harshly. "How can you look at me and lie like that? I look terrible. I'm aware of what this pregnancy and the war have done to me."

The heat of his gaze drew her forward like a moth to flame. She could feel the warmth of his body reaching out to her. She almost wished she could go back ten years to that carefree time in her life. Mandy could be Kent's child—hers and Kent's—and this baby she carried could be theirs, too. If she could go back in time, she'd give Ashley a better wife than she, one who deserved his love and devotion. But only fools believed in fantasy. Kent was a Yankee, her husband was dead, and her brother was seriously wounded and in danger of being imprisoned. That was reality. She couldn't bring back the past; she could only go forward, even though a dismal future awaited her.

"You're still beautiful to me," Kent said softly. "It's like a miracle finding you again. A Christmas miracle. I'd never hurt you."

They were standing so close to one another that Kent felt the child move inside her, a tiny thump against his abdomen, and a look of wonder crossed his face. Aware of what had happened, a slow flush crawled up Angel's face and she tried to back away, but Kent held her firmly.

"Angel, I'd give anything if that child growing

inside you were mine. But just because it's not my babe doesn't mean I won't help you or worry about you. I truly believe fate brought us together again for a purpose."

Angel seemed to retreat into a shell. "You're a Yankee."

"I'm a friend. Haven't I just proved that?"

She searched his face. "I . . . don't know."

"Trust me, Angel. Your brother is safe as long as he's here with you. So are you and Mandy." Leaning over, he kissed her forehead then released her with a reluctance that stunned him. "I have to go. I'll see you in a day or two."

Angel watched Kent ride away, her eyes misty with tears. The moment he had touched her, she knew the old attraction for him still existed. He had attained his dream and become a doctor, and she realized how wrong she had been those many years ago to deny him the opportunity to fulfill his life's ambition. But it was too late now to wish back the past. Much too late to wonder what might have been had he remained in Georgia as she'd demanded. There were dead spouses, children, and a difference in beliefs separating them. All she could hope for, pray for, was that Kent did not betray her brother.

"Do you trust him?" Blake asked anxiously when she returned to the cabin.

"We have no choice." She was so tired. Her back ached and the babe sat heavily inside her.

"I should leave."

"No! You're not well enough. I couldn't bear it

if something happened to you. I suppose we have to trust Kent."

"Doctor Turner won't let anything happen to us, Mama," Mandy piped up. "He's a very nice man. Look what he brought me." She held out her hand, revealing a fistful of hard round candies. "Would you like one?"

"I wish I still had your innocence and trust," Angel sighed, hugging Mandy close. "No, sweetheart, the candy is for you. I don't want any."

Kent returned to camp and spent the next hour checking on his patients in the hospital tent. All the wounded seemed to be improving, which said a great deal about his skill. Some of the men had come in badly mangled and near death.

Back in his tent, Kent stared moodily into space, his thoughts consumed with Angel and her predicament. Finding Blake with her only added to her problems and his own dilemma. He truly didn't want to turn Blake in, but neither did he feel comfortable lying to his own men. He was proud of his choice to serve in the Federal Army and hadn't regretted his decision.

He didn't believe in slavery, but he wasn't so naive as to think this war was being fought over the issue of slavery alone. He felt empathy for all those, Rebs and Yankees alike, who had to engage in battles and lose their lives over things they didn't even understand. He knew that many of the men who fought for the South had never owned a slave.

He wished he could do more for Angel and her

family than bring her food and medicine occasionally. Would she survive the war? he wondered dimly. What would happen to her when he left the area? He couldn't bear the thought of losing her again. He racked his brain for a way to keep her safe and came up blank. Each time he thought of something that made sense, he realized she wouldn't agree.

The next day Sergeant Norton returned for Lieutenant Keller. "Is the Reb prisoner able to travel?" he asked Private Dobbs as he strode into the hospital tent.

Private Dobbs gulped in dismay. He didn't want to be the one to tell the tough sergeant that his prisoner had escaped. "Perhaps you'd best talk to Doctor Turner first," Dobbs said uneasily as he motioned frantically for Kent, who had just walked into the tent.

"Sergeant Norton," Kent said, undaunted by the sergeant's fierce scowl.

"What's going on, Captain? Where's my prisoner? Headquarters is anxious to interrogate him."

Taking his arm, Kent guided Norton from the tent so they wouldn't be overheard. "I'm afraid your man has escaped. He knocked out a guard when I would have sworn he couldn't move a finger."

Norton fumed in impotent rage. "Escaped! How in the hell could you let that happen? Have you sent out a search party?"

Kent drew himself up to his impressive height.

"I suggest you remember who you're talking to, Sergeant. I'm still your superior. Of course I sent out a search party, but they've found no sign of the man." No lie there, Kent thought as he formed his answers to Norton's questions carefully.

"Sorry, sir," Norton mumbled, "but my superiors will have my hide for this."

"I'll write a letter of explanation, Sergeant."

"That's all well and good, but it won't make up for an escaped prisoner. My men and I will conduct a search of the area ourselves. If he's dead, we'll find him. If someone is giving him shelter, they'll have me to deal with." Having said those words, he turned and strode away.

Kent thought about riding out immediately to warn Angela, but a wagonload of wounded arrived and he was caught up in a battle to save lives. For a while, it was so hectic in the surgery tent that Kent had no conception of time. When he emerged into the dark of night, he realized that an entire day had slipped by.

Sergeant Norton was waiting for him in his tent. "I've found no trace of the Reb, Captain," Norton said. "We rode south, thinking he'd try to rejoin his regiment. Tomorrow we'll ride in another direction. Never fear, we'll find him. Dead or alive, we'll find him." He saluted smartly and ducked out of the tent.

Before Kent fell into an exhausted sleep, he thought of Angela and gave silent thanks that she was still safe.

Chapter Four

Angela didn't see Kent for two days and was surprised to find that she missed him. Blake had attempted to leave but had collapsed before he'd gotten out the cabin door, and she had convinced him that he needed another day or two to recuperate before he considered leaving.

"My message to General Hardee from President Davis is vitally important, Angel," Blake said earnestly. "He needs to know that General Lee cannot spare troops from the trenches around Petersburg to reinforce him against Sherman's march to Savannah. What's today's date?"

Angel thought for a moment, then said, "The eighteenth day of December."

Blake groaned in dismay. "It may already be too late. Two men set out with the same message. I pray the other man had more success than I."

Several days later, when Kent rode out to Angela's cabin, he found Blake much improved and anxious to leave.

"What news do you have of the war?" Blake asked, eager for any news at all.

"Sherman has moved into Savannah, and Hardee has taken his army north into South Carolina."

Blake looked stricken. "So it's truly too late. Is Sherman sacking the city?" He was concerned about his fiancée, who lived in Savannah.

"It's my understanding that the city is to remain intact. Sherman is presenting Savannah to President Lincoln as a Christmas gift."

Blake spat out a violent oath. The urgent need to deliver his message to General Hardee no longer existed. Evidently the other man had gotten through, and Hardee had seen fit to take his troops north since he could expect no help from General Lee.

"I must get back to my unit."

"Sergeant Norton is looking for you. This is the first chance I've had to get away. I wanted to warn you before you decided to take off. I expect him to give up the search soon and return to his unit. Perhaps you should wait another day or two. I'll let you know when it's safe."

"Perhaps you're right," Blake said, glancing uneasily at Angela. "I shouldn't leave Angela alone right now. I'll remain until she's safely delivered."

"A wise decision," Kent agreed, worried about Angel himself. "I may not be here much longer to keep an eye on her and Mandy."

"I'm not your responsibility, Kent," Angel reminded him.

Kent searched her face. "I've made you my responsibility. I care a great deal about you, Angel."

"I never thought I'd be grateful to a damn Yankee," Blake grumbled. "Will this war never end?"

Kent's answer was forestalled when Aunt Bessie ran into the cabin, panting and gesturing wildly. "Yankees comin'!"

Kent ran to the door, knowing precisely what to expect. Sergeant Norton had finally found Angela's cabin. "Go out the back door and hide in the woods," Kent told Blake. "I'll hold them off as long as I can. Stay inside," he told Angel and Mandy. "Let me handle this."

Kent was waiting by his mount when Norton and his men arrived. The sergeant appeared surprised to see him, and more than a little suspicious.

"What are you doing here, Captain?"

"I'm on a mission of mercy, Sergeant. There's a pregnant widow and child living in one of the slave cabins. Her home was destroyed recently, and I learned by accident that she was in desperate need of medical attention."

"Don't you have enough to do treating our own wounded without looking to perform good deeds?" Norton sneered.

"I'm a doctor, Sergeant. I go where I'm needed regardless of sides in this war. What are you doing here?"

"This is the only place we haven't looked for the Reb prisoner. I saw smoke rising from the chimney of that old cabin and decided to have a look."

"You might as well not take the trouble. You'll find nothing here out of ordinary."

Norton dismounted, handing the reins to one of his men. "I think I'll have a look, if you don't mind."

Kent positioned himself in front of the door. "I do mind. You'll frighten the child inside and terrify her pregnant mother. They were terrorized enough when their home was burned to the ground by Federal troops."

Norton stared narrow-eyed at Kent. "Are you forbidding me to enter that cabin, Captain? Can you swear to me that the Reb isn't hiding inside?"

Kent went still. Conscience warred with honor inside him. His conscience told him not to betray Blake and cause Angel more anguish than she could handle, and his honor demanded that he not betray the cause he fought for. A compromise was in order, one that would satisfy both his conscience and his honor.

"Believe me, Sergeant Norton, you won't find Lieutenant Keller in that cabin," Kent said succinctly. It was the truth. He had seen Blake slip out the back door scant moments before Norton and his men rode into the yard.

"You're sure about that?" Norton didn't believe him. If he recalled correctly, he'd never mentioned the prisoner's name, so how did the captain know it?

"Absolutely. You won't find the prisoner inside that cabin."

"Very well, Captain, my men and I will leave. It's not our aim to terrorize helpless women and children. But I'm not giving up. It goes against the grain to let some damn Reb get the best of me. I can't abide Rebs."

Mounting up, he and his men rode away. As soon as they were out of sight of the cabin, Norton ordered one of his men to hide in the woods, watch the cabin, and report back to him if he saw anything suspicious.

Angel came out of the cabin the moment Norton and his men were out of sight.

"I don't know how to thank you, Kent. I couldn't bear the thought of Blake dying in some despicable prison." She stepped close and shyly kissed his cheek.

Kent responded from instinct as his arms closed around her. As he stared deeply into her eyes, he realized that she looked much healthier than when he'd first seen her several days ago and hoped he'd made a difference in her life. He wanted to make up for all those years they had wasted, but the war was preventing him from making any kind of commitment—that and the sure knowledge that she'd accept nothing from a Yankee.

"I didn't do much," Kent replied. "There's still no guarantee that Blake won't be caught."

She felt wonderful in his arms, Kent thought. So warm, so ripe with new life. He wished desperately that she were his. His longing for permanency, for this woman, for love, overcame his hesitancy as he lowered his head and kissed her full on the mouth.

The moment Kent's lips covered hers, Angel lost all conception of time and place. Ten years dropped away and she was a young girl again, standing beneath the chestnut tree, kissing Kent and asking him to make love to her. His mouth was warm, sweet, and oh so tempting. She had felt genuine love for Ashley but nothing like this overwhelming surge of rightness, of desire, that she experience with Kent. It would be so easy to love him again, so easy . . . yet impossible.

Even as these thoughts raced through her brain, her mouth opened beneath the relentless probing of Kent's tongue. The small groan that escaped his lips brought her crashing back to reality as she remembered who and what she was and who and what Kent was. She was a woman about to give birth. She was a fiercely loyal Rebel who had lost a father and husband to the war. Kent was a Yankee. He was the man who had left her to pursue his life's dream. He was also a compassionate, caring man who deserved a wife and children of his own. Uttering a small cry of dismay, she broke off the kiss and shrugged his arms aside.

"Don't, Kent, this isn't right."

"It feels right." Kent grinned impudently.

"I'm a woman about to give birth."

He gazed pointedly at her protruding stomach. "Don't you think I'm aware of that? I am a doctor, after all."

"I'm a widow."

"I'm a widower."

"I have a daughter."

Kent sucked his breath in sharply. "I lost a daughter."

"You're a Yankee."

"I'm a human being. We're both human beings. What other arguments can you think of?"

"This . . . this is crazy."

"Those are the only intelligent words you've spoken in the past few minutes. Nothing is certain in these trying times. I could be called to Atlanta or God knows where else at a moment's notice. I worry about you and Mandy excessively, but I'm helpless to do anything about it. After this war is over—and it can't last much longer—I'll come back for you. Will you promise to wait for me? I want to take care of you and the children forever."

Angela stared at him in bewilderment. This was going too fast for her. Her first priorities were Amanda and her baby. Beyond that she couldn't think. Kent was confusing her; she wasn't prepared to think about another man in her life, not even one she had known long ago. Besides that, she didn't want to leave the South.

As if reading her mind, Kent said, "I don't intend leaving the South after the war. Doctors will be needed here during reconstruction, and I aim to help in any way I can. I hope you can live with a simple country doctor."

Kent's words made her smile. "You'll never be 'simple' anything, Doctor Turner. I admire your willingness to help the South, but your assumption is premature; the war isn't over yet. The South could still emerge victorious."

Kent's expression grew bleak. "You know as well as I that a Southern victory is virtually impossible. The South can't possibly recoup its losses or mount another costly offensive. Sherman has already reached the sea. Savannah has fallen. You must face reality, sweetheart."

The endearment caught Angel by surprise. It gave her a warm feeling in the pit of her stomach. "Yes, I suppose you're right, though it hurts to admit it."

Just then Mandy came running from the cabin. "Mama, are the bad men gone? Will Uncle Blake come back?"

"Yes to both questions, honey," Kent said, forestalling Angel's answer. "You've been a very good girl. Your mama is proud of you and so am I."

Mandy beamed, her little face glowing with delight. "Thank you for the candy, Doctor Turner."

"My pleasure, honey. Now will you do something for me?"

"Anything."

"It's time I returned to camp. Take care of your mother. I'll come back when I can, but it isn't easy to leave with wounded arriving daily."

"We'll be fine," Angel said. "Aunt Bessie is here with me. She's delivered many children over the years."

"Aunt Bessie is no longer young. Will you summon me if complications arise?"

"If I can," Angel said, aware of how impossible that might be. "But as I said before, I expect no difficulty. This is my second child."

"I'll take care of Mama," Mandy promised.

"Then I'll leave her in good hands," Kent replied as he mounted up.

"Kent, wait! Are you certain those men won't come back for Blake?" Angel asked anxiously. "Can I trust you not to tell them where to find my brother?"

"The only way I'll divulge any information is if I'm asked directly and point-blank where Blake is. I didn't lie to Sergeant Norton a little while ago. I simply said he wasn't inside the cabin at the present time, and he wasn't. I'm a man of honor, Angel. I respect my uniform too much to betray it. But I don't want Blake to end up a prisoner of war. I'll do my damnedest to protect all of you."

"Can you positively promise me that Blake will be safe here?" She needed more assurance than Kent was willing to give, and she knew it. But she couldn't help herself. Blake was the only member of her family left.

"Don't ask that of me, Angel. I can promise no more than I already have. I'll willingly offer nothing to Sergeant Norton that might harm you or your family."

Angel watched Kent ride away, feeling hopeful yet fearful. A sudden chill set her to shivering, and she hugged Mandy close a moment before returning to the cabin and the meager warmth it offered.

Later that evening, under the cover of darkness, Sergeant Norton's spy saw a lone man creep out of the woods and enter the cabin. He continued watching for better than an hour, and when the man did not leave he rode hell for leather to inform Norton.

To Kent's chagrin, he learned the next morning that Sergeant Norton had no intention of giving up the search for Blake Keller. In fact, he seemed more determined than ever, sending Kent a sardonic smirk before mounting his horse and riding off with his men. Unfortunately, Kent was unable to leave the newly arrived wounded long enough to ride out and warn Angela. Wounded soldiers, some of them Rebs, had arrived minutes ago, and Kent watched with a rapidly pounding heart as Norton left camp.

Blake was up and ready to leave before dawn. After yesterday's close call, he knew he couldn't remain with Angel. It was too dangerous. In the short time he had known Sergeant Norton, he'd learned that the man was ruthless and totally committed to destroying Rebels. He'd show no mercy to anyone found harboring an escaped prisoner, and Blake feared for Angel and his niece. It was best for all that he leave.

"Where will you go?" Angel asked, still not reconciled to Blake's leaving.

"Back to my unit. My message is of little value since Hardee gave up Savannah. It's best you don't know exactly where I'm headed, for I'll probably be carrying messages again soon for President Davis. If you write to Mary Ellen, tell her I'm alive and well."

"You're not well enough to travel," Angel cried,

hoping to delay him one more day.

"I'm putting your life in danger every minute I remain here with you. I have to leave, Angel. It tears me apart to leave you in these circumstances, but there is nothing I can do right now except pray that Kent Turner will look after you."

"I'll be fine, Blake. Take care of yourself, please. I need you." She hugged him fiercely.

After bidding Mandy and Aunt Bessie good-bye, Blake slipped out the back door just as mauve streaks made a timid appearance in a gray-tinged, overcast sky.

The first sign of trouble came when soldiers appeared on the horizon. Angela watched them ride in, identifying them immediately by their blue uniforms. Cautioning Mandy and Aunt Bessie to remain out of sight, she walked out to meet them. She wished now that Mose and his family hadn't already left for Atlanta. She felt alone, helpless and vulnerable. But she was more than grateful that Blake had left before he was discovered and taken prisoner.

Sergeant Norton didn't mince words as he glared down at Angel from atop his mount. "Where is he?"

Angel blanched. "I don't know what you're talking about."

"I think you do. You're harboring an escaped prisoner."

"No, you're mistaken. Captain Turner . . ."

Norton's eyes narrowed, suddenly seeing everything clearly. Captain Turner had lied to him for reasons unknown, and it made him madder than hell to think he'd been duped. What was this woman to the doctor? he wondered as he came to an abrupt decision. Since he'd been lied to, he had no qualms about what he was going to do.

"Who do you think was the one who told me where to find the Reb?" Norton asked nastily.

Angel gasped in shock. "No, Kent wouldn't . . ."

Norton sent her a sly smile, wondering about the relationship between the Union doctor and the pregnant Reb. Whatever it was, he hoped his deliberate falsehood put an end to it. "Wouldn't he? Captain Turner is loyal to his uniform. Why would he protect a Reb?"

Why indeed, Angel thought disconsolately. She had no reason at all to trust Kent or any other Yankee.

"You'll not find anyone inside the cabin but my daughter and her nurse."

"Forgive me if I don't believe you," Norton sneered as he stomped past Angel and thrust open the door.

"Wait! You'll frighten my daughter."

Norton paid Angel little heed as he entered the cabin, followed by several of his men. When Amanda saw them, she gave a frightened shriek and hid behind Aunt Bessie's ample skirts. Angel went to her immediately, trying to dispel her fright as Norton and his men began a thorough search of the cabin. Deliberately destructive, they tore everything apart out of pure meanness. When one of the Yankees turned up a frayed piece of gray uniform, Norton brought it to Angel, thrusting it under her nose triumphantly.

"Do you still deny giving shelter to a Reb prisoner?"

"I have nothing to say," Angel said stubbornly.

"Where did he go?"

Angel stared at him mutely.

"Your lover isn't protecting you any longer. He's already told us about the Reb."

Angel gasped. "My lover?"

"Why else would Captain Turner try to protect you?"

Angel laughed harshly. "Have you looked at me recently, Sergeant?"

Norton sent her an assessing look and shrugged. "You weren't always breeding. Are you going to tell me where the Reb went?"

Angel's chin rose defiantly, and she kept her mouth tightly closed.

Norton's temper flared. These proud Southerners angered him beyond reason. They had nothing of value, yet they acted as if they were too good for the likes of an Indiana farm boy. Well, he'd show them just what an Indiana farm boy was capable of. He turned to his men, his face contorted with wrathful vengeance.

"Fire the cabin."

Angel felt the child lurch in her womb, and she staggered backward. "No, you can't! It's our only shelter. We have no place to go."

"You should have thought of that before you took in that wounded Reb. You know the law. I suggest you gather your belongings if you don't want to see them go up in smoke. Not that we'll be destroying anything of value." He sent her a look of utter disdain. "This place is worse than the sty where we keep our pigs."

Unable to move, to believe this was happening to her again, Angel watched in a daze as a flame was struck and the kindling beside the hearth was set ablaze. The dry tinder caught fire immediately and spread to the surrounding walls in a matter of minutes. Aunt Bessie was the first to move as she gathered up blankets and threw them out the door. Shocked from her lethargy, Angel finally joined her, grabbing what food she could find and stuffing it into a pillowcase.

"Get your kid and that darky out of the cabin," Norton ordered gruffly as he and his men left the burning hut.

The fire was spreading rapidly and flames were already shooting through the roof. Angel shoved Mandy through the door and she and Aunt Bessie followed close behind, coughing from the dense smoke. Sergeant Norton and his men were already mounted. Without a backward glance, they rode off into the gloomy dusk.

Recognizing Angel's shock and fearing for her and the child she carried, Aunt Bessie urged her away from the blazing inferno. Clutching one another for support, they watched in mounting horror as their cabin burned to the ground.

Chapter Five

Numbed by all that had transpired, Angel could think of only one thing: Kent had betrayed her and Blake. Kent had led the Yankees to her brother. She thanked God that Blake had already left before that vicious Sergeant Norton arrived to apprehend him. Just when she had begun trusting Kent again, he had turned against her.

"What we gonna do now, chile?" Aunt Bessie asked, her bottom lip quivering uncontrollably. "Why would dat Yankee doctor do dis to us?"

"I don't believe those bad men told the truth, Mama," Mandy said, refusing to believe ill of Kent. "Captain Turner wouldn't hurt us, I know he wouldn't. You don't believe those bad men, do you?"

"I don't know," Angel said dully. She did know, but she couldn't bear to destroy her daughter's trusting nature. How could she tell Mandy that a man she trusted and admired had brutally betrayed them? That he'd lied and sent men to burn down their shelter, humble though it might be?

"How we gonna live?" Aunt Bessie lamented as she surveyed the destruction created by the Yankees. Not only had their cabin been destroyed, but all the other cabins that had once housed Bogart slaves were leveled as well.

The child lurched in Angel's womb, and she clutched her belly. She was so close to her time and so frightened for her child, for Mandy, for herself and Aunt Bessie. What would become of them now?

A cutting wind lifted her skirts and she felt blowing snow sting her ankles, reminding Angel of their perilous situation. "First we need to find shelter, Aunt Bessie," she said with courage that came from false bravado. Her loved ones depended on her; she couldn't break down now.

Aunt Bessie looked at her as if she had just lost her mind. "Ain't no shelter hereabouts. Dem Yankees done burned everything for miles around."

"Not everything," Mandy said, suddenly remembering something of vital importance. "The cabin that belonged to the Hamiltons' overseer is still standing at the edge of the woods. The Yankees must not have found it. I saw it one day when I went with Mose to check on his traps."

The Hamiltons were the Bogarts' closest neighbors. Their plantation had been set ablaze and the womenfolk had fled south to Louisiana to live with relatives. The slaves had scattered, and the overseer had gone to war with the Hamilton men. The cabin, if it still existed, was no more than a mile or two from where they now stood.

With one accord, they each took up a precious bundle that had been salvaged from the burning hut and started walking.

As soon as he could leave his patients, Kent struck out for the old slave cabin. He needed to see if Angel was safe. He wondered if Blake was still at the cabin when Sergeant Norton had returned. If only he could have gotten a message to Angel to warn her. As if his thoughts had conjured up the sergeant, he and his men suddenly rode into view. They stopped and waited for Kent to approach.

"Well, well, Captain, fancy meeting you out here." The sly smirk on Norton's face gave Kent an uneasy feeling. "It's hardly the kind of weather to enjoy a pleasant ride," Norton continued amiably. "Have you no sick or wounded to treat?"

"You take care of your job and I'll handle mine," Kent said curtly. He didn't like Norton and made no bones about it. Too many men in this war fought purely for the pleasure it gave them, and Norton was one of those men.

"Going out to see that little widow lady down the road?" With trepidation Kent watched Norton and his men exchange amused looks. What did they mean?

"That, Sergeant Norton, is none of your concern. Perhaps I should ask what you're still doing here.

Isn't it time you returned to your unit?"

"Damn right, sir," he said with a nasty inflection. "That's where we're headed now. We've done everything we can here. I'm convinced the prisoner is no longer in the area"—he sent Kent a furious glare—"but we got even."

Kent went still, his face frozen in harsh lines. "Got even? What do you mean?"

"You'll find out soon enough," Norton said with sly innuendo. Then, giving a silent signal with a slash of his raised arm, he spurred his mount and thundered down the road, his men hard on his heels. Kent watched for all of ten seconds before tearing off toward Angela's cabin.

He saw the thin spirals of smoke rising in the air long before he reached the smoldering cabin. His heart beat furiously in his chest, and the breath left his lungs in painful spurts, fearing what he'd find. Within minutes he came upon what was left of the slave cabins.

"Angel!" His voice echoed hollowly in the cold breeze.

Leaping from his horse, Kent ran to the smoldering hut, desperately seeking a clue to this tragedy. It took precious little time to decide that Norton had done this terrible deed, and he cursed the war that condoned such cruel acts. After diligently searching the smoldering ashes and finding no bodies, Kent allowed himself to breathe normally again. Never had he been so terrified. But knowing that Angel and Mandy were alive still did not ease his fear. What had happened to them? They weren't with Norton, so where were they?

The light dusting of snow covering the ground gave him his answer. Three sets of footprints, one of them much smaller than the other two, trailed south. Remounting, Kent followed the tracks over frozen fields, across a narrow stream partially frozen, and toward a forest of tall pines and dense brambles. He saw the cabin nestled snugly against a backdrop of trees. Dismounting, he reached the door in six strides and flung it open without bothering to knock. Relief shuddered through him when he saw Angel, Mandy, and Aunt Bessie huddled around the hearth, trying to warm themselves at the meager fire they had started from the scant supply of wood they found inside.

Angel heard the door open and whirled to face the intruder. Her face, gaunt with shock and exhaustion, hardened when she saw Kent framed in the doorway.

"Did you come to gloat?" she asked harshly. "Did you enjoy seeing our home destroyed?"

Kent closed the door softly behind him and walked into the room. "Why would I gloat? I was nearly out of my mind with worry when I saw what had happened. Who did this to you?" He reached Angel and tried to take her into his arms, to offer comfort, but she twisted away, looking at him as he were a disciple of the devil.

Her face was mottled with rage. "You know who did this. You sent them. Fortunately, Blake had already left before Sergeant Norton and his men arrived. I think he feared betrayal."

"My God, you believe I betrayed you? You always did think the worst of me. I told you

I would protect you, Angel, and I meant it. I wouldn't have sent Norton to the cabin even if I were forced to admit that I had seen Blake and treated his wounds."

"Don't lie, Kent," Angel sobbed, nearly at the end of her meager strength. "Sergeant Norton made sure I knew you had told him where to find Blake before he set fire to the cabin."

"Sergeant Norton is a lying bastard," Kent spat. "He suspected I knew more than I was willing to tell him. It piqued his perverse nature to lie to you. I didn't betray your brother, Angel."

"*I* believe you," Mandy said shyly.

"Children are trusting souls," Angel declared hotly. "They see only what they want to see. I'm not so gullible. You forget, I knew you long ago and learned you weren't trustworthy."

"How can I help?" Kent asked. Angel was clearly distraught. Since he didn't want to do anything to harm her child, he abruptly changed the subject. When she was calmer, he'd try to explain more fully that he was in no way involved with Norton's attack.

"I want nothing from you."

"We needs firewood," Aunt Bessie said, too practical to refuse help when it was desperately needed. "And water from de well."

"I've brought some food," Kent said. "I'll carry it inside."

"I'll help," Mandy said, skipping outside with Kent.

Two hours later, a fire burned merrily in the hearth and the room was fragrant with the odor of bacon and beans. Angel sat at the table sipping tea, a gift from Kent, and staring into space. Kent sat across from her, watching her closely, worriedly. He glanced around the room, aware that it was much larger and held more amenities than the slave cabin in which she had been living. There appeared to be a second room, possibly a bedroom, just beyond a door at the rear of the cabin.

"What place is this?" he asked, hoping to coax Angel from her lethargy.

When she didn't answer, Mandy rushed into the void. "It belonged to the Hamiltons' overseer. Mose and I came across it one day while we were out checking traps. I guess it's so far from the big house that the Yankees didn't find it when they burned the other buildings."

"We's gonna be all right here," Aunt Bessie said, trying to sound convincing.

Angel sent the old woman a sharp glance. "Unless Captain Turner sends the Yankees to burn us out again." She sounded tired and defeated, and Kent's heart went out to her. True, the cabin was in better shape than the old one they had occupied, and it was closer to the field hospital, but he couldn't banish the thought of Angel's child being born in such mean circumstances, with no one in attendance but a feeble old woman.

"You know I'd never do that, Angel."

Angel's chin rose fractionally. "I know nothing of the sort. Yankees are capable of anything. *You're* capable of anything."

Kent sighed wearily. Had nothing he'd said

gotten through to her? "I'd like to talk to Angel in private, Aunt Bessie. Would you take Mandy into the other room?"

Aunt Bessie hesitated, then did as Kent asked. Once they were alone, Kent knelt beside Angel, taking her hands in his. She tried to pull them away, but he held them fast, surprised at how cold they felt despite the warmth filling the room.

"Look at me, Angel." He lifted her chin until their eyes met. "I swear I didn't betray you and Blake. I care for you too much to allow someone to hurt you. If I had been pressed, I would have found some way to remain true to my uniform without betraying Blake's hiding place. I did it once; I could have done it again."

Angel searched his face, desperately wanting—needing—to believe him, but too much stood in the way. "It doesn't matter," she said wearily. "You've defeated us—is that what you want me to say? Very well, I admit it. You've beaten us. Sherman has reached the sea, and the South will surely fall. Why should you care what happens to me and Mandy?"

"Have you heard nothing I've said? Seeing you again after all these years has made me realize that I've never stopped caring for you. It nearly broke my heart when I learned you had married. I never forgot that magical night beneath the chestnut tree before I went off to England. You gave me a very special gift that night."

Angel flushed and looked away. She had been such a child then. But she still recalled how Kent had made her feel that night. Being loved by

him had been a never-to-be-forgotten experience.
Unfortunately, she had allowed her hurt and anger
to create a rift between them.

"After I heard you'd married, I found Jennifer,"
Kent continued, "and your image began to fade
from my mind, though it was never entirely
forgotten. When Jennifer and our child died, my
world fell apart. Finding you again has been like
a dream come true. I accept now that fate willed
our meeting at a time when you needed me most;
why can't you?"

"Why should you care? I'm carrying my dead
husband's child," Angel stated dully. "I have a
daughter whom I love dearly."

"I have nothing and no one," Kent said in a
choked voice. "My parents died in England, and
I am an only child. Let me share your family. I
want to take care of you."

She stared at him. "It won't work for many
reasons."

"Tell me why."

"First, you're a Yankee. Second, I don't trust you.
And last but surely not least, how do you expect
to take care of a family when you're likely to be
moved from place to place at any time? You said
yourself you're to be transferred to Atlanta soon."

Lord, why was she even considering his outrageous suggestion that fate had meant for them to
meet again? She could never be certain that he
hadn't betrayed them, and she was too tired to
think clearly. What she truly needed was time
alone to think. To decide what was best for her
family.

At one time, her fondest dream had been to spend the rest of her life with Kent. She had loved him. Though young, she had willingly given him her body, her soul, her loyalty. He had taken what she offered and then abandoned her. She had married Ashley because he was there and Kent wasn't. She had learned to care for her husband, to appreciate his sweetness, but she knew now that she had never forgotten Kent Turner, the man who had valued his profession more than he valued her.

"I must go where I'm ordered," Kent contended, "but that doesn't mean I can't provide for you and your children. I could send you North, or take you to Atlanta—there are any number of things I could do to ensure your safety. You've only to say the word, sweetheart. I worry about you. You're very near to your time."

As he spoke, Angel felt a sharp pain in the small of her back and fought the urge to place her hands where the pain was the greatest. She was indeed close to her time. She knew it, felt it with every breath she drew, yet pride prevented her from accepting anything from a Yankee—from Kent.

"I need time to think," Angel said as another twinge snaked from her back to her abdomen. "I think you should leave, Captain Turner. As you can see, we have adequate shelter. There is nothing more you can do for us. Go back to your patients. They need you more than I."

"Are you sure you're all right? You look unnaturally pale."

"I suppose it's the shock of being burned out again. Don't worry, I'll be fine. I've gotten along thus far without you and will continue to do so. Please leave now."

Before she could protest, Kent drew Angel gently to her feet and into his arms. He kissed her tenderly, then pressed his hand firmly against the hard bulge of her stomach, needing to satisfy himself that the babe within rested easily. The steady thump, thump against his palm assured him that all was well, at least for the time being.

"You're mine, Angela. You were always mine," he whispered in a voice filled with passionate promise. "Finding you again is like a miracle. Your children are an addition to my life that I would welcome gladly, if you but say the word."

Angel's scathing retort died in her throat as Kent searched her face for the space of a heartbeat, then turned abruptly toward the door. "I'll be back," he called over his shoulder. "Send Aunt Bessie if you need me."

Angel stared at the door, amazed at Kent's stubbornness. Didn't he understand that they couldn't relive the past? Didn't he realize that there could never be anything between them? Not even friendship was possible as long as he wore a blue uniform.

"Is de captain gone?" Aunt Bessie asked, coming into the room moments after Kent left.

"Yes, he's gone. Where is Mandy?"

"Sleepin'. De poor chile is purely worn out. What you gonna do, Angel?"

"About what?" Angel asked dully, fully aware of what Aunt Bessie was asking.

"About de captain. He seems right fond of you

and Mandy. I know somethin' happened between you a long time ago, but maybe you aughta put de past where it belongs."

"I can't think right now, Aunt Bessie. Besides, you don't understand about me and Kent." She winced as another pain struck somewhere in the vicinity of her back.

"You awright?" Aunt Bessie asked anxiously. "Is it de baby?"

"No," Angel lied, thinking it too soon yet to mention the nagging pain in her back. "I think I'll join Mandy in bed. It's been a long day."

Kent found it difficult to concentrate the following day. No new patients had arrived, leaving about a dozen wounded soldiers remaining at the field hospital. He'd heard that Hood's army was still moving south, pursued by Federal troops, and that a skirmish had occurred near Columbia, Tennessee, three days earlier.

Later that day, a messenger arrived from Atlanta with orders for Kent. Kent was given ten days to report to his new post as director of the military hospital in Atlanta.

Angel felt ominous misgivings about the child she carried. She was experiencing pain—sometimes sharp, sometimes vague, but always there, always reminding her of the imminent birth of her child. By her calculations, the babe could come at any time, and she mentally prepared herself for the grueling prospect of giving birth virtually unaided but for an old woman. She went to bed on the evening of December 23rd thinking of Kent and wondering if she would survive the ordeal of childbirth alone. She awoke during the darkest hours of the night, aware of crushing, unrelenting pain. Not even Mandy's birth had produced this much pain.

She arose at dawn, and Aunt Bessie knew by the look on Angel's drawn features that she was in labor. For Mandy's sake, Angel tried to suppress her discomfort as she busied herself with fixing a meager breakfast for her daughter. Aunt Bessie wasn't fooled one bit by Angel's false cheerfulness and prepared quietly for the birth, unaware that it was the day before Christmas.

"How long you been hurtin'?" Aunt Bessie asked sharply.

"Since yesterday," Angel answered honestly. "But the pains didn't get severe until during the night sometime. I don't imagine it will be long now."

As the day wore on, Angel's pain increased in severity until she could no longer hide the tearing, searing contractions that tore at her fragile body. She took to her bed at noon, with Aunt Bessie in attendance. Mandy was sent outside to gather firewood. When she returned, her mother's moans of agony frightened her so badly that she ran into the bedroom, appalled when she saw Angel's writhing form and contorted features.

"Don't die, Mama, please don't die!" Mandy cried, rushing to her mother's bedside.

"Hush, now, chile, yo mama ain't gonna die. You go on now and wait in de other room."

205

Reluctantly, Mandy left the room, far from placated by Aunt Bessie's words. It didn't look to her as if her mama was going to be all right.

"Why isn't the baby coming?" Angel gasped between pains. "Why is it taking so long?" Mandy's birth had been easy and relatively uncomplicated.

Aunt Bessie's eyes filled with helpless tears. She had examined Angel and ascertained that the baby was turned wrong, making the labor long and difficult. Trouble was, she didn't know how to go about fixing it. She wasn't a midwife. True, she had brought many children into the world, but all had come spontaneously and without complications or mishap. None of the women had been as fragile as her Angel. She was frightened.

Angel was growing weaker, her moans coming nonstop, interspersed with muffled screams. Mandy knew a fear more potent than her years could handle. She wanted to help her mother and immediately thought of Kent. She recalled that Kent had said to send for him if they needed him, and she could think of no greater need than saving her mother's life. Her mind made up, Mandy quietly left the cabin. She knew exactly where to find the field hospital and set off at a brisk run, her little legs churning beneath her, her arms pumping wildly.

Kent worried about Angel excessively. His consuming fear was that her child would arrive and neither would survive. He couldn't help thinking about his wife and how devastated he had been to lose her and their child. Childbirth was safer than it had been in years past, but it was still dangerous. Deaths still occurred despite the improvements in medicine.

Kent had just left the hospital tent when he saw a small body hurtling through camp. He stopped dead in his tracks, recognizing Mandy immediately. The blood froze in his veins, imagining all kinds of dire emergencies that might have brought Mandy to him. All of them involved Angel.

"Captain Turner! Captain Turner!"

Kent caught her in his arms as she rushed toward him. "Easy, Mandy, what's wrong? Is someone in trouble? Is it your mother?"

Out of breath and unable to utter a word, Mandy merely nodded her head.

"Take it easy, honey. Breathe slowly. That's it. Now, tell me what happened."

"It—it's Mama," Mandy gasped, clutching desperately at Kent. "The baby is coming and she's dying. Help her, Captain Turner. Please help her."

Dying. Kent's gut clenched with grinding fear. "Don't worry, honey. I'll help her." He only hoped it wasn't too late. "Did Aunt Bessie send you? Is she helping your mama right now?"

Mandy swiped ineffectually at her teary eyes. "I came here on my own. Aunt Bessie is with Mama and I didn't want to bother her. You can save Mama. I know you can. I don't believe you did anything to hurt us or Uncle Blake."

The trust Mandy placed in Kent was awesome. He hoped he could live up to the kind of faith Mandy possessed. It gave him one more reason to want to take care of Angel, Mandy, and the new baby forever. Besides that, he loved them, even the unborn child.

"I'll hitch up a wagon, Mandy, and we'll be on our way. I may need to bring Angel back to the field hospital, where more sophisticated care is available." If something was drastically wrong he might have to perform surgery to remove the child from Angel's womb, and he preferred to do it in well-equipped surroundings.

Fifteen minutes later Kent and Mandy were careening down the road in a wagon used to transport wounded men from the battlefield. Nothing mattered now but reaching Angel in time.

Chapter Six

Though the distance wasn't great, it seemed forever before the cabin at the edge of the woods came into view. Each second seemed like an hour, each minute an eternity. Should something happen to Angel and her child, Kent didn't know how he would bear it. He jumped from the wagon before it came to a full stop, forgetting Mandy in his haste to reach her mother. He heard Angel's moans as he burst through the door and rushed inside the cabin, his fear a ravening beast inside him. He continued on to the bedroom, thrusting the door aside and stepping into the room.

The first thing Kent noticed was Aunt Bessie's face, ashen with exhaustion and worry, and her relief when she saw him. Then he looked toward the bed, where Angel's swollen body arched and writhed in agony.

"Hot water!" he ordered crisply, "and soap." He flung off his jacket and threw it aside, trying to recall everything he'd learned about childbirth and its complications. He bent over Angel, placing his hand on her stomach as another powerful contraction ripped through her. After it passed, she opened her eyes and looked up at him.

"What are you doing here?"

"I've come to help. How long has this been going on?"

"Since yesterday, Captain," Aunt Bessie answered, "but de babe don' wanna come." She approached the bed, offering a basin of steaming water, soap, and a towel. "I done all I could, but it ain't enough."

Kent stepped to the basin, immersing his hands and arms up to his elbows and scrubbing vigorously. When he had finished, he approached the bed, kneeling down and taking one of Angel's limp hands in his.

"I'm going to examine you, Angel. I'll try not to hurt you, but I need to know why the babe isn't coming."

Angel was beyond caring; she just wanted this to be over.

"Is Mama going to be all right?"

Kent whirled, startled to find Mandy standing behind him. In his rush to reach Angel, he had forgotten all about the child. He beckoned to Aunt Bessie. "Take Mandy into the other room, Aunt Bessie," he said gently. To Mandy, he said, "Your mama isn't going to die, honey. I won't let her." He prayed to God he'd be able to keep his promise.

When they had left the room, he turned back to Angel, all his energy and considerable knowledge focused on the woman he had never stopped loving. Years had passed, time had dulled his memory, but love had never died.

The examination was swift and painful despite Kent's gentle hands. When he had finished, he rocked back on his heels and stared at Angel.

"Am I going to die?" she asked, gritting her teeth against the stabbing agony of another contraction.

"No, don't even think about such a thing. Your baby lies in an awkward position within the birth canal. There is a slim possibility that it could turn without manipulation. I want to give it every opportunity to do so before I take drastic measures. An hour or two should tell the tale. Can you manage that long?"

She stared at him, her face pale, her eyes huge. "If the babe doesn't turn? What then?"

"Then I will do what nature did not and turn the babe myself," Kent said confidently. "If that fails, there is always a surgical means to remove the child. I'm going to take you to the field hospital where there are surgical tools available to aid me. Can you manage?" he asked again.

"Are you sure this is necessary?" she asked. "Can't you just do what needs to be done here?"

"I can only remain away from camp a short time, and I'd feel better with a fully equipped surgery to rely upon. We'll take it slow and easy. The camp is but a short distance away. Mandy made it easily on foot, and I have a wagon."

"Do what you think necessary," Angel gasped, hovering on the edge of another contraction. "I don't want my baby to die."

"No one is going to die," Kent promised. "Trust me."

"Trust . . . you . . . How can I?" Her eyes were glazed now, fully controlled by pain. "You . . . led the Yankees . . . to Blake."

"No, Angel, I wouldn't do that. I don't know how Norton learned about Blake, but it wasn't from me. Now, let's get you into the back of the wagon."

Kent carried Angel to the wagon and laid her gently on the mound of blankets placed there by Mandy and Aunt Bessie. Mandy cuddled next to her mother, and Aunt Bessie climbed up beside them. Kent picked up the reins and set the horse into motion. Though he tried to pick the route least likely to jar his passengers, Angel's moans spurred him to haste.

"Better hurry, Captain," Aunt Bessie urged when Angel arched sharply upward. "Dis babe wants to get born."

"Almost there," Kent said as the camp came into view.

Private Dobbs met the wagon as it pulled into camp and ground to a halt. "Captain Turner, no one knew where you had gotten off to, sir." It wasn't the first time the captain had been missing from camp, but Dobbs was not one to question an officer. Especially one as dedicated to his patients as Doctor Turner.

"I'm back now, Dobbs. Help me get my patient to surgery."

Only then did Dobbs notice the three women inside the wagon. He hastened to lift the child down, then turned to help the old woman as Kent lifted Angel into his arms.

"The woman is in labor, Dobbs, and in trouble. I'm taking her to surgery. Show the child and her nurse to my tent and find them something to eat."

"Yes, sir. Anything else?"

"Stay close in case I need you," Kent said in a voice meant only for Dobbs's ears. "I may have to perform surgery to save the life of mother and child, and I'll need an assistant."

Kent strode toward the surgery, unmindful of the curious glances following his progress, or of the speculation and gossip flying back and forth among the men under his command. When Dobbs returned from settling Mandy and Aunt Bessie in Kent's tent and stationed himself outside the surgery, men crowded around him, asking questions to which he had no answers.

"A baby, you say?" one soldier asked as he tried to peer inside the surgery. "Here? Now?" Dobbs nodded his head and those around him fell silent, perhaps recalling families they had left behind or children they had never seen. "Don't that beat all."

Then a strange thing happened. From every corner of the camp men came. Some hobbling on crutches, some sporting bandages, some wearing rags that could scarcely be called uniforms. And still they came, whispering among themselves, Yankees and Rebs alike, finding a common bond in the miracle of childbirth.

"It's Christmas Eve," someone said, his voice taut with hushed reverence.

A murmur went through the ranks, rising in excitement as the significance of the holy occasion and imminent birth of a child struck the men who had thought of nothing but killing for so long.

When Dobbs tried to disperse the gathering, the men refused to budge. Yankee and Rebel alike sank to the ground in front of the surgery. As the day lengthened into night, someone started a fire and the men huddled close, waiting. The chaplain, who had arrived to investigate the strange gathering, grasped the mood immediately and joined the group, awed and not a little amazed at the sense of good will present in the mixed gathering of Yankees and their Reb prisoners, drawn together by the renewal of life and inspired with new hope for the future by the birth of a child.

Angela was weakening, and it worried Kent. The child still had not turned naturally, and he mentally reviewed all he knew about surgical birth.

"Kent."

Kent bent close; her voice was barely a whisper. "What is it, love?"

"I'm going to die."

"No," he denied fiercely, "you're going to live. I'm going to turn the child in the birth canal. If that doesn't work, I'll perform surgery. Brace yourself, love—this may hurt, but the child will have a better chance of survival if it comes naturally." He moved to the end of the cot.

"Kent, wait! If I should die, what will happen to my child? To Mandy?"

"You're not going to die."

"Please, Kent, I have to know."

"I'll try to find your brother."

Angel shook her head as vigorously as her meager strength allowed. "It's not good enough. Lord only knows when or where you'll find Blake. They need someone to care for them now."

Kent saw that she was deadly serious. "Both you and your child are going to be fine."

"Promise you'll look after them, Kent, promise me."

"I'm not their father, love. I have no say over what happens to your children." He fell silent for the space of a heartbeat, staring at Angel intently. "But there is a way, if you will agree. You could marry me before the babe is born, then I will in truth be the father."

"Marry you? But you're a Yankee."

"A moment ago you were begging me to see to your children's welfare, Yankee or no. I love you, Angel. I've never stopped loving you. There's a chaplain in camp. Say the word, and I'll ask him to marry us immediately."

"And you'll care for the children as if they were your very own?"

"Forever."

"Call him," Angel gasped, lost in the throes of another contraction.

Kent acted with alacrity, moving swiftly to the door of the tent and speaking quietly to Private

Dobbs. The startled private nodded his understanding as Kent ducked back inside the tent.
Within minutes, Captain Myers, the chaplain,
slipped into the tent.

"This is rather irregular, Captain," Myers said,
looking at Angel with compassion. "Wouldn't it be
better to wait until after the child is born?"

"No, please!" Angel pleaded as waves of pain
ebbed and crested. "You must marry us now,
before the child comes."

"It's what we both want," Kent said earnestly,
"and please hurry. There isn't much time."

"We need a witness."

"Private Dobbs!" Kent called. Dobbs appeared
immediately. "We are in need of a witness."

"Witness, sir?"

"Mrs. Bogart and I wish to marry. Will you act
as our witness?"

The private's confusion was clearly evident, but
he did not hesitate. "Yes sir, happy to, sir."

The ceremony was necessarily brief, and afterward Angel felt a kind of peace she hadn't
experienced in a long time. She knew she was
marrying the enemy, but none of that mattered
now. The welfare of her children took prece-
dence over her hatred for Yankees. And despite
everything, she knew she could trust Kent to take
care of Mandy and the new baby should she not
survive the ordeal of childbirth.

Kent had no illusions about Angel's reasons for
marrying him, but they did not matter. He had
never stopped loving her, and he loved her still.
Somehow he would overcome her aversion for

him and what he stood for and make her love him. More importantly, he now had a family of his own to love and care for forever. And one day, God willing, there might be a child of his own, not that he wouldn't love Mandy and the new babe as if they were his very own.

After the chaplain pronounced them husband and wife, Kent shooed everyone from the tent and prepared himself for the ordeal ahead. Ever scrupulous about cleanliness, Kent scrubbed his hands and forearms, then turned back to Angel.

"This will hurt, sweetheart, but if I can turn the babe in the birth canal, it may not be necessary to remove the babe surgically, which is a risky procedure."

Angel gritted her teeth, her strength rapidly waning. "Do what you must, Kent, but do it fast. I don't know how much more of this I can take. Just don't forget your promise to look after the children if—if I don't make it."

"Don't talk like that, Angel. You're going to make it. I don't intend to marry and bury a wife all in the same day."

Kent moved to the end of the cot, took one last look at Angel, then did what he had been trained to do, allowing his expertise as a doctor to guide him. Once he divorced himself from the knowledge that Angel was the woman he loved, his professionalism took over and he was able to perform his job with the detachment necessary for success.

Angel gave one piercing scream as Kent turned the child, then went limp. After that things progressed rather quickly. In a hurry to be born, the babe was more than ready to present itself.

"Help me, Angel," Kent urged softly as he pressed gently upon her belly. "Push with the pains. It won't be long now before you'll have your babe in your arms. I know you're tired, sweetheart, but you can do it."

His voice, so coaxing, so caring, so richly confident, provided Angel with the courage and fortitude to produce the extra effort necessary to birth the child. Angel felt a great pressure, and following Kent's directions, she pushed the babe into his waiting hands.

"It's a boy, sweetheart! We have a son. A fine healthy son."

The thin wail of a newborn babe filled the tent, wafting out into the cold, clear night where men were milling around the campfire with an air of expectancy. The cry grew stronger and they smiled at one another, Yankee and Rebel alike, regardless of political beliefs or regional differences.

Suddenly Mandy appeared amidst the tangle of men, her eyes alight, her little face suffused with joy as she looked toward the tent and saw Kent standing in the opening holding a tiny bundle and smiling, indicating that all was well.

Her answering smile was as wide as all outdoors as she turned to the men and announced jubilantly, "It's Christmas Eve! I knew Saint Nicholas wouldn't forget me. He's given me a new baby to love!"

The men exchanged incredulous looks, most having forgotten that Christmas still occurred during bad times as well as good. Suddenly a young Yankee, wounded and wearing a bandage around his head, gazed up into the star-studded sky and said in a hushed voice, "Well I'll be danged. It *is* Christmas Eve. And just like the Good Book says, a child is born."

The silence was deafening as each man envisioned another Christmas, another time, a wife, children . . . peace.

Mandy, whose mind dwelt strictly in the present, rushed up to Kent to peek at the babe. She spoke quietly to Kent a moment then turned and announced quite grandly, "It's a boy!" Then she rushed past him to see her mother. Kent turned and followed her inside.

Chapter Seven

Despite her weariness, Angel smiled when Kent placed her newborn son in her arms. She was amazed that she had survived the ordeal and credited Kent with saving the lives of both her and her babe. When Mandy crept up to the bed, Angel welcomed her joyously as the child gazed raptly at her new brother.

The heartwarming scene produced a lump in Kent's throat and he swallowed convulsively, suddenly recalling that he was now a part of this wonderful family. Would Angel remember the brief vows they had spoken? he wondered. Would she regret marrying him now that she was safely delivered of her child? Thus far she had made no move to include him in the intimate family reunion and he hung back, observing, waiting. . . . Aunt Bessie was warmly welcomed when she tiptoed into the tent to assure herself that mother and child were well. Still Kent waited.

Outside the tent, something exciting and wonderful was taking place. A wounded Reb soldier searched through his pockets and found a coin. Rising unsteadily to his feet, he limped to the tent, standing hesitantly in the opening, his hand outstretched, offering the only gift he could find on his person. Kent saw him first and looked at Angel. She had also seen him and offered an encouraging nod. The soldier entered gingerly and approached the cot. Angel smiled at him and held the babe so the soldier could look at him.

Tears came to his eyes as he gazed at the tiny, wizened face. "Thank you, ma'am," he said in a choking voice. Before he turned and left, he placed the coin still clutched in his fist beside Angel on the cot. "It ain't much, ma'am, but I want the babe to have it."

Private Dobbs, still stationed at the door, saw what was taking place and whispered to those nearest him. Word passed quickly, and within minutes each man began searching his meager possessions for a gift to present to the child. A Yankee soldier approached the tent next, holding a whistle he had carved in his spare time. It had been made as a gift for his own child when he returned home. But he could carve another.

Angel stiffened perceptibly when she saw the despised Yankee offering her son a gift. Then her face softened, and she relaxed visibly when she saw the tender way he gazed at her babe. She thanked him softly, agog with the wonder of what was taking place this Christmas Eve, in this insignificant place, inspired by a child who meant nothing to these war-hardened men.

One by one, the men milling outside the tent found some token to offer the newborn. Whether valuable or not, each gift meant something to the man who offered it. One Yankee, sporting only one arm and the stub of another, unwound a silk scarf from his neck, a present from his mother, and placed it on the cot next to Angel and the babe. Angel could see how difficult it was for him to part with and she tried to return it, but one look at Kent changed her mind.

She realized then that these men were giving from their hearts, offering a tiny part of themselves that made them feel good no matter how insignificant their gift. Any birth, even one as unimportant as her child's, was a miracle, and Angel recognized the need for each man present to celebrate the renewal of life. In times of death and destruction, the spirit yearned for peace and harmony, and a child's birth signified a rebirth into better times. Especially during the holy time of Christmas.

The line of men moving in and out of the tent continued as the babe slept peacefully in Angel's arms. Those who could not walk were supported by others; more often than not Yanks helped Rebs and Rebs helped Yanks, the color of their uniforms all but forgotten. A grizzled Yankee sergeant with frozen feet literally crawled to the cot and gently touched the downy cheek of the babe, a look of utter astonishment softening his features. A career soldier, he had never married.

"I ain't never felt anything so soft, ma'am," he said reverently as he pulled a gold button from his uniform and placed it on the cot. He gazed raptly at the infant for a moment more, then turned away as another soldier appeared in the doorway to take his place.

In the brief interval before another replaced him, Angel glanced over and saw Kent looking at her and the children with such longing that she felt her heart contract with something akin to pain. Were it not for Kent, she wouldn't be holding her child right now. She reached out her hand to him. His face glowed as he stepped close to the bed and took her hand in his. But there was no time for words as another soldier moved into the tent. Kent motioned him closer.

"Mama, look!" Mandy squealed in delight.

The soldier, a Yankee orderly, carried the cropped top of a small pine tree. It was about eighteen inches high and decorated with bits of gauze tied into bows, tiny acorns, and gold and brass buttons torn from the jackets of men fortunate enough to still have uniforms. It brought tears to Angel's eyes. It was the first Christmas tree they had had in years. After the war heated up, she had been unable to provide her daughter with the kind of Christmas she deserved. It had been all she could do to find food for their stomachs after the men in the family left to fight.

The tree was placed upright in a pitcher on a nearby table where Mandy could gaze at it to her heart's content. And still the parade of men and gifts continued. A few had even found something in their belongings for Mandy, so that she would not feel left out.

One of the last gifts offered was a makeshift bed for the babe. A Yankee soldier had found an empty crate, lined it with blankets and placed it on the floor beside Angel.

Finally, only one man remained who had not made an offering of some kind to the newborn. He was a young Reb soldier, so young that his cheeks still bore the downy fuzz of youth. His head and one eye were swathed in bloody bandages. He had deliberately hung back, finding nothing worthy enough to offer to the child. No one seemed to notice, but he could not help feeling the lack.

Suddenly a thought came to him, and his one good eye misted with happiness and his mouth curved into a smile—his first since he'd been captured and brought to the Yankee field hospital to be treated for his wounds. Slowly he made his way through the throng of men still clustered around the tent. Darkness and his grave wounds made it difficult to see clearly. When he stumbled forward, Private Dobbs grasped his arm and guided him toward the tent. Immediately a path was cleared for him.

He ducked inside the tent and paused, leaning heavily upon Dobbs's arm. "I—I have nothing of value to give," he stammered in a voice that betrayed his youth.

Angel blinked away a flood of tears; the boy was pathetically young, barely out of kneepants. War had made a man of him before his time. It was sad, so terribly sad.

"You're alive, that's gift enough," Angel said softly.

The youth's one good eye settled on Kent. "I wouldn't be alive but for the Yankee doctor. He's a good man, ma'am. He wouldn't let me die even though I'm a Reb. And—and I still have one good eye. But there is one thing I can offer. I hope it pleases you and the babe."

He cleared his throat, raised his head, and began to sing, his voice as clear and true as a choirboy's. At first the lilting strains of the familiar Christmas hymn were barely audible, but as the melody drifted on the night breeze, the men outside grew quiet, and into the hush his voice rose with renewed vigor and tremendous sweetness. By the time the last haunting strains died away, there wasn't a dry eye in the camp. Abruptly the Reb turned and walked away, his head high, his step firm.

One by one the men drifted away, Reb and Yankee alike, some with arms linked, helping those less fortunate, many speaking of family and home with men they would not normally confide in, given the circumstances of war. But it was Christmas Eve, a time of peace and goodwill, and into their midst had come the miracle of birth. A child was born. In a field hospital where death visited often and the maimed sought solace, the wail of a newborn had brought hope.

As the last strains of the Christmas hymn died away, Angel slept.

*   *   *

Angel awoke the following morning as the camp was stirring to life. The first thing she saw was Kent sitting in a chair beside her. It was Christmas day and relatively quiet throughout the area, though reports indicated that fighting was still taking place around Nashville. Confederate reinforcements were reported within five miles of the Tennessee River.

"Didn't you go to bed?" Angel asked, startling him.

"You're awake. How do you feel?"

"Like a woman who has just given birth." At the mention of her child, a worried frown creased her brow and she searched frantically for her son. "My baby . . ."

"He's fine, Angel. He's sleeping soundly in his bed. Have you given any thought to a name for our son?"

Our son. Kent's words gave her pause for thought. What had she done? Would she live to regret her hasty marriage to a Yankee doctor?

He took her hand in his, caressing her wrist with his thumb, feeling the rapid beating of her pulse. "You do recall marrying me, don't you, sweetheart?" She nodded absently. "In fact, you were quite insistent upon doing it immediately."

Her gaze dropped, settling disconcertingly upon that place where he caressed her wrist. She caught her bottom lip between her teeth. "I'm sorry. I didn't mean to put you in an awkward position. Is . . . is our marriage valid?"

Kent gave her a dazzling smile. "Legal and

binding. You can't take it back even if you want to." He frowned at her. "You don't, do you?"

Angel stared at him. "I don't know what I was thinking of. I thought I was going to die."

"I understand, but I'm not sorry we married. I hope I never give you cause to regret it." He bent and kissed her forehead, thinking her the most beautiful woman he'd ever seen, despite the harrowing ordeal of a difficult birth. "I'll be a good father to your children, I promise."

Angel didn't doubt him for a moment. If men who hated each other could put aside their animosity to celebrate the birth of her child, then she and Kent owed it to themselves and to the children to learn to accept each other's beliefs and overcome the obstacle of their conflicting ideals.

"What do you suppose happened last night, Kent?" Angel asked thoughtfully. "My babe is nothing to these men, yet they acted as if a miracle of some sort had occurred."

Kent knew exactly what Angel meant. He had been no less surprised than she at the outpouring of love and goodwill generated by the birth of her child. "When men are far from home and hearth, their thoughts are often with their loved ones— especially at Christmas, a time when families gather to celebrate."

"That still doesn't explain . . ."

"You might call it a miracle of sorts. For a short time the men were able to forget their troubles as life renewed itself in the most basic way. It was a special time, Angel. I'll never forget it, not if I live to be one hundred."

Angel sighed heavily and closed her eyes. She had so much to think about. So much . . .

Kent turned from the cot quietly so as not to awaken Angel. She needed the rest. On his way out, he stopped to gaze at the infant sleeping peacefully in his makeshift crib. Kent loved this child already. He had coaxed him from Angel's body and caught him in his hands; he had been the first to see or touch him. The boy might have been sired by Ashley Bogart but he, Kent Turner, would be the man who raised and nurtured him. As for Mandy, she was the daughter he might have had if his own baby girl had not perished with her mother.

When Angel awoke later, Kent carried her from the surgery tent, which was to be dismantled for moving, to his own quarters. She seemed stronger and ate a hearty meal before nursing the babe. Then Kent arranged for Mandy and Aunt Bessie to occupy a vacant tent.

The following day, Angel was up and moving gingerly around the tent, caring for her child. She had seen little of Kent since giving birth, for in addition to caring for his patients, he had the added responsibility of seeing the field hospital dismantled in preparation for the move to Nashville. Therefore, Kent was somewhat surprised when he returned to his quarters that evening and found Angel fully dressed and sitting on a stool nursing the babe. He came to an abrupt halt, mesmerized by the sight of mother and child. Angel looked up and smiled at him.

"He's almost asleep. Would you like to put him in his bed?"

Kent complied eagerly, somewhat disconcerted as his hand brushed the soft flesh of her bare breast, which she hastily covered. Before he drew away, he looked deeply into her eyes. She met his gaze evenly, without flinching, and Kent was heartened. That she did not shy away from him was a good sign. He placed the child in his bed and came back to Angel. Taking her hands, he pulled her to her feet.

"You should be in bed. I want you well for our trip to Atlanta." He swept her from her feet, carried her to the cot, and sat down with her in his lap. Then, still looking deeply into her eyes, he began unbuttoning her dress. She grasped his hands.

"Kent . . ."

He shoved her hands aside. "Don't. We're husband and wife now. I'm not going to hurt you. I'm a doctor; I know how long it takes a woman to recover from childbirth."

Carefully he lowered the oft-mended dress from her narrow shoulders, vowing to dress her in the finest silks when this senseless war was over. "You're lovely," he said, staring at the fullness of her milk-swollen breasts clearly revealed through her thin chemise. "I pray that one day you'll want me as much as I want you. When that day comes, we'll truly be husband and wife."

Then he kissed her, and Angel was shocked at how eagerly she responded. It was almost as if she were swept back ten years and she and Kent were standing beneath that chestnut tree where he had

229

told her he was going to attend medical school in England. The intervening years fell away as if they had never been. She was Kent's, always Kent's, forever Kent's, just as she was meant to be. In her mind, she relived the extraordinary experience of that first and only time he had made love to her, and knew that one day she wanted to experience those same feelings again.

She had been such a child then. She had selfishly demanded that he abandon all his dreams and cling only to her. She had foolishly thought that giving herself to him would change his mind, alter the course of his destiny. He hadn't wanted to make love to her, but she had been so insistent that he'd been unable to resist. She saw it all quite clearly now. She had been so angered by his leaving that she had married in haste, refusing to wait for him. But no matter how sweet and dear a husband Ashley had been, he had never measured up to Kent.

When Kent broke off the kiss, his expression was somber. "Were you remembering?" he asked as he laid her down gently on the bed. "I was. I've never stopped loving you, sweetheart. The years have brought a depth and meaning to my love that it did not have all those years ago. Life doesn't offer many second chances. Our love can prosper and grow in our newfound maturity. The children need a father, and I'm eager to be that man."

"If I hadn't been such a spoiled child years ago," Angel said on a sob, "we could have been together all this time instead of . . ."

"No, it wasn't meant to be," Kent countered.

230

"Everything that has happened since our parting years ago was meant to be. It has made us both stronger, more resilient, better able to cope with the changing world around us. I regret those lost years, but the time left to us will be sweeter for them. I love you, Angela, more than I thought possible."

Grasping his face between her hands, she smiled into his dark, glowing eyes. "I know you didn't betray Blake. I'm sorry for even thinking it. Mandy already loves you and—and so do I."

She kissed him of her own accord, seeking the richness of his mouth with the tip of her tongue as she deepened the kiss. Kent groaned and broke off the kiss with an abruptness that startled her. He gave a shaky laugh. "I'm only human, sweetheart. This has gone far enough." He laid her gently back on the cot and covered her with the blanket. "Have you given any thought to a name for our son?" he asked distractedly. Her words and the heated kiss that followed had shaken him more than he cared to admit.

"I thought we'd call him Nicholas, after Saint Nick, since he was born on Christmas Eve. If that's all right with you."

"Perfect, my love. Just as you are. I hope you have no objection to being a country doctor's wife."

"Not as long as you're the country doctor."

They smiled at one another in complete understanding. The South as they had once known it was gone forever, but the future of the reunited lovers had never looked brighter.

Epilogue

Atlanta—March 1865

The room was cast in shadows. Angel glanced out the window, wondering when Kent would return from work. She had seen precious little of him since he had brought her to Atlanta. He had found them a house in the nearly deserted city and reported to his new post at the hospital. She knew he was kept busy saving lives and mending broken bodies, but deep inside she felt that he was waiting for her to make the first move toward making their marriage one in deed as well as fact.

She walked to the dresser mirror and stared at herself. Since Nicky's birth, her figure had returned to its normal slim proportions and she looked better than she had in years. Her complexion was clear, her green eyes sparkled with health and vitality, and she owed it all to Kent. He had saved her life in more ways than one, and she had yet to show him how much she loved and appreciated him.

Angel looked at the bed and smiled. They had slept side by side every night since arriving in Atlanta, yet had shared no intimacies. It had taken her body a long time to heal from childbirth, and Kent was allowing her all the time she needed. She knew he was waiting for her to tell him when she was ready to be his wife in every sense of the word, and she loved him all the more for not pressing her.

Absently, she picked up the nightgown she had laid out earlier, noting with satisfaction that it was nearly transparent and quite enticing. With full recovery had come the knowledge that she wanted her husband, wanted him as a woman wants a man, and tonight she was going to show him exactly how much. Aunt Bessie and the children were sleeping, a bottle of wine waited on a nearby table, and she was more than ready to become Kent's wife. She undressed quickly and pulled the nightgown over her head lest she lose her nerve.

Kent arrived home too late to take supper with his family. He had hoped to leave the hospital before the children went to bed, aware that he had spent far too little time with them since arriving in Atlanta. His one consolation was that it wouldn't be much longer before the war was brought to conclusion. The South was all but defeated, and everyone expected Lee to surrender his army to

Connie Mason

Grant soon. Then he and Angel could get on with their lives and help rebuild the South.

His weary steps carried him up the stairs toward the bedroom he shared with Angel. Would she be waiting for him? he wondered hopefully. It had been nearly three months since the birth of her son, and she looked wonderful, as slim and shapely as he remembered her. Sleeping beside her night after night had been torture in the extreme, and his wait had seemed interminable. Though professionally he knew her body was ready to accept him, he waited for her to make the first move. He wanted her to come to him, not out of duty but because she wanted him as much as he wanted her.

Each night he held her in his arms, enjoying the scent and warmth of her body, savoring the small intimacy of touching and holding. They had kissed often, but he had forced himself to stop before it went too far, and it always left him frustrated and wanting her more than ever.

Kent paused before the door to the nursery, turned the knob, and quietly entered the dimly lit room. Both children were sleeping soundly. He approached the crib first, bent down, and placed a kiss on Nicky's golden head. He was sucking his thumb vigorously and Kent knew that the little fellow would awaken in three or four hours to be changed and nursed. That thought brought a smile to his lips. He gained a great deal of satisfaction watching Angel nurse the greedy little fellow while he pretended to be asleep.

Next he moved across the room to gaze down at

234

Mandy. She slept as deeply as her brother, her long golden hair spilling around her pillow. She looked so like her mother that it was uncanny. He stroked her smooth cheek with the back of his hand before leaving as quietly as he had entered. Closing the door behind him, he moved on down the hall to the room he shared with Angel. He hoped she was still awake, for he had something to tell her, something he hoped would please her.

Angel heard Kent's footsteps on the stairs. She knew when he went into the nursery, for he had done so each night that he arrived home too late to take supper with them, and she knew just as surely that when he entered their room, his eyes would seek her out immediately.

She had doused the lamp moments before, relying on the golden glow from the fire to light the room. As Kent's footsteps neared, she stood nervously in front of the hearth, unaware that the light behind her cast her body in shimmering golden tones, illuminating every lush curve and indentation through her thin gown. Kent opened the door and stepped inside. A log popped, drawing his gaze to the hearth. He saw her and his eyes widened. His heart thudded to a stop and the breath slammed from his lungs. It was difficult for him to believe that this glorious creature was truly his.

"Angel . . ."

Angel licked her lips and swallowed convulsively. She felt as nervous as a virgin. "I've been waiting for you, Kent."

Kent gave her a heart-stopping smile. "Had I

known, I would have run all the way home. Are you saying what I hope you are? If so, I've waited a long time for this moment."

Angel opened her arms and Kent responded with alacrity. Then they were kissing. Kissing as lovers too long parted. When Angel began tearing at his clothes, he eagerly helped her, stripping them both and carrying her to the bed.

"I was hoping you'd be awake, but I never expected this. Are you sure, sweetheart? Lord knows I want you, but only if you want me."

"I want you, Kent. I've never forgotten how tender and gentle you were the first and only time we made love. Or how you made me feel things I never knew existed. I want to feel those things again. I love you."

Kent chuckled. "I'm glad Aunt Bessie insisted on cooking Hoppin' John for our New Year's dinner. She said it would bring us good fortune. If you love me, then I'm the most fortunate of men. I have a feeling this is going to be a lucky year for us. I might as well tell you now instead of later that I paid the taxes on your property today, and as soon as the war ends we'll move back to Rome. I intend to be the best country doctor in the South."

"You're already the best doctor in the entire country. Now I'm ready for you to show me that you're the best lover."

"Gladly, my love, and if I don't measure up we'll do it over and over until I get it just right."

She nuzzled his neck. "Ummmm. And we'll eat Hoppin' John every New Year's Day so we'll have good luck forever."

Hoppin' John

In the South, Hoppin' John is the traditional dish served on New Year's Day. It originated in Cajun country and is supposed to bring good luck during the new year for those who eat it on that day.

    One cup dried black-eyed peas
    Six cups water
    One dried hot red pepper or hot pepper flakes
    One smoked ham hock
    One medium onion, chopped
    One cup long-grain white rice

Wash and sort peas. Place peas in a pan, add water and discard any peas that float. Gently boil, uncovered, with hot pepper, ham hock, and onion until the peas are tender but not mushy, about one hour. About two cups of cooking liquid should remain. Add the rice to the pot, cover and simmer over low heat for about twenty minutes, never lifting the lid. Remove from heat and allow to steam, covered, for another ten minutes. Remove cover, fluff with fork. Makes six servings.

Four slices of bacon cut into small pieces can be substituted for ham hock. Brown bacon with onion, then continue as in above recipe.

NELLE McFATHER
SUSANNAH'S ANGEL

To the cast of *As The World Turns*,
my favorite soap opera—especially to John and Lucinda.

Chapter One

Christmas Eve, 1859

The excitement of Christmas was in the air, and Susannah Armstrong could hardly contain her joy in the anticipation of wonderful events to come. Not the least of her happy expectations was that of greeting her older brother, Ward, who would be arriving that very night from the Citadel, where he attended college as a mighty senior.

Susannah knew she was expected in the kitchen to help her mother and their black cook Beulah in the last-minute preparations for the sumptuous meal that would be served that evening. But she had to relish the secret, jittery emotion accompanying the knowledge that Ward would be bringing his roommate, Morgan Dancey, on his holiday visit.

"Morgan Dancey." Susannah said the name out loud, recalling the tall, handsome young man who had been visiting the Armstrongs on holidays since she was twelve. Her brother had teased her the last time about having a crush on his Yankee roommate, but had ended on a serious note.

"You're too young to be thinking about boys, Susie-Q, especially boys from New York." He had pulled her pigtails playfully and tickled her in the ribs.

Well, she no longer wore pigtails, Susannah thought with a sniff as she went upstairs on the balcony to watch the sunset off Catshead Peak. She was sixteen years old now and didn't have to go to bed early with her younger siblings to dream about Santa Claus.

She wondered if Morgan Dancey would notice. He had told her once, quite solemnly, that her hair was as glossy and thick as that of his favorite mare back home. The boys in Darien, Georgia, had certainly started noticing her.

She looked out over the river, shivering under her wrap. Morgan had told them the previous Christmas about the snow they had in upstate New York and about ice-skating on frozen ponds, and Susannah had been a little jealous.

Georgia Christmases hardly ever were cold enough to do more than stoke up the fires. But Susannah loved her native land and was fiercely devoted to the house her ancestors had built with their bare hands. Catshead was like a real person in her mind, its long windows sometimes sleepy-eyed with shades, its huge brick-and-iron stove always warm and full of enticing smells, the pulsing, beating heart of the house. Decorating for Christmas at Catshead was a massive undertaking which consumed weeks of serious preparation. Every room was filled with bowls of holly and fragrant evergreens. Every mantel, every surface held decorated pine-log candleholders that were lit at the first blush of sundown. The baskets of pinecones dipped in scented colored wax would add delicious colors and smells to the huge Yule log which would be brought in and lit ceremoniously on this Christmas Eve.

Susannah hummed the music she had painstakingly learned just two nights before. An Armstrong Christmas Eve could not be ended without a session around the square piano that had been brought at great cost and trouble from the Highland birthplace of her mother's grandparents. Susannah gently stroked the smoothly grained wood, smiling happily at the surprise she had in store for those who would be gathering for the family musicale. "I'll bet Morgan Dancey will be impressed at how I can hit all the high notes perfectly now." Indeed, Susannah's voice teacher, Miss Gibbs, had been awestruck by her pupil's perfect rendition of the new song she was teaching her.

Leaving the piano and taking a last look at the giant tree that would be covered with gay decorations as soon as the young people returned from gathering mistletoe, Susannah took a last approving look around her. What a splendid holiday they would have together! She retied a red bow at a perkier angle and looked at her handiwork. The curving stairs with their twisted green vines on the railings invited her to go up and see the rest of the house.

Catshead Peak was an unusual structure, as solid as it was charming. Two-storied, with one-storied wings, built wide and low to the ground, it was considered the finest house in the area. Handcarved wainscotting, cornices, and mantels were the touted features, but Susannah loved best the tabby-covered exterior, feeling that its mixed shells and sand linked her to the very essence of the marshes themselves.

"Yoo-hoo!"

Susannah turned, startled from her reverie, to be greeted by her mother. As always, the daughter marveled at the youthful beauty of the older woman. Since she had her mother's coloring and features, it was just like looking into a mirror which held the future. "I'm sorry, Mother. I was daydreaming out here. I know there's lots to be done, and I was just on my way."

"No hurry, sweet pea. Beulah's running the kitchen show like your great granddaddy did his regiment of the Black Watch. What kind of daydreaming is my sweet daughter doing?"

Susannah put her hand over the arm that Dorothea Crandall Armstrong placed around her. "I was thinking about Ward and wishing he'd hurry and get here. He insists on our waiting for him to get the mistletoe down and trim the tree, and I'm just getting a little anxious."

"Are you sure you were thinking about your

brother?" Dorothea smiled into her daughter's face, which was almost heartrendingly lovely in the softening rays of sunset. "I seem to remember a certain little girl tagging along after a certain young man almost everywhere he went a Christmas or two ago."

"Oh, Mother." Susannah blushed. "I was just trying to be nice to our guest. The poor boy doesn't have any family except that old aunt who packed him off to school when he was barely old enough to talk."

"Well, be that as it may, you have to remember you're a young lady now, and Ward's friends are older and will be going their own way." Dorothea plucked a pinestraw from her daughter's long dark hair. "Goodness gracious, have you been riding pell-mell through the woods again?"

"I just rode up the Savannah highway for a little while, hoping to meet Ward on his way home."

"You mustn't do that anymore without telling us," Dorothea said, her gay smile fading. "There are so many changes in the wind now." She and her husband Angus had, in fact, stayed up the night before discussing whether or not to join the Darien residents who were working up a petition against slavery. "Now go down and make yourself useful. Beulah is grumbling about not having any help cutting up the oranges for the ambrosia."

"I will, but I'd rather be decorating the tree. Do you suppose Ward met up with one of his Charleston girlfriends and forgot all about coming home?"

Dorothea laughed and gave Susannah a playful

slap. "If he's anything like his father, home comes first, women later. Now get along with you. Ward will be here when he gets here."

Susannah stopped by on her way to the kitchen to make sure everything was in place for the Christmas Eve gathering in the huge living room toward the back of the house. Catshead Peak was unique in another architectural sense: it had a series of floor-length windows across the front, but the entire back of the house was without windows. Her father had explained that this provided solar warmth for the winter when Susannah had asked why they had no windows looking out on the back of the house.

Beulah looked up from the pot she was stirring when Susannah entered the steamy kitchen. "Um-um. Come taste this. See can you tell me if it needs more salt."

"Perfect," Susannah said after she'd sipped the succulent oyster stew that the black cook had made every Christmas Eve since she could remember. "Ward said he tried to get the chef in Charleston to use your recipe, but it just didn't taste the same."

Beulah looked pleased. "Yo' brother's gone grow fins after all the seafood dishes I got planned for 'im. Never seen a boy could eat shrimp and oysters like that brother of your'n. Now, honey, you git to cutting up them oranges and make sure they ain't no pits in there. I got to git busy on the Lane cake for tomorrow dinner."

Susannah spread a towel in her lap so the juicy fruit she was peeling wouldn't soil her frock. "I guess you want me to read the recipe out to you so you can keep your eyes on the stew while you mix things up." Susannah knew the old negro couldn't read, but she had never let on that she knew.

"That'd be nice. Yo' mama said she got that recipe passed down from her grandmama, 'long with some others." Beulah got out a huge crockery bowl and a wooden spoon and started deftly picking out the spices as Susannah read off the ingredients for the traditional Christmas cake.

"All right, here goes. One cup of butter, two cups of sugar, cream thoroughly."

She nibbled a slice of orange as she watched Beulah's deft hands at work smoothing out the mixture. "Okay? Now sift three and a quarter cups flour, almost a teaspoon of salt and three and a half teaspoons of baking powder—three times, Beulah. Mama says that's important for some reason."

"You sure it's that much baking powder?"

"I'm sure," Susannah said firmly. The recipe she was looking at had that part underlined.

"Now what?"

"Add your flour a little bit at a time, along with a cup of milk, half plain, half cream, beating smooth all along."

"Whew." Beulah wiped her sweating forehead with the back of the hand that held the flailing wooden spoon. "Hot for December, ain't it? 'Bout time for the flavoring, ain't it?"

"Yes'm. One teaspoon vanilla."

"Git them eggs out, will you, and break 'em up for yo' ole mammy."

Nelle McFather

"Yes, ma'am." Susannah loved the ritual of separating the yellow from the white and did so with the required eight eggs until Beulah fussed about how long she was taking in the process. "All right, all right. I've got them, but you have to do the whipping. I always get them too dry."

Susannah handed over the bowl of egg whites for Beulah to whip into stiff peaks, preparing in the meantime the three large cake pans with light grease. "Okay," she said, licking her lips at the sight of the creamy mixture being poured into the pans. "Now for the filling. Want me to soak the stuff for you while you're getting that in the oven?"

At Beulah's nod, she got out the two cups of coconut they'd grated that morning, along with a cup of chopped pecans and equal measure of chopped white raisins. Pretending to swig as she took out the kitchen whiskey, she poured a half of a cup into a bowl to soak these ingredients in.

"I could use me a sip of that," Beulah said, pausing at her task of beating the egg yolks, to which she'd added the softened butter and sugar. "Thanky. Which white icing you think? I kind of like the plain one—you know, with the white syrup, the egg whites and sugar, and not much else. We'll wait and do that tomorrow morning. Boy, this whiskey really adds a nice flavor." She put all the layer filling mixture ingredients in the top of a two-layered pot on the wood stove, adding the whiskey-soaked items after the butter, eggs, and sugar had thickened slightly. "This is gone be the Lane cake to end all Lane cakes."

248

"You say that every year," Susannah pointed out.

"Well, that's cause I'm the cook to end all cooks—black, white, or polky-dotted."

"You can say that again," came a deep voice from the door.

"Ward!" Susannah nearly broke her neck—and the bowl of oranges—getting over the door to hug her tall, handsome brother, hardly noticing the dark-haired young man who came in right behind him.

It was too bad that she was too wrapped up in her enthusiastic welcome of her brother, since she would have enjoyed seeing the look of surprise—and something more—on the face of Morgan Dancey as he saw Susannah again for the first time in two years.

Well, well, he told himself. The little sister has grown up. "Ahem! I believe I'm entitled to one of those hugs." Morgan's green eyes were teasing as he held out his arms. When Susannah went into them a little shyly, he swooped her off her feet and whirled her around. Susannah didn't know which was making her dizzier: having the strong arms and laughing face so close or being spun like a rag-doll.

"Put me down this very instant," Susannah demanded. When her captor acquiesced, she smoothed her hair and dress a bit huffily and tried to regain her earlier grown-up dignity. "I'm not a little girl anymore, to be tossed around like you and Ward used to do to me."

"I can see that," Morgan said, his teasing

Nelle McFather

manner vanishing and a speculative admiration taking its place. "Please, Ward, tell me what we have to do to keep the local bucks away from your sister."

"You ain't got no worry in that department, Master Morgan," Beulah put in fiercely. "One of them boys come sniffin' around my baby, somebody ain't fit to shine her boots, he'll git sent packin' so fast he'll think a hurricane's got holt of 'im."

Ward and Morgan laughed and the former gave the black woman another bear hug that had her squealing that he was squeezing the stuffings out of her. Morgan took advantage of the distraction to whisper to Susannah, "Looks like you've got a good protector, and I won't have to take on the whole Darien male brigade."

The implication made Susannah's heart flutter, just as the way Morgan was looking at her made her quite aware that he no longer looked on her as just Ward's little sister. "We'd better go get that mistletoe before it gets too dark."

"Right." Ward took one last look into the pot of oyster stew and rolled his eyes in ecstasy. "Hmmm. I have died and waked up in heaven's kitchen. And do you realize, Morgan, that this goddess of the stove has made her famous shrimp timbales as well as that divine dish of doomed bivalves?"

"Watch what you be calling my stew, now—y'hear?" Beulah made as if to chase them all out of the kitchen, brandishing her long wooden spoon. "Now git on with your business, young'uns, so's I can finish this supper."

They went out laughing. Ward dashed upstairs to kiss the younger children, calling out to his friend and sister, "Have to let the children know I'm home and brought them lots of gifts to add to the loot Santa is bringing them tonight. Be down in a jif! Susannah, you know where the best trees are on the promontory. Get my rifle off the back door rack and show Morgan around."

As he followed Susannah around the tree-shaded point that overlooked the river and marshes, Morgan commented on the strange custom involving mistletoe. "We didn't do this the other Christmases I came to visit."

"You were paying court to Celia McIntosh on one of those occasions," Susannah reminded him with some asperity. "Another time, you and Ward went off with some of his friends and came home drunk as skunks."

"Umm. I remember that time well. Haven't touched any Spanish brandy or cognac since. Well, you were missing the first two years, I seem to recall. You were upstairs with visions of plum pudding dancing in your head."

Susannah stopped under one of the huge trees, where the telltale globes of mistletoe hung from the highest limbs. "All right, here's your chance." She handed Morgan her brother's gun. "Try to hit the twig closest to the limb so it'll fall straight down."

Morgan missed and then missed again. "Hell, I've had better luck practicing on moving ducks."

"Here, I'll do it." Susannah lifted the gun to her shoulder and took dead aim. The large mass of mistletoe plummeted almost to Morgan's feet.

"Well, I'll be double-damned. Where'd you learn to shoot like that?"

"I've been practicing shooting since I was six. My daddy says a girl needs to learn to protect herself instead of letting some man do it." She calmly unloaded the gun, handed it back to Morgan and motioned to Ward, who was walking up. "This ought to be plenty, oughtn't it?"

"Sure thing. Boy, Dancey, you're a crack shot. Usually takes me two or three trees to get one down that clean."

They put sprigs of the fabled greenery over every doorway in the house, with Susannah moving quickly away every time before she made herself vulnerable to the traditional kiss. She laughed when Ward jokingly kissed his friend on the cheek, howling at the look of disgust on Morgan's face as he scrubbed it. "Well, it looked like about the only way you were going to get bussed."

"I'll get you for that, Armstrong," Morgan said with mock menace. "And you, too, little minx," he told Susannah with a different sort of threat in the words.

Susannah felt her cheeks redden at the image of Morgan's mouth on hers, a quiver of unknown emotion going through her entire body at the idea of a kiss from the man she'd dreamed about from the moment she'd laid eyes on him.

The young people were soon joined by Dorothea and Angus Armstrong, who complimented them on the fine job they'd done on the huge Yule log, which was merrily blazing away in the tabby-built fireplace. "When you get ready to trim the tree, I'll have Beulah send in the eggnog."

"First, the boys have to do their yard of cranberries and popcorn." Susannah ran to get the bowl containing the decorative strings that would be draped over the finished tree. "We each have to do a yard; that's the rule."

Morgan looked skeptical when Susannah handed him the needle and the basket of unstrung tidbits. "Seems like I haven't been doing my part until this Christmas."

"That's because my daughter has taken over the business of making sure that every family tradition we've ever followed is followed to the letter." Angus hugged his wife on one side and pulled Susannah into his other arm's embrace. "Ever since she was a little girl, our Susannah has loved the stories passed on about family traditions and how they got started."

"The mistletoe, of course, is used in most homes at Christmas, but we insist on shooting it out of the tree because one Highlander ancestor broke his leg trying to climb up for it."

"The popcorn and cranberries have to be strung by everyone because that keeps our family circle intact and healthy."

Morgan turned from finishing his task, looking rather proud of himself for completing the yard before Ward did. "I feel honored to be a part of that circle tonight." He looked at Susannah, whose hair seemed haloed by the flames behind her. "I hope I always will be," he added softly, just to her.

"Ahem! Am I gone have some help from these

strapping boys carryin' this punch bowl into the dinin' room, or do I got to hold it all the blessed night?"

Ward and Morgan rushed to relieve Beulah of her burden, and before long everyone was sipping at the delicious thick eggnog that the black woman made from hand-churned ice cream and peach brandy that she made every year by burying jars filled with fruit and sugar. Somehow, the jars were always found just in time for Christmas eggnog.

"Perfect!" Dorothea raised her cup to her cook. "First toast is, as always, to the lady who has made every Christmas a bigger pleasure than the one before. To Beulah, who rules our kitchen and our taste buds like the benevolent queen she is."

"Hear, hear." Ward filled everyone's cups again. "To our honored guest, whose time at the Citadel, like mine, will soon come to an end. May his visits to our home never cease."

"I'll drink to that," Angus said cheerfully. "Forget going back to that frozen country up North, fellow, and just stay down here with us in the South."

"I wish I could, but I guess Ward can tell you what they teach us at the Citadel about serving your country. Loyalty is the *sine qua non* that no successful military can operate without. And my loyalty lies with my own part of the country, just as Ward's does with the South."

They were all quiet when the young man's words were spoken. Susannah was reasonably sure that they were all thinking about the same thing— the uneasiness that had followed the incident at Harper's Ferry, when abolitionist John

Brown was captured by U. S. Marines and later hanged for treason. Ward had told her how he and Morgan had almost fought over the issue, on which they held opposite views.

"Well, it's Christmas Eve, and I for one am eager to trim the tree and have that wonderful supper Beulah's been promising us."

Ward looked at his mother with relief. He knew that Morgan was not very good at keeping quiet about sensitive issues. "Capital idea! As promised, I painted a new miniature to hang on the tree." He brought out a tiny painting of Catshead Peak itself, and everyone oohed and aahed. Susannah secretly hoped that her brother would forget a professional military career and develop his brilliant talent with oil paints and brush. "It's beautiful."

Susannah contributed a knitted stocking with all their names knitted in. She had hung on the fireplace two smaller ones for the young children, but this one would be for Beulah, who was just as anxious on Christmas morning as the little ones. She made sure, too, that there were gifts for the children in the black quarters down in Darien. Crates of oranges and grapefruits were even now sitting on the porch ready to be delivered to "Roosterville," as the quarters were called. The black children always awaited that event eagerly.

Angus and Dorothea Armstrong together hung an envelope which held a substantial number of dollar bills, which would go to the little Darien mission house to make sure that there were no homeless or hungry people in the area.

"Well, I'm not to be outdone," Morgan said

proudly as he produced a wrapped object from his coat pocket. "This is my contribution to the Armstrong household on this Christmas Eve." He looked at Susannah and said softly, "I noticed how very much you looked like an angel when you were standing with the fire lighting your hair like a halo. I carved this especially for you, Susannah. It's your own private angel, who has the power to keep this family together and safe and to look over all of you for all the Christmas Eves yet to come."

Susannah felt tears come to her eyes as she saw the delicate creature slowly revealed in Morgan's brown hand. "She's beautiful!" she breathed, seeing the dainty wings and sweet face so beautifully crafted from applewood. "Oh, Morgan, you've given me the best present in the world—my very own Christmas tradition, one I can pass on to my children and they to theirs." She carefully hung the angel as high on the tree as she could reach. "I already feel it—her wings guarding us and protecting this family. Thank you," she added simply.

When they had finished trimming the tree and poking among the gifts beneath, putting the rocking horse Ward had bought for his little brother in full view, arranging the stuffed doll for the youngest Armstrong, they all marveled at what they had wrought. "Somehow she's very real," Susannah whispered, looking at the angel, whose burnished wings seemed poised to fly.

"Mother says she's dying to hear the new hymn you promised to sing," Ward said, coming over from the piano. "And then we'll be ready for the carollers when they come, not to mention that yummy supper Beulah's been working on." He smacked his lips gleefully, making his mother cuff him for poor manners.

With a last look at the beautiful tree, Susannah went over to sit down at the piano. "Are you ready?" The room became as quiet as a field of new snow as she began to sing "Ave Maria." When her voice touched the pure high notes of the solo which had been recently adapted from Bach, her mother touched a handkerchief to her eyes and Morgan had to turn away lest unmanly emotion erupt in view of the others.

When she'd finished, there was no applause, no murmur of appreciation. Everyone in the room was stunned by the magnificence of the beautiful song that would become a classic Christmas hymn for years to come.

Like Susannah's angel, "Ave Maria" had lifted every heart in the room with the ethereal spirit of Christmas.

Chapter Two

Christmas Day always started early in the Armstrong household and this year was no exception. When Susannah came into the room from which whoops of joy had been erupting since dawn as the small ones discovered what Santa Claus had brought, she smiled to see Morgan's dark head right next to her little brother's brown curls as they worked on putting together the wooden logging truck (complete with logs) he'd been brought.

"Well, I certainly am glad to see that big boys still believe in Santa Claus," she said, bending down to give her little brother a kiss and to admire her little sister's new doll and tea set.

Morgan looked up at her, his eyes kindling at the appealing sight she made with her hair tied up girlishly with pink ribbons that matched the woolly robe that had been on her bed that morning from Mama Claus. "They sure do. Especially right now, looking at you. I always begged Santa to bring me a real live doll on Christmas morning— and he did."

"Where's Ward? Don't tell me he could sleep through all the noise." Susannah still wasn't comfortable with the change in her relationship with her brother's friend. She was not the flirt that some other girls her age were.

"He is having coffee with your parents in their room. Something about bringing them up to date on career plans and a certain young lady they've found out about."

Susannah's dimples peeked out. "I told them Ward had a sweetheart, but they didn't believe me. What about you?" Susannah very carefully poured her coffee from the Limoges pot on the morning tray and stirred in sugar without looking at the man on the floor.

"Sweetheart?" Morgan laughed and shook his head. "Not me. I plan to be a career officer and that's no life for a woman."

Beulah came in with some of the coffee rolls that she made specially for Christmas morning. "You folks better eat up, since that turkey ain't gone be ready, and none of the other fixin's neither, till three or fo' o'clock." At the groans from the younger crowd, who realized that meant there would be no handing out of gifts until after the main meal, she scolded, "Now, listen to you! Got mo' presents spread out on this flo' than Carter's got little liver pills and you wantin' mo'—mo'— mo'. Come on, Miss Priss, you left that ambrosia

Nelle McFather

half made and still have the sweet taters to hep me with, not to mention the giblet gravy."

"Can I help?" Morgan got to his feet eagerly, obviously ready to give up his place amongst the toys in order to be with Susannah.

Beulah looked him up and down, a little smile working at her lips. She hadn't just fallen off one of the rice barges that moved up and down the river. She knew when a man was falling in love— and just how deep.

This one was serious, all right. Beulah pondered her role in this romance and decided that it wasn't the best thing in the world for her baby to fall in love with a boy who came from a different background and was planning to go back at the first chance. "Well, I tell you how you kin hep. There's a stack of wood out back that my sorry nephew was s'posed to cut up for stove kindlin,' and it's still sittin' right there needin' the ax taken to it."

When Morgan got his jacket and went off enthusiastically in the direction of the woodpile, Beulah nodded to herself. *Now we'll see what the boy's really made of.* That pile of wood was high as her head and hard and green to boot. "Come on, miss. We got us a lot of work to do."

The ambrosia was finally mixed up in the huge bowl that had come down to Dorothea when the old aunts in Scotland had at last closed the ancestral home and shipped what remained in it to the Darien branch of the family. "That's it, Beulah, I've put the coconut in, the nuts and cherries, and must've picked out a thousand orange pits."

"Good. Be sure that whipped cream peaks nice

before you put it in the spring room. And I got the sweet taters all cooked and cut up so all they needs is mashin'. Just remember when you put the raisins in to leave one end without, since your mama sez they remind her of eatin' bugs."

When Susannah had finished, the black woman took the casserole away to the big safe in the pantry. "Don't forget about the wishbone, Beulah. I haven't gotten it for two years straight."

"Well, maybe your luck will change. But I got it bleached and tied with the little red ribbon, so whoever gits it in his helpin' of rice will be the lucky one."

Susannah wondered about that as she chopped up the cooled-off giblets and liver from the huge turkey and put them back in the gravy pot along with sliced boiled eggs. She was feeling extra lucky this Christmas.

The activities slowed down as dish after dish was completed and stored either in the pie safe or the spring room, making room for another tradition. Angus Armstrong would come in soon after the kitchen was clear of all the womenfolk to make his famous sage cornbread dressing. He was scornful of the lightbread dressing which some of the newer transplants to Darien stuffed into their birds.

Ward made an appearance in the kitchen and nibbled at everything that wasn't safely stowed away. He reminded his sister that they needed to gather up the candy and fruit that they always took down to the Negro quarters, and she went upstairs to dress for the occasion.

Morgan, meanwhile, made an impressive hole

in the pile of firewood and Beulah, softened up by his industriousness and blistered hands, rewarded him with one of her famous long biscuits. Under Susannah's tutelage, Morgan hollowed out the innards and filled the biscuit with fresh-churned butter and gallberry honey.

Morgan confided to Ward on the three-mile wagon ride from the Bluff that if he lived in the South permanently, he'd probably be as big as Sir Raleigh, the Hereford bull that grazed on Catshead pastures.

Susannah liked sitting next to Morgan in the back of the wagon, where they both dangled their feet and waved to people as they rode into Darien. Susannah pointed out all the landmarks, many of which had been destroyed in the disasters of 1823 and 1824. "The old Eagle Hotel, the Mansion House, Baisdon Academy on the Bluff—the '24 hurricane got 'em all, those that weren't already ruined by the big fire the year before. But you saw the Oglethorpe Oak, which once sheltered a whole company of British soldiers. It'll always be with us," she added proudly.

She let Morgan lift her down from the wagon when they reached the community of shanties where black people lived and worked for the shipping companies that had made Darien prosperous. "Wait till you see their faces when I give them the candy. The older people love the fruit, but the children never have candy and it's a sight to behold."

She handed out handfuls of wrapped candy and peppermint sticks to the eager dark hands pushing into their midst while Ward and Morgan unloaded the crates of oranges and grapefruits and divided them among the shyer older residents of Roosterville. When it was all over, and all the goodies were distributed, Morgan made a move to help Susannah back to the wagon but she whispered, "Not yet. Old Aunt Bessie and Uncle Lijah are making their way out of their house to thank us. Just wait till you see what they do." She stepped forward to greet the ancient black couple, who were perhaps the oldest inhabitants of Darien, bowing to the Negro man and kissing the wrinkled cheeks of the grizzled old woman at his side.

"Merry Christmas, Aunt Bessie, Uncle Lijah. I hope this year will be good to you and yours."

"Bless you, chile. This be your young man?" Faded eyes that nonetheless held sharp inquiry perused Morgan's face.

"He's my friend. And you remember my brother Ward, of course." Susannah brought the latter up by the hand and was glad to see that her brother did not fail to show the expected courtesy to the dignified old pair.

"We have nothing to return to you in the way of gifts but one of our old songs. The children have no thoughts of anything but the candy you brought them, but perhaps they will listen too and learn something about the old ways from your grandfather's time."

With that, the older residents gathered in a semicircle behind the two old leaders, and when Aunt Bessie's quavery voice started the Negro spiritual, "Go Down, Moses", each joined in the chorus. Old Lijah's worn baritone still could belt out the words behind his wife's soprano, and soon the entire contingent were joining in and singing from the bottom of their hearts, swaying and clapping to the rhythm.

"Swing Low, Sweet Chariot" had Susannah, Ward, and Morgan joining in. People, both black and white, kept coming up and joining in, leaving their houses, calling over friends, until it was as though an entire chorus was formed, with nobody knowing who was leading the singing anymore.

Finally, Aunt Bessie waved the singing to a faded echo of the belting "Beulah Land" and looked Susannah straight in the eye. "They say you have a voice straight from the angels, and I'd not like to leave this earth without hearing it."

Without hesitation, Susannah held out her hand to Morgan, who along with Ward hoisted her to the front of the wagon. As a hush fell over the gathered children and adults, she started singing "Ave Maria", first softly and then with a fire that came from within at having such beautiful music inside her. The hush that came over her audience brought tears to her eyes.

"Merry Christmas, everybody," she called out shakily, aware of Morgan squeezing her hand so hard she could feel his heavy Citadel ring biting into it.

"Merry Christmas, Susannah." And then, as though it had been planned ahead of time, the children came forth and started singing the Stephen Foster song, "O Susannah!", and by the time the wagon rolled away from Roosterville, they were all joining in, laughing and clapping to the lively song that would forever be Susannah's very own hymn.

The mood persisted throughout the scrumptious dinner that had everybody gasping for more room to digest all the delicious dishes.

Morgan was the lucky recipient of the wishbone, which he chose to break with Susannah. She accused him of strong-arming the winning half that allowed the victor to make a silent wish.

"Oh, no. This is a wish for all of us." Morgan closed his eyes. "I wish for every Christmas in your Southland to be as warm and happy, as filled with family love and joy and giving and music as this one has been."

They all seconded his wish, Susannah especially, since she was getting old enough to realize that nothing ever stayed the same for very long.

But if she had her wish, Christmas at Catshead Peak would always be like this.

The solemnity at the end of dinner ended when Ward came up behind Morgan and held a sprig of mistletoe over his head. "Another kiss?" he asked with false mincing tones.

At that, Morgan grabbed the sprig with the speed of light and put it over Susannah's head. Before she could move away or protest, he had kissed her square on the mouth. To the cheers of those seated around the table, the kiss lasted for much longer than it should have, leaving Susannah not only flustered but wondering what would have

265

happened if Morgan had caught her alone under the mistletoe.

Growing up, with all the new feelings it generated in the company of a young man who already held a piece of her heart, was more complicated than the several-layered Lane cake Beulah was even now bringing in with coffee—and just as delicious.

Susannah was still floating on a cloud of happiness when, on New Year's Day, the Christmas holiday was officially brought to a close. She couldn't even feel sad when the beautiful tree was dismantled—leaving it up one minute past midnight, into the new year, brought terrible luck. Nor did she mourn the removal of the charred remains of the Yule log, since an unseasonal drift of warm air from the Gulf had made the days preceding New Year's quite pleasant and balmy.

She made sure her angel found its way into the box of treasured ornaments that would be stored away till next Christmas. The New Year's Day meal of blackeyed peas and hogjowl (for luck) and crisp green collard leaves (for money) would be followed by one final event.

"Don't laugh when you see my father in his kilts, or cover your ears when he brings out his bagpipes," Susannah warned Morgan as they took their morning walk along the Bluff. "As for the replication of the special ceremony of the war between the Indians and the Highlanders, I'll thank you not to make fun of it. They are dead serious."

"I'll try not to," Morgan said, having much less difficulty with imagining that bizarre reenactment than keeping his thoughts off the kiss that had haunted his dreams. "Are you hinting that I don't fit in with your ancestors?"

Susannah stopped and looked up at him, her heart stopping at the way his green eyes positively glowed in the new tan that had been acquired from long rides along the sunny banks of the Altamaha. "You fit in with me," she said softly. "I know you come from a different place, have different ways and ideas, but somehow I feel you're my . . . brother."

With a cry, he took her into his arms and held her so tightly that she couldn't breathe—and didn't need to. "I don't want to be your brother," he growled fiercely, his hands tangling in her hair and forcing her head back so she must look up at him, directly into those luminous eyes. "I want you to be my sweetheart, my lover, my . . . wife."

"But you said there would be no place for a wife, a family, in the life of a career military man." Susannah's heart beat so rapidly that she spoke in little gasps.

"That was before I heard you sing that song. The words and music have found their way into my heart and soul, never to be dispelled, just like my dreams about you."

He lowered his head to hers and, as they stood there under the historic umbrella of Oglethorpe's Oak, they seemed to be caught up in a moment that was eternally isolated, nothing to do with what was to come or the events that would center on the spot they stood upon.

Their kiss transcended all that lay between them—the differences, the years of playful teasing, the knowledge that their worlds and ways could any day now diverge. When Morgan finally raised his mouth from the sweet lips that had opened in tender moistness to his demands, he could hardly speak for the strength of his emotion. "I love you so, Susannah. I didn't know it until I saw you this time, but I have loved you from the beginning." He lifted her chin, his finger traveling the lips he had so recently possessed, sending chills over Susannah's body. "You are my beautiful love, and no matter what the world does or comes to, you belong to me."

Susannah and Morgan found a shady spot overlooking the promontory area where the symbolic games, harking back to the 1700s when Indian and Highlander discovered a meeting ground in their love for fancy dress and whooping physical activity, were to begin.

"The first thing you'll see is a parade up and down by those portraying the Indians in their breechclouts and eagle feathers. Then you'll hear the skirling of the bagpipes as the descendants—including my father—display their tartan kilts and bare knees." Susannah giggled. "Ward refuses to take part, saying he'll not get out wrestling with make-believe Indians who like nothing better than hiking up a man's kilt to find out if it's true what they say about the Highlanders."

Morgan was in a young man's fog that left

little room for anything but enjoyment of having Susannah sitting next to him in disturbing nearness as she pointed out the highlights of the competition. "I'm sorry to miss seeing your brother in bare knees, but have to admit I find another member of the family more enticing at the moment."

Susannah smiled to herself, seeing some of her friends from town on a nearby blanket looking at her and whispering among themselves. She'd already noticed how that flirt Pansy McIver was giving Morgan Dancey the look that was supposed to render men in the area powerless to her charms. More satisfyingly, she'd noticed that Morgan hadn't paid the little twit one iota of attention. "Don't miss this, now. This is the most exciting part of the competition."

"My God, they're bringing out the cannon! Susannah, don't tell me we're going to have a real fight."

Susannah laughed. "Well, they are real cannon, but they won't be fighting each other. The aim is to see who can shoot closest to the opposite bank of the river. Believe it or not, no one has ever succeeded in getting even halfway across."

They watched as the formal charges were made to the two teams of men manning the artillery. Susannah plugged her ears when the torch was lit and held to the firing end of the war machine. "Tell me when it's over. Ooh! Look at that. Daddy's team's missile came almost to the bank!"

Morgan sat quietly as the men cheered, wondering if this playing at war was as innocent as

269

it seemed. Though the Indians had been friendly to the settlers of the area, and vice versa, he knew from his studies of military history that the battleground held a fascination for men who often needed very little motive to enter it. "What will the victors win as their spoils?"

Susannah turned her head sharply at the serious tone of her companion's question. "Why . . . why, the pleasure of being the best, I suppose."

"The best. The best and the finest. They're on both sides of a real battle, you know, the best and the finest."

Susannah looked at Morgan, puzzled by his new solemnity. "You sound so glum, as though you are seeing some . . . some terrible prophecy in this silly playing at war."

"I find nothing silly about war." Morgan leapt to his feet, realizing that he was putting a damper on his companion's mood. "Come on. I'll race you to the picnic tables."

Susannah cocked her head at him. "And if you win? What are the victor's spoils?"

Morgan held her hands and kissed each lingeringly, making Susannah shiver at the touch of his soft lips at the tip of each finger. "Another kiss— in the moonlight, this time, without one of your family coming to fetch us for another meal."

Susannah laughed. "Are you trying to tell me that Southerners eat too much?"

"No, only that if I have one more rich dish put in front of me, I will have to have all my uniforms let out." He looked at Susannah's tiny waist, so enchantingly delicate that he lifted her, circling her middle easily, from the blanket to the bare ground. "How do you do it?"

"Why, Mistuh Dancey, would you have a Southern belle reveal *all* her secrets?" Susannah fluttered her eyelashes in such a close parody of the luckless Pansy that Morgan chuckled.

"Here I had you all pegged as an angel, and you're really a little devil."

"That," Susannah told him with a bewitching grin, "is one of my secrets."

It was time for good-byes, and nobody was quite ready for them, especially Susannah. She had said farewell to her brother amidst the family huddle of kisses and hugs and excited crying from the young ones.

"Dear little Sis, I almost hate to see it, how you've grown up on me and turned into a young lady."

Susannah dabbed at her eyes with a handkerchief as she embraced her brother. "You won't do anything foolish, like sign up for some crazy volunteer post or take off after the Pike's Peak crowd?"

"I promise." Ward patted the canvas bag on his shoulder. "I love the book, Sis. Can't wait to read it." He had been pleased with the copy of *The Ordeal of Richard Feveral* which Susannah had with some trouble ordered from the publisher. "As for you, keep that pretty chin up and don't take anything any fellow tells you seriously. Remember, they're all just like me inside."

She kissed him again. "If they are, then I'll be just fine."

"I think there's someone waiting to say a special good-bye to a special young lady," Dorothea whispered to her daughter. "He's under the oak, looking very gloomy at all this Southern keening and wailing. I think if your young man had his way, he would have slipped off at dawn without a word of leavetaking." Dorothea leaned closer and whispered even more softly, so Angus couldn't hear. "I think, too, he is a fine young man and"— her eyes were teasing—"if I weren't so attached to your father, I might have a go at him myself."

Susannah slipped up behind the tall figure who stood on the bluff looking down at the geese picking at invisible insects in the marsh mud. "I know you hate these long-winded Southern goodbyes."

Morgan turned, his face revealing how much leaving Susannah meant to him. "It's just that I don't know when I'll be down here again." He swallowed hard. "I graduate this June, you know, and I'll be going back East."

"But there's a wonderful steamer that comes right to Savannah and I could meet you and—"

"Oh, Susannah!" He held out his arms and she ran into them. "That's your song, all right," he said, his words muffled in her hair. "I'll never hear any song without thinking about you, about that angel voice, about that—"

"Devil inside." Susannah opened her mouth as he kissed her.

"I will come to see you," he vowed fiercely. "We'll write to each other." At her nod on his shoulder, he held her even closer. "You're my sweetheart, Susannah. I don't care what divides us—nothing can keep us apart, can keep me away from you. Remember that—nothing!"

"There's always next Christmas," she ventured softly.

"Yes, and I'll be here unless the devil himself keeps me from it." He raised her face and searched her eyes. "There won't be any other man, will there? You promise you'll belong to me, be my girl, wait for me and then be my wife someday?"

She nodded. "No man could ever take your place in my heart, no one!"

They stood under the sheltering arms of the ancient oak and quietly savored the last moments before parting, wondering how they could bear to leave the spot where they'd just sealed their troth.

"As long as that old oak stands, we belong to each other," Susannah whispered. "Oh, no, they're calling you. Oh, Morgan, please be safe. I have my angel to look after us, but you have only yourself."

"Believe me, I'll look after myself so I can come back to my sweetheart, whole and healthy." Morgan cupped Susannah's tear-stained face in his hands, kissing away the dampness. "And that goes for Ward, too. I'll see to it that he's safe, always, as long as we're friends. He's my brother, the brother I never had and always wanted. As long as there's a breath in this body, Ward will always come home to his family."

"I believe you."

Morgan kissed her on the top of the head. "And you believe in angels, right?"

"I believe in angels," Susannah said brokenly.

She did not go back with him to the others, nor watch as, with final hoorahs, the two young men took their leave for Charleston. Instead, she watched a flock of herons rise into the early morning sky over the marshes. They looked like confetti fluttering over the wake of a passing hero.

Chapter Three

Susannah missed her new sweetheart terribly but took comfort in the long letters she received almost weekly from Charleston. She spent so much time answering them that her father teased her about writing a book like *The Mill on the Floss*, which Susannah had devoured avidly upon its release.

Young men were beginning to come courting, and Susannah discouraged them as gently but firmly as she could. Finally, her mother called her into her bedroom for a mother-to-daughter talk one evening after supper.

"Susannah, darling, I know you think right now that Morgan Dancey is the only boy in the world, but believe me, you will meet others before you finally choose the man you want to spend the rest of your life with."

Susannah shook her head. "Like that silly James Cochran, who keeps pestering me to go to dances with him?" She snorted indelicately. "All he can talk about is the newest dance steps or the latest party and who flirted with whom and which horse he plans to ride in the next jump meet."

Dorothea put her arm around the girl. "That's very normal, if you ask me. James is a fine young man, with a great future ahead of him in his father's lumber business. You could do worse." Dorothea squeezed the unyielding shoulder. "Perhaps he's not as involved in causes as your friend Morgan and doesn't read everything he can get his hands on and write you ten-page letters about it but . . ."

Susannah flung her mother's arm off. "You've been reading Morgan's letters to me?" she accused her.

"Of course not. I think I'd have to be blind, though, if I weren't aware that every time the post arrives, you vanish with those thick letters from Charleston and don't emerge for an hour. Even Angus has commented about how you seem to be a lot more up on literary and political issues since you and young Dancey began your correspondence."

"Is that something awful? To have a . . . friend who thinks I have a mind even though I'm a girl—a Southern belle?" Susannah's eyes flashed as she thought of James Cochran's patronizing remark to her when she'd talked enthusiastically about the new Winchester rifle and how it would probably change America and the way men fought.

"Girls don't know anything about war and rifles," he'd said scornfully, "or about men, either." To add insult to injury, he'd tried to sneak a kiss from her.

With satisfaction, Susannah recalled how she had bounded from the porch swing so fast that it had spilled, landing the insufferable Master Cochran on his behind.

"Of course it's not awful, honey. You know how your father and I are about discussing everything in the world, from the latest books and music to the way we want our children to grow up."

"You want me to grow up just like you did, right in the middle of the family and the place we've always lived, marrying somebody who's part of the same kind of life, somebody like Daddy."

"You could do worse," Dorothea said with a smile. The seriousness returned. "Darling, I'm not trying to discourage your friendship with young Dancey. He's a fine young man. It's just that he comes from the North, where people have different ideas from ours, where family and land aren't part of the blood ties that mean so much to us. . . ."

"Where people don't have slaves like we do."

It was Dorothea's turn to show flashing anger. "Now, just a minute, young lady. I'll not sit still to be tarred and feathered by your young man—speaking through you—for tolerating a practice that was never instigated by Southerners in the first place. Thank God your father and I are not dependent on slave labor. We've never owned one, as Beulah and the others will tell you, but there were some sound economic reasons that caused that dependency. I don't like the idea of people owning other human beings any more than your Master Dancey does, but neither do I approve of children and poor immigrants being worked to death in Eastern mills."

Susannah's anger died down. She hadn't thought about the parallels her mother was pointing out. In her next letter to Morgan, she would ask him a few pointed questions about this matter of the pot calling the kettle black. "Mama, I don't want us to argue. All I want is to be happy like you and Daddy always have been. And you've always said that arranged marriages are all very well, but that you wouldn't take anything for the adventure you've had with the man you picked just for love."

"I said that, did I?" Dorothea murmured ruefully. "Well, mothers don't always know best, do they? Here I am trying to warn you about getting too close to a young man who's going to be leaving the South as soon as he graduates, and you probably won't even see him again!"

"Not until we go up for Ward's graduation."

"Oh, dear. I suppose I'll have to act happy about the Charleston belle your brother's picked out to attend the dance."

"And about the young man who's asked me to be his partner."

Dorothea shook her head. "I should have known. Well, I'll have to ask your father about that. You're very young to be going to such a grown-up affair."

"But not too young to be courted by James

278

Cochran," Susannah countered slyly.

"Sometimes I think there's a little bit too much of me in your blood." Dorothea sighed, getting up to join her husband for the stroll they always took along the bluff to watch the sun go down. "The March winds are blowing. Be sure to close your window before going to bed. And don't stay up too late writing to that beau of yours!"

It was a kind of concession, Susannah realized, her mother's referring to Morgan as her "beau." Well, there would be other concessions, she determined, such as her father's agreement to let Susannah attend the senior festivities at The Citadel that June.

She thought about seeing Morgan again, then went out on the balcony to cool the flushed cheeks that such reverie brought. The silhouettes of her parents on the bluff overlooking the river and marshes brought tears to her eyes.

"Why can't they understand?" she whispered, watching the pair below pointing out various sights in the marsh as they strolled along arm-in-arm. "I just want to be with the man I love, forever and ever. Oh, Morgan," she whispered, squeezing her eyes shut as she visualized the two of them enjoying the end of the evening as lovers, like the couple on the bluff. "They can't keep us apart, no matter what happens. Nothing will ever keep us apart!"

She opened her eyes and gave a little cry when she looked down at the marsh and saw the omen that only appeared during troubled times. The first occasion had been just before her grandmother's death, the second just prior to the fire that nearly gutted her father's bank in Darien.

Nobody but Susannah, or so they claimed, ever saw the black heron standing dark and still on the spit of crag jutting from the marshes. Only Beulah believed her when she told everyone about the sight.

"Oh, lawsy," the black woman had moaned, crossing herself and rolling her eyes back in her head. "I'se scared you got a touch of the shinin', chile."

She would never say more, but it didn't take Susannah long to figure out that seeing the black heron was a sign of something ominous ahead.

This time, she feared, it had something to do with the man she loved.

The spring seemed long in coming, but once it finally arrived, Mother Nature joined in the celebration with all her resources. Susannah had never seen so many dogwoods rampant in white splendor, so many spikes of wild pear trees and luxuriant azaleas roiling with color.

"It's because I'm in love," she proclaimed happily, dancing on her way to her room to try on the dress she would be wearing in Charleston to dance with her handsome beau.

She still couldn't believe that Angus Armstrong had agreed to let her be Morgan Dancey's partner for that soon-to-come fairytale event. She had held her breath when he called her into his study that Good Friday, the day after the cream-colored, hand-lettered invitation with her name on it had arrived.

"Yes, Daddy?"

"Sit down, Susannah." She knew how serious the occasion was when her father solemnly poured out two cut-glass goblets of his best sherry and handed her one. "Your mother tells me that this young man Dancey has serious intentions where you're concerned."

Susannah took a very large gulp of sherry before answering. Her throat constricted, her eyes big on her father's, she nodded. "Yes, sir. He's . . . he's always made that plain."

"And you probably would go into some sort of deep decline, if not into a convent, if I said no to these arrangements for this dance."

"Not into a convent, no, sir." The sherry, added to shaking her head vigorously, made the room spin around.

"I suppose you know that your mother and I have certain . . . reservations about the suitability of this—ah, match."

"Yes sir, I'm aware of that. But you just don't know Morgan like I do, Daddy! He's kind and he's wise, and he thinks the country is strong enough to survive anything, and he wants me to be part of his life and I—"

"Whoa. Hold on. You're drinking that sherry entirely too fast and your tongue's tripping over it." Angus ran his hand through his thick dark hair. "If I agree to letting you go to this boy, do I have your word as an Armstrong that you'll not disgrace the family by eloping to New York with him or some such nonsense?"

"Oh, no! I would never do such a thing!" In truth, Susannah had not thought of that possibility. Surely Morgan wouldn't have such an outrageous plan in mind . . . would he? She cleared her throat. "Daddy, cross my heart and hope to die, I would never do anything to disgrace you and Mama. I'd kill myself first!"

"Well, I hope that drastic a step won't be necessary." A gleam came into his eyes. "Maybe if I took Beulah along and let her be your constant chaperone. . . ."

Susannah's horrified look made him start laughing so hard that he choked on his sherry and his daughter had to pound his back. Before it was over, they were both laughing about the thought of Beulah trailing around behind Susannah as she accompanied Morgan on the traditional promenade down Senior Walk and trying to keep up with them on the dance floor.

And here she was trying on the most beautiful dress she'd ever owned in her life. In just two weeks, she would be wearing it while dancing in the arms of Morgan Dancey!

"Do you like it?" Her little sister had come in and flopped across the end of the bed to ogle her big sister in the cloud of white organdy whose flounces were caught up in pink ribbons and silk roses. "What do you really think, Belinda? Isn't it the most beautiful dress you've ever seen?"

The small girl, whose heart-shaped face promised to someday rival her sister's in beauty, studied the vision before her with the solemnity of the precocious connoisseur. "I think," she said finally, "that if Beulah sees how much you stick out over the top, she'll probably have a hissy and you won't go to Charleston after all."

Susannah turned hastily to the mirror to see if there were validity to her young fashion critic's prediction. Her frown turned slowly into a smile as she observed how her bosom curved alluringly out of the low-cut front, the expanse of white chest and bare shoulders making her neck appear as long and graceful as a swan's. "It is a bit daring," she said, practicing biting her lips to bring additional color into them and pulling down a curl to see how a ringlet might look against her throat. "Tell me, do you think Morgan would like my hair better up, like this?" She pulled the dark locks up atop her head and postured. "Or like this?" She shook the masses out over her shoulders and posed, her hands on her hips like a saloon girl.

"I think you ought to shave it off and wear one of old Chief Tom-Tom's feather headdresses that they have hanging up in the barber shop."

Susannah chased her sister around the bed before she finally caught her and whacked her with a down pillow. Belinda soon had her own pillow defense, and when Dorothea walked into the room, attracted by the shrieking and laughing coming from upstairs, they were flailing away at each other.

The older woman stopped and leaned on the door jamb to watch, a smile tugging at her lips to see the frivolous horseplay. It pleased her

283

inordinately to see that her precious Susannah
had not yet completely left behind her girlhood.

It was wonderful having Ward home for the
summer, even though he was playing hard at
being the banker that his father wanted him to
be. Susannah teased him about that, reminding
him that he had to go four years through college
to get a job in his own daddy's business.

"Don't worry," he told her. "I'm planning to go
to Fort Sumter as soon as the officer's slot they
promised me opens up. I don't plan to stand
around behind iron bars counting money, sis."

He was a little resentful that Morgan Dancey
had been immediately inducted into the Federal
Army and was already earning lieutenant's wages
in his Mt. Vernon post.

"Morgan wrote me that he thinks he'll be able
to come see us again this Christmas." Susannah
was still dreaming about the time she'd had in
Charleston, and from the letters she got weekly,
Morgan had not forgotten it either.

The recent letter burned against her breast,
where she'd stuck it when Ward had come up
on her suddenly as she read the sweet missive
for the hundredth time:

Darling Susannah, O Susannah,
How I miss you. I shall never forget the
look on my classmates' faces when you
walked with me down the Senior Arbor
Promenade, looking so beautiful I wanted to
clasp you in my arms and run away with you

to places where no other man could see you except me. And that night when we danced— and danced—and everybody kept wanting to break in but I wouldn't let them and you felt as sweet and airy as a perfumed cloud in my arms, I thought about how lucky I was. Dear heart, I want you to be my wife so badly that I struggle daily to keep myself from risking the brig to go back and get and bring you here. Some officers are married and how I envy them, going home to sweet wives instead of to churlish captains or stark quarters.

How I long to see you! The Christmas we plan together seems so far away at the moment. This time I'll be the one to shoot down the mistletoe. I've gotten to be quite a crack shot, though I still prefer the idea of shooting down mistletoe to shooting a fellow man. I hope, I pray, this country isn't ever going to come to that. But it scared me in my history studies to learn of battles against the British, who were actually of our own blood, and of the chilling inhumanities that were perpetuated, brother against brother.

Ward hardly writes to me at all anymore. This troubles me, since the last time we were together we argued about states' rights and whether said states had a right to withdraw from their own country. I love Ward like a brother, but he won't admit that such a divided country could never stand against an outside force that threatened it. He loves our country as passionately as I do; we just see some things differently. But one thing we don't see differently. You, your family, and Catshead must always be safe and protected. On that issue Ward and I are totally in agreement.

It's time for dinner. Unappetizing though it may be, I must keep up my strength. Please tell Beulah I'd trade everything in my bunk locker for just one of her old homemade biscuits with butter and honey. I'd trade more than that for one kiss from my sweet honey.

Must go, my darling. I'll count the days till we're both home for Christmas. Home is, by the way, wherever you and I are together.

Much love,
Morgan

Susannah counted the days as well, willing the time to go by so that she and her sweetheart could be reunited.

December 21, 1860

Susannah had helped Beulah air every room in the house, polished the dining room table and chairs to a high polish, and was still full of energy when it was all done. "I declare," she told the black woman when the latter collapsed with a cup of Luzianne by the kitchen stove, "I think I could go all day and night getting ready for Christmas. With Morgan and Ward coming home like always, I just know it's going to be another wonderful year."

Beulah had heard some things in Roosterville that didn't sound wonderful to her old ears, but she just grunted something in reply.

"What did you say?"

"I said, it ain't gone be the same this year. You saw the black heron last spring. You know somethin's in the wind."

Susannah disregarded the chill that came over her with the reminder that she'd seen the black heron. She tried to ignore, too, the sense of anxiety she'd felt on her trips into Darien. The old men were huddled around stoves in the usual gathering places, but the usual chitchat and gossip wasn't about local matters. "People are worried about politics, as usual, but how can that spoil our Christmas?"

She found out how very soon after, when her father came home looking like a storm cloud and called her into the living room before supper.

She didn't like it that her mother was there too. That meant that her parents had agreed on something concerning Susannah, something that she was bound not to like.

"Mama? Daddy? Please tell me quickly. Has something happened to Ward?"

"Not yet," Angus Armstrong said grimly. "Though it could any day now—to all our boys with Confederate loyalties who're at Sumter."

"Angus, don't delay this. Susannah needs to be

told exactly what's happening and how it can affect her and all of us."

"Lincoln's election was the start, honey. You heard about it, how it's almost cut the country in half."

"Yes, but . . ." *Please don't let that keep Morgan apart from us.*

"Well, today South Carolina seceded from the Union." Then Angus dealt a second blow. "Honey, we'll be right behind. Georgia won't leave her sister twisting in the wind, nor will Tennessee or Alabama or—"

"Daddy, we can't do that! Morgan says that if we start splitting up our country, then we'll—"

"Never mind what Lieutenant Morgan Dancey says. He's now on the other side and what he says doesn't count." At Susannah's horrified look, he added more gently, "Don't you understand, honey? Your brother will resign from his post and join his own side if it comes to that. Your sweetheart, Morgan Dancey, will be his enemy on the battlefield if we go to war. Could you live with that, loving a man who's out there leading his men against your brother and the men from your own state?"

Susannah's stricken face brought her mother to her side. "Angus, you're being too harsh. Darling, you understand how sorry we are— we like your young man so very much, but your brother . . . darling, he's our son. We can't have someone visiting us in our home who might one day be pointing a musket at your very own brother."

Susannah looked at them both as though she didn't see them. Then, almost wildly, she ran from the room.

The day the black heron had prophesied was here.

Chapter Four

December, 1864

Nothing would ever be the same again in Darien,
Susannah thought despairingly as she guided the
remaining Catshead wagon into the scarred little
town. Most of the old businesses were gone, but
there was one hastily rebuilt general store, where
she would try to procure enough supplies from
the meager stocks to get her family through
Christmas.

She couldn't bear to look at the desolate remains
of her father's bank, of the two hotels, of the
friendly houses that had once lined the shaded
streets. Those who lived on Baisden Bluff, out
of town, had escaped the horrendous night in
1863 when a ravaging band of freedmen and
runaway slaves had put the torch to the little

village, burning everything in it to the ground.

Susannah still shuddered to think of that night. People had fled to seek refuge with those living on the Bluff, and they all watched hopelessly, helplessly, as the glow of fires below illuminated the destruction of everything in their lives.

The Oglethorpe Oak had survived, miraculously putting out growth months after its magnificence had been charred. It was a symbol of the South, Susannah thought. Like the oak, her land and people would survive somehow and put out new growth.

But it was pretty desolate right now. Word was that the South was losing the war and Sherman was topping his destructive March to the Sea with an invasion of Savannah.

Her brother Ward was among the Confederate troops defending that city. Susannah and her parents prayed for his safety day and night but knew his life was in more danger than it had been since the fatal shot on Ft. Sumter that had triggered the war.

She thought about Morgan, who could very well be on the other side of the Savannah conflict. "No, you mustn't think about him. It's disloyal to Ward and to the South, and you mustn't include him in your prayers."

She couldn't prevent that, though. Even after she'd written to him, sending back everything except the carved angel which she could not bear to part with, he had written entreating letters to her, even from the posts that he occupied in the Union Army. Susannah could hardly bear not to answer the letters, knowing his anguish as he found himself moving geographically closer to her, yet further apart than ever.

But he was a lieutenant in the Union Army, her enemy now. It was partly from her anguish over these feelings that she had allowed herself to be talked into an engagement with James Cochran six months after the war began and all of the young men of Darien, including James, were going off to war.

She had genuinely grieved when word came of James's death in the fateful battle of Gettysburg, but she had almost been relieved to realize that with the demise of her fiancé, there would be no more pressure to marry someone she didn't love.

"Oh, here you are daydreaming again," she scolded herself, "and Lord knows there's enough to do to try to make this a halfway decent holiday. After all, we can always hope that Ward will be home for Christmas." Susannah felt tears trickling down her cheek as she turned the buggy up to the house where Beulah would be waiting anxiously to see if the general store had been able to provide sugar for at least one cake for Christmas. Ward would not make it home, she reminded herself tearfully, maybe for the same reason that James Cochran wouldn't be home for Christmas.

Susannah wiped her face. Everyone at her house was worried enough about Ward without her coming in crying about him. "Beulah, they didn't have any sugar, but Mister Phinney had a jar of old sorghum that he let me have." Susannah slung her bag on the kitchen table and called again. "Beulah, where in the blue-eyed world are you?"

"I'se in heah, in the pantry, tryin' to figger out what we do for supper tonight. Yo' daddy and mama is gittin' mighty tired of sweet potatoes and co'nbread, and to tell you God's truth, so'm I."

"Well, we're luckier than most. At least we've still got our house standing. Any luck on little brother's trying to run down that gobbler that ran off with all the hens? He'll be needing some fattening up, and we've only eight days left before Christmas."

Beulah came out of the pantry, her face set in disgust. "I tell you, if I ever run across any of them darkies that made off with our best cow, I'll skin 'em alive. You realize we ain't got milk for eggnog nor nothin' fit to drink on the Lord's day of celebration?"

Susannah sighed and sat down at the kitchen table. No turkey, no laying Rhode Island Reds, no cow—just sweet potatoes and turnips. "Daddy and I'll go out and shoot us a couple of wild ducks. And we'll just make do with the brandy you left buried through last Christmas. It'll be plenty strong enough by now."

Angus Armstrong spoke from the door. "That's good to hear. The stronger the better, because bad times have just turned to worse."

Susannah half-rose from her chair, her face full of fear. "Daddy, not Ward. You haven't heard something about Ward over at Savannah. He's not . . . he's not . . ." She couldn't make herself say the awful word "dead."

"No, Susannah, not that I know of. Your mother says she feels that he's still alive, in spite of what we've heard." As Susannah waited, her face blanched, he said brokenly, "Savannah's fallen, over a week ago. They just hadn't let anybody through to tell us. And that damned Sherman, that bastard, they say he sent a telegram to Lincoln making him a Christmas present of Savannah."

Susannah wept. Proud Savannah fallen! That meant it was only a matter of time till the North would claim victory over the defenseless shell of an army that the Confederates had left. "Oh, Daddy, what if Ward's been taken prisoner? They say our boys can't last in that prison they take them to up in New York." Susannah couldn't help it now. She started weeping in real sorrow.

"Now, now, Susannah," Beulah comforted her, the tears coursing down her own cheeks. "You know that brother of yourn, how he could out-smart ever' bully tried to take 'im down when he was growin' up. Have faith. We gone have Christmas, if we have to harelip Annie and the whole state of Georgia and fight that debbil Sherman to boot."

Angus Armstrong looked at Beulah with grati-tude. He had deeded her and her family and the other loyal Negroes their own little houses and plots of land soon after they'd come to work for the family. Unlike other freedmen like those who had burned Darien to the ground, most of the people working at Catshead Peak had remained fiercely loyal. "I'll do my best to scare up some fancier vittles for the holidays, but come what may, we'll celebrate."

"That we will," Beulah said firmly, wiping away

her own tears, then Susannah's, with the corner of her apron. She lifted her *chile's* face and kissed it. "We's countin' on you and your brother and sister to git that tree up and decorate it just like allus, and I want to see that there angel swingin' right from the highest limb, and I don't want to see no more tears on that pretty face till that brother of yourn comes marchin' home."

Susannah smiled and nodded. She'd forgotten about the angel. Somehow just thinking about it made her feel better.

Everybody at Catshead made a brave effort to make that Christmas Eve seem as normal as possible. Susannah and her mother brought out all the decorations and festooned every surface with the fresh greenery and holly that had always filled the house on the occasion.

Susannah and her father brought home a wild duck, laughing when Beulah grumbled over the dressing of it, saying, "There ain't no way to make a quacker come close to lookin' like a fat turkey." But the black woman fell right into the spirit of it, tying the bird's trussed legs with gay bits of ribbon and glazing it over with some of the brandy they'd dug up that morning.

The tree went up amid cheers from the younger children, who would be allowed to stay up for the first time as the adults had their traditional libation by the Yule log. When the decorations for the tree were brought out, Susannah and her mother fought back their tears when they looked at Ward's little painting of Catshead, but they went on to cheer the younger ones' contributions of pinecone dolls made to represent each member of the family.

Dorothea handed the tissue-wrapped angel to Susannah as they reached the bottom of the box. "Here, my darling, I think you should place this one in a very, very special place."

Susannah held the carved angel for a long time, thinking about how Morgan Dancey had given it to her and about the things he had said when he presented it. "Bring him back," she whispered, putting the smooth carving to her lips and closing her eyes. She meant her brother Ward, but she knew that deep inside, she had another's name in mind as well. "Bring him back home safe and sound on this Christmas Eve."

Angus came up to her and put his hand on her shoulder after she'd reached up to attach the angel to the tree. "Honey, don't place your hopes on that too much. Praying for miracles is well and good, but we have to have faith that miracles only happen when they're meant to, not because we want them so much."

"I know, Daddy, but I know, too, that if there is any way that Ward can come back to us, he'll make it. I just know it."

"Keep thinking that, honey," he said, squeezing her shoulder hard. "Now, how about some carols around the piano? Beulah's bringing out the peach brandy, and I think it's time we gave thanks for still having our home, for being safe and well, and for having a chance to celebrate Christmas."

Susannah led the choruses of "Silent Night", "O

Little Town of Bethlehem", and "Hark the Herald Angels Sing", wondering if the echo she seemed to hear from all around came from the silence of the Bluff on this hallowed night.

In fact, those echoes were from far away, on the banks of the Altamaha River not far out of Savannah, where two fatigued units, one Confederate, one Union, ragtaggle remnants of their fighting battalions, rested on opposite sides of the river. Occasional sounds of gunfire had marred the star-filled night, which most soldiers thought of with images far-removed from battle.

But then the sounds of gunshot and cannon splitting the air ceased, and another sound drifted out over the moon-streaked river. So faint at first that the other side must strain to hear it, a Southern tenor voice began singing "Silent Night." Then others on the same side joined in, singing all the verses.

Susannah would have wept to hear it. On the opposite side, the Union soldiers, many wounded and waiting for deployment home, others too weary to move on with their units, joined in the singing.

There was no diversity of accents or tone, no lack of harmony. Both North and South knew all the words, and each soldier had his own dreams of home and family, of Christmas Eve back where he came from, of a peace that seemed far removed from the battlefields, to think about as he sang.

Those Union troops who had left Savannah quickly to join forces with Admiral Dahlgren's fleet lying off the coast had gone, but some Federal officers and foot soldiers had stayed behind to check the outlying areas of Savannah for pockets of rebels, for snipers, and for Union wounded who'd been overlooked during the pullout. Those on the Altamaha's banks who had joined in with their enemy's singing were among these; some were on lone missions, such as the soldier moving quietly around the area where skirmishes had occurred long after the main battle was fought and won.

"Soldier?" whispered a weak voice, and Lt. Morgan Dancey moved toward the sound. He moved faster when he saw the prone body struggling for breath against the gurgling spurts of blood that were spouting from the wounded man's mouth onto the cold ground, made colder by a pool of blood.

"Sir!" Morgan bent quickly to lift the head whose open eyes held the promise of approaching death. It was his captain, a young man from Maryland who had fought valiantly in the front lines with his unit, never turning back to seek safety when he might have. Morgan had sought news of his superior but had learned he was missing in battle, had been thought dead. "Captain Breyer—my God, I must get you to safety, to the medical camp."

"Too late for that, Dancey." The dying captain coughed. "I heard the singing. I think it kept me alive. I swear I could see my wife at the pianoforte, holding my little girl in her lap while they sang together for me."

"Don't try to talk, sir." Morgan cradled the head of the man he'd fought under, his heart constricting at the rattling sounds that accompanied the strained words. "You're going to get to see that wife, that little girl again. The war's almost over. You'll be going home almost any day now."

"Home." The laugh ended in a paroxysm of coughing. "I'm afraid I'm not headed for the home you're talking about, Dancey. Home. I hope you get to yours."

"Thank you, sir. But right now, I'm here helping you make it to yours."

"No, no, you can't do that. That blasted Reb's bullet has taken care of that. Damn. Those Rebs are something. You know that even with us kicking their asses all over Ft. McAllister and back, even with having their whole damn state of Georgia turned into barbecue, they . . ." His voice sputtered into blood, and Morgan used his kerchief to wipe it off the trembling chin. "They had a big boiling pot of what they called Chatham Artillery punch. Hear that, Dancey? Can you believe it—these Rebs, being shot and killed right and left, had themselves a party? Put all their whiskey, whatever they had, together, let it stew into the devil's brew, and had themselves a party?"

"Don't talk any more, sir. I'm going to try to move you now. I've got a wagon and I can get you to somebody to fix that wound."

"No, no, I'm done for. I'm just trying to figure it out, how men out dying and killing, can still find it in their hearts to want to party and drink whiskey. Have I missed it? Was I on the wrong side?"

"No, sir. You were on the right side. So were they, according to their lights. But only one side can win, and that's us, sir. We won this war, Captain. We won it. And you were one of the reasons for that, you and a lot like you."

"But what did we win?" The dying man's eyes looked around him, at the still woods which held carnage and desolation. "What did we win, Dancey? These backwoods full of mosquitoes and Confederate widows?"

"Don't worry about that, just think about getting well and seeing your family again. Let me get you out of here."

"No." The captain turned his head. "I won't leave this place alive. But there's one over there, lying behind that clump of bushes over there that might make it. Help him if you want to help somebody. We talked about our families while we were lying here waiting for somebody to find us. He's got a chance. The shrapnel's in the thigh, but he got the bleeding stopped before he passed out. Help him. He's a Reb, maybe the one that shot me. Or maybe I'm the one that shot him. Doesn't matter now. He's from close by, stands a chance. Help that Reb over there, Dancey, help him make it back to his home and family. Somehow that'll mean something to me, knowing that somewhere a family will have their soldier come home for Christmas. . . ."

"I couldn't help a Reb! That would be treason, Captain. You're delirious. You don't know what you're saying."

"I know exactly what I'm saying. I don't stand a chance, but that boy over there does. My wife and daughter won't see me again, but if another man's family can have him back, somehow it'll make it up for this idiot business we got ourselves into."

"I can't do that, sir. I'd be shot as a traitor, helping the enemy."

"I'm your superior, ain't I? All right, soldier, I'm making it an order." The weak voice took on authority. "I hereby order you, Lt. Morgan Dancey, to take that boy home. Tonight. Whatever it takes."

The hand clutching Morgan's made a fierce clinch and then relaxed. The eyes that had been fixed on the Christmas Eve heavens went blank. The Union captain was dead.

Morgan gently placed the limp hand over the dead man's chest and closed the lids of his eyes. For some reason the words of Hamlet's friend Horatio, spoken after the Danish Prince was dead, came into his head and he found them a fitting epitaph.

"Good night, sweet Prince, and may flights of angels see thee to thy rest."

Angels. The thought of Susannah's Christmas tree came over him, and he wondered if she still had the carved angel, still hung it on the traditional tree.

A moan from the direction his captain had pointed reminded him of the order that had been the last one ever to be made by the dead man. He owed it to a respected superior to try to carry out what had been his last command.

"All right, Reb, I'm coming to help you, but if you try any tricks, I'm warning you . . ."

Morgan held his musket loosely but at the ready.

He wasn't new to the desperation of wounded Rebs who would do anything to keep from being captured and taken away from their beloved South.

The moan didn't sound threatening. "Water," rasped the hoarse voice. "If you've got any water, I'll think of you as an angel of mercy, Fed or friend."

"Well, I'm no angel, but I'll give you some water. And then we're going to talk about what's to be done with you."

The wounded Rebel was so caked with blood and mud that Morgan had to wipe off his cracked lips to smoothe the way for the canteen of water. "Thank you, whoever you are. I hope you're enjoying your Christmas as much as we are."

Morgan chuckled with him. "Bad leg there, fellow. Hope you're not planning on dancing any jigs with your girl this Christmas."

The soldier had fainted, probably from the relief of having water, and Morgan was in the dubious position of holding an unconscious Confederate in his arms, not a situation a strictly trained military career officer relished.

He wondered if he had the moral if not military obligation to follow his superior's final orders. To delay a decision on that, he used some of the water to wash the Rebel's stubbled face. "You could use a shave, Reb," he muttered as the bathing revealed reddish-brown whiskers and—

Morgan almost cried out in the night when he realized who the Rebel was, but restrained himself just in time.

He didn't need to be caught coddling Lt. Ward

Armstrong, who had singlehandedly wiped out one of Sherman's elite scout troops.

"Well, I'll be damned. Well, I'll be double-damned."

Orders from the Captain or not, he had only one choice.

Susannah pulled her fleece-lined cape closer around her as she took a walk along the bluff after supper. There was no sign of the black heron, she was glad to see. In fact, with the dying embers of sunset, there was little sign of any marsh life. "No doubt the ducks have spread the word that anything edible had better take cover." She looked back up at the house with the candles showing in the windows and hoped that they would, indeed, guide weary travelers home.

"Oh, Ward, if only I could have fought at your side. Why couldn't all of us have shared the fight? Why should just our finest young men be the ones to battle for our South?"

She could almost hear what her brother would have said to that. "Sis, women are too emotional to be involved in war. They would take it personally, be too soft on the enemy. Can you imagine a girl shooting another girl and then not rushing over to be sure she hadn't hurt her?"

Maybe men ought to be more that way, Susannah thought, looking down at the river which had once been alive with barges laden with supplies bound for the seaports.

With Savannah fallen, the South's ports were no longer viable.

"Susannah! Su-sannah!"

"I'm coming, Mama." Susannah pulled her hood up and walked back to the house, hurrying when she saw her mother and father standing at the door. "Is something the matter?"

"No, we thought we ought to call on the Bennetts, who just found out they lost their twins in the Savannah fight."

"Oh, Keith and Lian," Susannah mourned. "Please tell them I'll call on them tomorrow, but I know they need you more than me since Ward was their closest friend. I'll look after the children, don't worry."

"Thanks, darling," Dorothea said with a sad little grin. "Try not to worry. Chin up and all that. Ward would want us to do that."

"I know." Susannah waved them off, then went into the house to look at the sputtering fire which lit up the tree. The angel caught the light as it always seemed to, and she looked at it, wondering if she were imagining the spark of light in the carved eyes.

"He said we would always be safe and protected, that you would see to it," she whispered.

She sat at the foot of the tree and let the warmth from the Yule log take the chill from her bones as she waited for the midnight hour.

Chapter Five

His mission would be dangerous, Morgan knew, perhaps more dangerous than any he had undertaken since the onset of the war. He would be in the line of fire not only from the scattered outposts of fleeing rebels, but from his own side as well.

He looked at the man lying vulnerable and wounded, knowing that even without the Captain's charge to him, he could never have sentenced his old friend and brother to live out the last days of the war in a cold prison up north.

"Ward," he whispered, "Can you hear me? Are you conscious?"

"I don't think so," the Southerner's voice said faintly. "I think I might be dead because I'm hearing a voice from a long time ago, one that I thought I'd never hear again."

Morgan laughed softly. "You're too damn' stubborn to die, you upstart Rebel, you. It's not heaven you're in, old friend—you're still in the hell that this war has thrown us all into, and if we're going to get you out of it, you've got to try to listen to me, stay conscious, and do what I say. Otherwise, we'll both be buzzard carrion like the other poor souls out here."

Ward tried to sit up, looking around frantically. "There was a man dying, lying over there. He . . . he tried to make me hold on, even though he was suffering more than I was. Help him, Morgan. Forget about me—help that man over there."

"I'm sorry, Ward, Captain Breyer is gone. If it makes you feel any better, he was just as concerned about you."

Ward fell back, pale and drained from the effort he'd just made. "I hope you'll tell his family someday that he kept me alive till you came."

"I will do that. Now look, old friend, you mustn't use up your strength talking. We have a long way to go, and it's not going to be the cakewalk at the Citadel Senior Prom."

"Darien?" Ward's whisper held the joy of revived hope. "You're going to take me home?"

"Make that *try* to take you home," Morgan said grimly. "Can you imagine what would happen if I got stopped between here and there, how I would explain having a Reb in the back of a Union soldier's wagon?"

Ward's grin was weak but carried some of the old salt. "Knowing you, it'll be a piece of cake. Cake. Morgan, I'll bet they're waiting for us at

Catshead, just waiting for us to come home and have some of Beulah's cake."

"Dream on, ole buddy. In the meantime, I'm trying to figure out how I can pass you off as a wounded Union officer that I've got to get past the checkpoints just the other side of Midway."

"Well, this reb uniform won't help."

Morgan's mind lit up. "You're right! Damn, I wonder how many court-martials I'd face if anybody found out about what I'm doing here."

"When the war's over, it'll be over. Nobody is going to be looking at acts of kindness between brothers."

"I hope you're right." Morgan took off his coat and placed it over the shivering man on the ground. "That's just temporary. I have something more permanent in mind."

With apologies to his dead superior, he gently removed the bloodstained jacket from the stiffening body. "This was your idea, remember, Captain Breyer. I'm sorry to do this, but you're past feeling the cold. Dammit." He looked down at the now vulnerable corpse. "I can't do this. I'm taking you for a decent burial, the devil take it. Those vultures aren't going to have a go at a man like you."

With that, Morgan put the Union dress back on the dead Captain and placed the crumpled hat atop the still head.

Then he went to fetch the wagon. When he reached Ward, he whispered, "Plans have changed. You have to be very careful from here on. No matter how much that leg hurts, you can't let out

307

a sound, can't make a move, because you're going to be acting dead as a doornail."

Ward groaned as his friend lifted him into the back of the wagon. "I think I may be before too long. Did you practice your medical career very long before deciding to be a juggler?"

"Funny, really funny. Try keeping the jokes to a minimum. Union checkpoints don't have much of a sense of humor since you blew up one of their biggest units."

"Remind me to tell you about that sometime," Ward said, gasping with pain as Morgan adjusted his leg so that it would not feel all the jolts of the road from Savannah. "I didn't learn the strategy of that attack at The Citadel, believe me."

"I'm putting poor Breyer on the blanket next to you. Now, remember, if anybody stops us, you pull his body on top of yours so that none of yours is showing. I know it's grisly having to use a dead soldier for cover, but we have no choice."

"Somehow I don't think he'd mind." Ward passed out as soon as the wagon started up, hitting a trench and flinging him and his silent companion from side to side.

Morgan looked back long enough to be sure his charge was still breathing, then breathed a quiet curse as he set the wagon in motion along the back trail running parallel to the major highway, the first one in Georgia, which connected Savannah to Darien. "I feel like Charon, ferrying the dead and the half-dead across the Styx," he muttered, wondering where he would fit into those two categories before the night was out.

His first challenge came not far past Midway. A ragged threesome stepped forward, their muskets held menacingly. "Halt! Who goes there?"

Morgan prayed that the stirrings he heard from the wagon meant that Ward was taking care of concealing himself as they'd discussed. "Lieutenant Morgan Dancey, soldier. I've had orders from my unit commander to take a deceased officer from our section to the outpost set up near Darien."

They were satisfied by his explanation, but gave Morgan an anxious moment when two of the soldiers stepped around to the back of the wagon and held up their lantern to examine the tumbled heap atop which Captain Breyer lay limply.

"What's beneath him, Lieutenant?" one asked, quickly moving his lantern aside from the staring death's mask that its beams had found. "You're not trying to smuggle out some of our short supply of bedding along with the corpse, are you?"

Morgan laughed. "If you call pine straw a precious commodity, I am. The Captain wasn't dead when we started, and I stopped to provide padding when the bumps and jostles seemed to be speeding his end along too uncomfortably."

"Well, it's an end he's made, all right," the soldier said, shuddering and crossing himself. "All right, be on your way, but watch out for the heavily wooded areas approaching Darien. There are Rebs in 'em trying to protect their poor burned-out excuse for a fort."

Morgan's heart constricted at the words. Darien

309

burned! What about Catshead, what about Susannah and her family? He hoped Ward wouldn't react to the revelation that the town beneath his precious Bluff had been ruined.

"I'll be careful, soldier. I won't get on the main road till I'm sure it's safe."

They exchanged salutes, and Morgan gently flicked the reins, fighting an urge to slap the lean horse into frantic motion to close the distance between here and what he was afraid he might find at the end of his mission.

Susannah poked at the Yule log, making sparks fly off the charred cylinder, lighting up the room briefly and then settling down to the smoldering glow that she felt equaled her heart's hope. "Mama and Daddy are right. Miracles don't happen just because we want them to."

She lifted the stockings on the fireplace, one by one, comparing their near-emptiness with her own life. "The Christmas that Santa Claus couldn't make it," she whispered, thinking about the sparse presents that would await the younger Armstrongs the next morning. "Oh, Ward, I just wish you could be here, teasing me like you used to, making me laugh. . . ."

She knelt at the Christmas tree and fingered the stocking she'd knitted all those Christmases ago. "Poor Beulah. She'll act like the hickory nuts I put in here are pure gold, and Mama will pretend that the scarf I trimmed with old scrawny rabbit's fur is something special."

She looked up at the angel and said softly, "You

just hang up there, looking down and acting like you know something I don't. Why do I keep thinking you're smiling as though you had some wonderful secret? Why do I keep thinking about you at all? Why shouldn't I throw you into the fire and let you burn like most of our town did, make you suffer for reminding me of all the good times?"

Susannah knew the answer to that. The angel was all she had left of her sweet memories of Morgan. She could never toss it into the fire, no more than she could toss away her thoughts of the man who still haunted her dreams.

"Susannah?" Belinda stood at the foot of the stairs, rubbing her eyes, her rag doll Taffy tight under her arm. "I . . . I had a bad dream."

"Oh, darling, come let me hold you, make the bad dream go away." Susannah held her little sister close, rocking her, glad to have someone else's dreams to deal with besides her own. "Want to tell me about it?"

"I dreamed Ward came home, and he didn't have any legs." Belinda sobbed and burrowed her head in Susannah's shoulder. "I dreamed he kept saying it was all right, that if he was home, he didn't need any legs. Oh, Susannah, will we ever see him again, do you think?"

"Yes. Yes, Lindy, we will. Look up at that angel. Do you know what she just told me?"

"No," the child said, wiping her eyes on Susannah's dress sleeve.

"She said that if we believe in miracles, they will happen. I swear to you, that's what she told me."

"That angel can't talk. She's just made out of wood."

"But she was carved with love. When Morgan made her, he had all of us in mind—you, Ward, me, our daddy and mama and even that little devil brother of ours."

Belinda was almost laughing through her tears. "She wouldn't have any good thoughts about him, would she?"

Susannah laughed and cuddled the smaller girl close. "She's supposed to make all of us safe and protected, especially this time of year. Don't you feel it? Look at her, how the light from the fire makes a spark in her eyes, like she's real." Susannah was glad that Belinda did not know that her older sister had contemplated turning the wooden angel into cinders just a few moments earlier.

"I just want to see Wardie," Belinda murmured.

"You will, precious, you will."

The two sisters sat there in the flickering shadows of the waning Christmas Eve, both praying that somewhere, somehow, their beloved brother was in safe hands.

"My God, Ward, if you pull another stunt like that, we're both dead. Did you do that on purpose, sitting straight up like that when I pulled up alongside that bunch of blacks?"

Morgan was still reeling from the shock of turning the wagon off the cow trail they'd been following to encounter a group of Negroes who were moving their belongings on an old mule, goin' no'th, they said.

When he had challenged their leader, not being able to make out in the dark to which side the contingent might belong, a quavery-voiced old Negro had said, "We jist gittin' outta heah, Mistuh Soldier. Don't shoot, don't shoot!"

Whereupon Ward, rousing from a fit of fever, sat up and moaned terribly. The awful sound, combined with the sight of Captain Breyer's corpse, had terrified the entire group.

When the crew of unfortunate refugees scattered, one coming back to collect the mule, Morgan chided, "You scared those people to death."

"They scared me to death. Every time I pass out, I wake up to find some new terror facing us. How far are we?" Ward felt the throb of pain starting again and knew the fever that had abated with the water he'd been given earlier was rising sky-high again. But he tried to sound calm, realizing that Morgan had all he could handle without hearing that his passenger was burning up with a dangerous fever that had not yet reached its peak.

"We're not far now. Maybe an hour. Ward, you don't think when we come up, your father will shoot first and ask questions later? Ward?"

The voice came weakly from the back of the wagon. "Don't worry about my dad. It's Susannah you need to worry about. She can hit a squirrel's eye from more feet away than you and I can see."

Susannah, Morgan thought, his blood racing at

the thought of seeing her again. He knew she'd been engaged but, thank God, wasn't married. What would it be like, seeing her again, after all that had happened? "Ward, I hope your sister isn't going to give me a hard time when I see her. Ward?"

The labored breathing of the feverish man in the back made him speed up the horse. If he should arrive at Catshead with not one, but two dead men, he might as well put a bullet to his own head.

He stopped at a ditch to give the horse water and, feeling the burning heat of Ward's forehead, dribbled a few drops into his parched mouth, then poured the rest of the container over his matted head.

"God, I'm no doctor, I've probably killed him," he muttered, getting back on the road.

The hell with taking the cow trails that were supposedly safer. He had to get his friend home, and the fastest way was to get on the main road. Militia be damned. If anybody tried to stop him, he'd give the horse a hard switch and run them over, Rebels or Feds.

Belinda had finally been persuaded to go back to bed, and Susannah was thinking seriously about doing the same thing. She looked at the old granddaddy clock, which showed how close it was to being the midnight hour, and she sighed.

"I'm as silly as Beulah, who's been keeping the candle in Ward's room burning night and day," she muttered, getting up to poke at the waning Yule log. "Don't go out, now," she warned, poking vigorously until the lethargic flames flared up bright again. "There. At least the young ones can wake up in the morning to a warm Christmas, even if there's not a lot under the tree for them."

And no Ward. She looked up at the angel and whispered, "It's not your fault. It's the people down here who are to blame. If it were left to the angels, Ward wouldn't be out fighting in some dreadful war. . . ."

The dogs were setting up a furious barking. Susannah went to the window and pulled back the curtain cautiously. There was a wagon pulling up the front drive. "Oh, my lord, it's the Union soldiers come to pillage what they didn't get before!" She ran to the foyer where they kept their new Winchester in the corner ready to fire.

She blew out the lamp on the table and slipped out the door, waiting till the wagon with the blue-uniformed driver came to a halt, both soldier and horse looking weary enough to drop on the spot.

The gun wavered in Susannah's grip. She'd never shot a man, and somehow the idea of doing so when her target was weaving with exhaustion made her queasy.

"All right, Yankee trespasser. Drop your firearm where I can see it or I'll shoot."

Morgan held his face down and put his hands up, his heart turning to jelly at the sound of the voice he'd longed to hear for so very long. "I'm at your mercy, ma'am," he said in a gruff voice.

Susannah started at the note of familiarity in the voice, then dropped her rifle at the sound of another, totally identifiable voice. "Sis! For God's sake, don't shoot him! He saved my life!"

She ran around the wagon, her skirts held high, her heart pounding. "Ward! Ward, is it you?" When she reached her brother, she saw him struggling to sit up, then saw the dead man next to him and let out a little scream.

"It's all right, Susannah. Captain Breyer here may be my best friend in the whole world. Or maybe the next. But before you get your hands on that gun again, let me introduce you to my driver, Lieutenant Morgan Dancey."

Susannah stood gaping as the Union soldier on the driver's seat turned around and smiled as broadly as he had the energy to do. He tumbled off the seat just as Angus Armstrong, awakened by the ruckus, appeared at the buckboard—just in time to catch the exhausted form of Susannah's live but very tired angel.

They held a memorial service at the grave they dug for Captain Breyer, overlooking one of the prettiest spots on the bluff.

"I just wish his wife and child could be here. Isn't there any way we could let them know, Morgan?"

Morgan shook his head sadly. He still couldn't get over how much more beautiful the young woman at his side had become in the past few years. His arm around her itched to hold her closer, though the time was not appropriate. "I'll be sure that she's notified just as soon as I get back to my company."

Susannah felt a lurch in her stomach at his last

words. "I'm sure we can make arrangements after the war's over to have his remains shipped up there if that's what she wants. Morgan, will they put you in jail for treason? I mean, you helped a Rebel escape and used Federal property to do it."

"Something we'll always be grateful for, son," Angus said, his hand resting on Morgan's shoulder. "That boy wouldn't be here if it wasn't for you."

"He wouldn't be here if it wasn't for Captain Breyer," Morgan said, looking at the fresh grave with the spray of flowers on it. "And neither would I." He looked down at Susannah. "I guess you don't know how much that means to me, being here."

Angus patted his shoulder again and walked back to the house. The others followed, except for Susannah and Morgan, who had not been alone until now.

"I . . . I suppose you know that we'll never be able to thank you enough for what you did."

Morgan brushed away the dark curl that had blown over Susannah's cheek, thinking he had never felt skin so soft. "I'd do a hundred times more for you, Susannah."

"I . . . talked to Daddy last night after you were asleep. I asked him if, after the war is over, you and I could be friends again . . . if we could invite you back to Catshead some Christmas."

"Oh, Susannah!" He reached out and crushed her in his arms, pressing his mouth to her hair, then raining kisses down her face, over her cheeks, to her mouth. After an eternity, when they could both catch their breath, he said fervently, "I don't want to be your friend. I want to be your husband, your lover, the father of our children. I want us to work side by side to help heal the scars of this country, put it back together again, make us whole again. It'll take people like you and me, people who're willing to overlook their differences, to resolve America's problems."

"You sound like Patrick Henry or somebody," Susannah said with a smile. "Are you by chance planning to go into politics?"

"I might be," he said. "God knows, I've had enough of the military."

"Could you live in the South?"

"I could live any place if you're there, too."

"Vermont? I've always hankered to try out one of those sleigh contraptions." She laughed. "Or maybe we could visit your North every winter. I like the sound of the ice-skating and hot chocolate."

He held her close to him. "I don't care where we go. If we live down here, you can teach me how to shoot." After a very long kiss, he raised his head, sniffing. "My God, what's that delicious smell?"

Susannah sniffed the air. "It can't be. If my nose doesn't deceive me, that's the unmistakable aroma of Beulah's incredible Christmas Day molasses popcorn balls. So that's what she did with the sorghum!"

"Forget going back north. I'm staying right here after the war. I'll get roly-poly fat and—"

The soft punch in Lieutenant Dancey's stomach

reminded him that Susannah was a girl a man needed to stay in shape around.

The kiss she got in return reminded Susannah that Morgan Dancey was not entirely an angel, which suited her just fine.

Epilogue

Christmas, 1868

"Beulah! Mama! Susannah! They're coming! They're coming!" Sixteen-year-old Belinda Armstrong, her hair flying as she ran into the kitchen excitedly, skidded over the freshly mopped floor and was caught by the black woman just before she collided with the counter.

"Whoa. Hold on, chile. Cain't you see I'se puttin' the finishin' touches to yo' brother's weddin' cake?" Beulah stood back from her masterpiece, viewing it with satisfaction. Supplies of sugar still weren't plentiful, but she had her own private black-market sources.

There wouldn't be any duck parading as a turkey this year, either, she thought with glee, turning from her current task to the oven, where Tom

Turkey basted in crisp, golden splendor.

"Well, you just got to see 'em, Beulah. Ward looks plumb goofy, he's so happy about this wedding, and I declare that sister of mine acts like she's sixteen again." Belinda swiped a tiny swath of white icing. "I certainly won't wait till I'm twenty-five years old till I get married."

"Well, I wish you would. And if you take one more lick o' that icin', I gone take a few licks o' my own, and they won't be sweet."

"Mama says we've been cut by some of the mucketymuck in town for mixing up with Yankees. They didn't even answer the invitations, she said."

Beulah lifted the pot lid to the famous oyster stew that Ward would be expecting. "Well, we all know what they can do with them invites."

"Susannah says Miz Cochran, James's mama, crossed the street to head off speaking to her when she was in town last week."

"Yo' sister can handle herself jes fine, Miss Priss. Don't you worry 'bout our Susannah. That chile has allus knowed what she wanted and now she's gittin' it."

"If you're referring to me, I'm sure glad."

At the voice from the door, Beulah let out a squeal and ran into Morgan Dancey's arms. After he'd hugged her, he had it to do all over again with Belinda. "Gracious, are you a sight for sore eyes," Beulah said finally, wiping the sticky icing off her hands that she was sure had been transferred to young Dancey's dapper white suit. "Now where's that other boy? I gotta git all this mushy stuff over

Nelle McFather

with quick so's I kin git back to makin' up vittles fit for a weddin'. Two weddin's, that is."

"I'm right here, Beulah," Ward said, coming in the kitchen door. "My bride had a special place to visit, and I left her alone for a few moments."

There was more jubilation amidst hugging and kissing, and then Beulah made everybody leave, saying that if they didn't there wouldn't be any wedding, much less any supper on the table afterward.

Susannah was enjoying her last Christmas Eve as an unmarried woman, taking in the sunset off her balcony as she had done so many times before. She marveled at how quickly the horrible scars of war had been covered, if not healed, by nature. The white herons still took flight over the marsh, the gaggles of wild geese still sounded their calls, the drifts of sunset color still made their peace with the shimmering water of the Altamaha.

"Oh, Morgan, I hope we can be happy together after all that's happened." What if he regretted marrying a daughter of the beaten, struggling South? What if their marital arguments took on the ugly substance of different philosophies?

"It won't happen," she vowed fiercely. "Like President Andrew Johnson, Morgan and those who fought with him will try to help us rather than punish us. I have faith in him. Dear God, if I did not, this marriage would not be taking place!"

She looked down at the still figure kneeling on the point of the bluff and saw her brother hurrying to the side of his intended.

Peace returned to her heart. If Captain Breyer's widow could find it in her heart to love Ward Armstrong and want to marry him after their brief courtship, there was hope for the country.

The wedding would be held at the foot of the Christmas tree, Dorothea declared, since outdoor weather could not be relied upon this time of year. She was still reeling with the news of her son's engagement to a widow with a small child but had been won over by the shy young Janice Breyer, who obviously adored Ward.

"Now, everybody," Dorothea announced as they assembled around the tree, "I know we have an unusual Christmas happening here, but we have our traditions that we must follow. Janice, Morgan, you're not Southern by blood, but you're about to be by marriage."

"Amen," Morgan murmured, holding his bride-to-be close to him and winking at Janice, who was very happy to be part of this warm family. "Dorothea, if we don't have a toast with some of Beulah's famous eggnog, I shall be very disappointed."

"Angus and I are still in charge of this household—and Christmas festivities," she reminded him with mock sternness. "Belinda, you and your new little niece-to-be are in charge of passing around the eggnog."

They all lifted their cups in a toast to the bridal pairs and then to the South.

"And to the North," Ward said, remembering how one on the other side had not only saved his life, but would always be a part of his family.

Ward had plans for preserving the heroic memory of Captain Breyer so that his little daughter would always remember him.

"Hear, hear." Morgan stepped forward with his cup held high. "We can drink tonight and on holidays to come, but we all know that putting our country back together is going to take more than a toast."

"Oh, Morgan, do you have to get political?" Susannah whispered, nudging him.

He ignored her. "No, it will take something bigger than all of us—greater, nobler, and for damn sure, wiser."

Susannah nudged him again.

Morgan lifted his cup, turning in place to face the Christmas tree. "Here, my friends, north and south, east and west, is my toast. To Susannah's Angel!"

They lifted their cups to the glistening figure atop the tree, and Susannah could have sworn on the Bible she carried with her to the altar later that night that there was a heavenly chorus of "Ave Maria" resounding in the halls of Catshead Peak.

Author's Note

Dear Readers,

I hope you've enjoyed this story, which is based on very real circumstances, setting, and Southern traditions. Food is, of course, almost as important to people in the South as blood and plays a large role in all our celebrations of the holidays—especially Christmas.

The Lane Cake that Beulah makes every year is identical to the one our grandmothers, even great-grandmothers, made. Many other sweet dishes, like pecan pie and a multitude of other sinful desserts, would make a possum sit up and beg for seconds.

The traditional Christmas menu was and still is the same. Roast turkey, rice-and-giblet gravy, cornbread dressing, sweet potato casserole, whatever greens are in season (usually collards), ambrosia, and cake are still the favorite offerings at the big family dinner. The coastal South hostess always includes wonderful seafood treats, such as oyster stew and shrimp timbales. I've included one of the best of the recipes for the stew of "doomed bivalves," as Ward called them. (We usually have this for breakfast on Christmas morning.) A famous restaurant in New Orleans serves a very similar dish as a specialty.

Wonder who made it first?

Who cares! It's absolutely delicious.

Bon appetit!

Nelle McFather

Dr. Bob Reed's Famous
Mouth-Watering Oyster Stew

1 Pint oysters
2 Tbsp. butter (or to taste)
1 Tbsp. chopped or dried parsley
2 or 3 spring onions, sliced thin (include green parts)
1 Tsp. Worcestershire sauce*
Dash of Tabasco*
Pinch Cayenne pepper
Dash of ground black pepper
2 cups whole milk
½ Tsp. salt
Paprika

Heat oysters, butter, parsley, onions, Worcestershire, Tabasco, and peppers in a skillet over low heat and let simmer until oysters are done (sides curled, about ten minutes).

In a separate saucepan, heat milk (low heat) while cooking the oysters. Add salt.

Combine all ingredients and serve piping hot with oyster crackers if you like. Sprinkle paprika over each serving.

*Beulah didn't have Worcestershire or Tabasco, but I'm sure she added comparable condiments of her own.

SUSAN TANNER
A WARM SOUTHERN CHRISTMAS

The story is for my mom, Erlyne—
but the camellias are for Betty.

Acknowledgments:

I'd like to thank the ladies of the Lucedale-George County Public Library—especially Ms. Janet Smith—for their assistance in researching Merrill's past. Any errors or liberties taken with the history of Merrill are the fault of the author only.

Chapter One

Merrill, Mississippi, 1895

"This town is never going to let you keep those kids. You know that as well as I do, Luke."

Luke Tattersall studied the sheriff with narrowed eyes, seeing not his old friend, but someone sent to do an unpleasant job.

"I won't let you take them," Luke said finally, his voice as flat and uncompromising as the plank board table between them.

Sheriff John Marsh lifted one hand in a conciliatory gesture. "I don't aim to even try; you should know that, son." He sounded slightly hurt at the suggestion. Though there was a span of twenty years between their ages, the two had been close for years. Luke's father had been John's closest friend.

It had been John who helped to bury Luke's brother and sister-in-law just three weeks earlier. John who helped to tell ten-year-old Kane and six-year-old Gracie that their parents were never coming home. But not even John had had nerve enough to tell them why. That, and everything after that, had been left to Luke.

John shook his head. "The fact that I don't agree won't stop them, though. They'll go higher than me to do what they think is right by those children."

"You think they're going to talk to God about it?" Luke asked irreverently.

That irreverence was part of what marked the Tattersalls as being just slightly different—apart, as it were, from the other folk of Merrill. Being set apart was what John was trying to warn Luke about.

John ignored the quip. "There's all kinds of government laws seeing to the well-being of kids these days."

"Who's trying to take my kids?" Luke scowled ferociously. "Who's wanting them, John?"

The sheriff shifted uncomfortably. "Well now, Luke, I don't rightly know that anyone is exactly wanting them for themselves, so to speak. They just don't think a home with an unmarried man is the best that can be done for them."

"I'm their uncle," Luke argued. "The only family they've got left in these parts." And Luke would move heaven and earth to keep them with him. He'd promised them that.

"And Jake was their father," John said pointedly. "Would you really have thought him fit to have their raising if it was only Grace Ann who was gone?"

Luke flushed. "I don't drink, John."

The words hung angrily between them.

No, that was one flaw not a soul in Merrill would lay at Luke's feet. Whatever his failings, Luke Tattersall did not partake of hard liquor, not after watching the slow destruction of his brother over the past five or six years.

Slowly John got to his feet, looking around at the small kitchen, seeing the bare wood floor and unpainted shelves full of crockery and foodstuffs. But he saw the spartan cleanliness of the room, as well. Grace Ann had kept it just this clean. The sorrow of her death and the shameful way it had happened hit him again.

"I'm not here to fight you, son. I'm here to help. I'll do everything I can to keep this from happening, but . . ." His voice trailed away, and he gazed blankly through the uncurtained window, not seeing anything of the pretty Mississippi countryside beyond.

Luke got to his feet as well. "I appreciate the warning, I reckon."

John refocused on the younger man and stifled a grin. Luke sounded about as appreciative as if the sheriff had hauled a nest of rats into the house.

"Like I said—I'll do what I can, but it'd sure Lord help if you had a wife."

"A wife!" Luke looked stunned despite the fact that the idea of taking a wife had crossed his mind once or twice in the past few weeks. "And just who in Merrill do you think would be willing to take on the raising of two half-grown kids?"

"You did," John reminded him.

"They're mine. My brother's son and daughter. My flesh and blood."

John sighed, thinking maybe Luke was right. Though John could think of half-a-dozen girls who'd give every curl in their hair for a chance at having Luke as a husband, he couldn't picture any of them willing to take on the mothering of two half-grown children. Or any of their mamas willing to let them. The Tattersalls weren't exactly considered respectable.

The fact that Luke was little more than a dozen years older than his nephew was another problem. If Luke had been thirty or so, the difference in age between him and the handful of spinsters and widows in town wouldn't seem so great, and likely he could choose at will from among them.

John shook himself from his reverie to find Luke watching him with a peculiar expression.

"You tell those folks who are so all-fired worried about those two kids that I'm getting married." No one was taking his kids, no matter what he had to do to prevent it.

"You are?" John stared at him blankly. "I didn't even know you were courting." From all John had seen, Luke had been too busy supporting Jake and his family the past few years to allow himself the luxury of sparking a gal.

"I'm not." Luke's tone held a grim determination. "Yet."

"Now, Luke, Nadine is a pretty little thing, but I'm thinking she's not much for wife material.

Nor the Willis girl, either, for that matter." John knew both girls had shown every interest that their mamas would allow, speaking to Luke every time he so much as walked through town. Grace Ann had confided in John, wishing for a way that Luke could have a normal life without her and her children starving to death. Every dime Jake Tattersall had managed to get his hands on in the past five years had gone for whiskey.

"I'll have a wife come Christmas."

Maybe in six weeks' time, Luke's deep blue eyes and ready smile could convince some young lady to ignore the gossip, defy her parents, and give up her romantic dreams of a neat house with a white picket fence in exchange for skinned knees and freckled faces and a plain but well-built home just outside of town.

"Well," John said, looking dubious, "I wish you luck."

Luke saw John to the door, then poured himself another mug of strong coffee and carried it to the front porch. The afternoon sun slanted across the fields. He needed to be thinking about dinner. Kane and Gracie would be home from school soon, and they never walked through the door that they weren't hungry.

Despite what he needed to be doing, Luke propped one shoulder against a porch post and stared in the direction of town. Not that he could see much of it from here, just a fragment of white-washed building peeping here and there through the thin stand of trees. By the time October and the leaves were gone, he'd be able to see a lot more. Not that being able to see Merrill would make the

Tattersalls any more a part of the town than they were now. He reckoned nothing could accomplish that. Jake had managed to alienate half the folks thereabouts.

The thought of his brother filled him with a lingering sadness. At least he'd gotten over the anger. For a while, he'd been so furious that he'd wanted Jake alive just so he could have the pleasure of killing him. Now he was left with only the sorrow of Jake's wasted life and Grace Ann's needless death.

Pushing away thoughts of things he couldn't change, Luke tried to formulate a plan to find a wife. His mind ranged over the eligible girls in town, and he knew they were just that—girls. Ready, maybe, for the first honeymoon year of marriage, but far too immature for the raising of Kane and Gracie. Besides, he could remember most of them flirting as much with Jake as with Luke, regardless of the fact that Jake had a wife and two children. Young girls liked flirting with danger.

Nor did Luke think he could bring himself to court one of the several women who were both eligible and mature. The two spinsters were stiff and starched and rarely smiled; the widows—well they were more grandmotherly than anything else to Luke's way of thinking.

Luke couldn't think of one female in all of Merrill that he'd want to bring here to be wife to him and mother to Kane and Gracie. He rubbed his jaw thoughtfully. Maybe his sister Jeane would have a suggestion. He'd wire her tomorrow in the state of Washington. He'd ride over to the telegraph office in the next county to do it, just as he had when he'd had to tell her about Jake and Grace Ann. The worst of the gossip about his family had only recently begun to die away; he wasn't of a mind to stir it up any more than necessary.

He had a feeling it was going to be almost as hard to find the words this time as it had been when he'd wired her three weeks ago. Tears had burned his eyes when he'd read her grief-stricken response. There had just been no easy way to tell her that their brother had killed his own wife in a drunken rage and then—when his whiskey-soaked brain realized what he'd done—killed himself.

She'd wanted Luke to bring the children to her, but Luke wouldn't do it—selfishly, because he didn't want to lose his entire family, and unselfishly, because he didn't think the children could bear being uprooted just now. Merrill was all they'd ever known.

Maybe Jeane would know of someone there in Washington suitable for a wife and willing to travel to Merrill for the opportunity. But, Luke wondered, what kind of a woman would want to marry a man she'd never even met?

"What kind of a man wants to marry a woman he's never even met?" Wide grey eyes stared suspiciously into Jeane Tattersall Rand's neat features.

"The kind who's willing to wire enough money to get you out of Seattle," Jeane retorted. "Last night you said you'd sell your soul for the chance."

Stephanie flinched at the reminder and resumed pacing the length of her friend's neat little kitchen. Last night she had been ready to sell her soul— now all Jeane suggested she do was sell her body. Still, Jeane's words caused familiar feelings of desperation to wash through her soul. She had to get away. If she didn't, she feared she might really find herself married to a man three times her age, a man with calculating eyes and cold hands.

Not that her predicament wasn't at least partially her fault. She'd admit that much. At twenty years of age, she'd run off the few young men willing to overlook the scandal of an aborted elopement three years earlier. Maybe if she'd had a doting papa, her lack of prospects for a husband wouldn't have mattered so much. But her papa was definitely not doting, and he wanted her off his hands. He'd promised her to Karl Hendricks without so much as a blink of his eyes.

"What's your brother like?" Stephanie tossed the question over her shoulder as she paused to stare out of the window at the muddy street. She hated the fact that she'd even asked, and her mind continued to search for another way, any other way to escape. If there was one, surely she would have thought of it in the month since her father had told her to prepare for a wedding she didn't want to a man she would never willingly marry. But how could she possibly consider the intimacy of marriage with a man she'd never met?

"Handsome as the devil with blue eyes and shoulders as broad as a lumberman's," Jeane returned quick as a wink, picturing Stephanie's lively brown curls next to Luke's dark hair, or more likely his chin. That was about where the top of Stephanie's head would reach on her brother. "Always laughing or smiling . . . at least until Jake got so bad. There wasn't much to smile about by the time Henry and I left with the logging company. I missed Jake and Grace Ann and the kids a lot." Her voice slowed with real longing. "But I've missed Luke most of all these three years."

"If he's so wonderful, why does he need his sister to find him a wife?"

For a moment Jeane bit her lip, but she knew there were things that Stephanie would need to hear if Jeane wanted her to seriously consider traveling the length of the continent to marry Luke and raise Kane and Gracie.

"Sit down, Steffie."

The quiet in Jeane's voice pulled the other girl's attention from the empty street and brought her to sit in a chair across the table. Slowly, Jeane poured them each another cup of tea, using the time to gather her thoughts.

"Merrill is a very small town . . . a good town with good people, but still a small town with small town ways of thinking and small town gossip." Her lips twisted. "And we Tattersalls seem to provide a lot for them to gossip about."

Stephanie wrapped her cold fingers around the cup, feeling less need to drink the liquid within than to absorb the comforting warmth it gave. She listened, her expression cautious.

"All of Merrill respected our daddy, but only a few people actually liked him. He was a hard man, hard and fair. I've heard it said by more than one that Daddy would walk ten miles to pay a man a nickel if he owed him, but he'd expect that same man to walk that same ten miles if he owed Daddy."

Jeane sighed and sipped at her tea, barely even tasting it. "Jake never quite lived up to Daddy's expectations. He got Grace Ann pregnant when they were both just sixteen." A sad smile touched her lips. "Aaron was the prettiest little boy I've ever seen." The smile faded. "He died of rattlesnake bite just after he turned two. He was with Jake when it happened. Grace Ann was expecting Kane then. She never blamed Jake, but Daddy did—and that was when Jake started drinking. Not too much by some folk's standards, I reckon, but Daddy was a teetotaler. One drink was too much as far as he was concerned."

"What about your mama?" Stephanie's heart hurt for these people she didn't even know.

"Mama died when Luke was born. Daddy never married again. He just raised us by himself. Then Daddy died in a hunting accident a few years after we lost Aaron, and Jake really started drinking. He still managed to work and feed his family, but you could tell it was getting harder and harder for him to stop lifting that jug whenever he'd get started."

"Did your daddy ever forgive Jake?" Stephanie couldn't help the whispered question.

"Never. And Jake never forgave himself. Fortunately for Grace Ann and the kids, Luke finished school and got work at the sawmill about the time Jake got to where he couldn't stay sober long enough to keep a job anywhere. Luke's been more or less supporting them ever since, though I've helped whenever I could."

Jeane stopped talking and twisted her cup around and around in her hands. Stephanie had the feeling she didn't want to finish telling what she'd started. But now Stephanie had to know. She placed her hand on Jeane's to still her nervous movements and peered into a face pale with newly remembered grief.

"How did Jake and Grace Ann die, Jeane?"

Tears filled Jeane's eyes. "Grace Ann always managed to find whichever of Jake's drinking buddies was hosting the evening's fun, and she always went to get him when she thought it was time for him to come home." One tear fell. "I think she honestly worried about him getting lost or hurting himself on the way back. This particular night, Jake wasn't ready to leave when Grace Ann showed up. They—they had an argument, an ugly one, and Jake hit Grace Ann. He never had before."

Jeane stopped for a moment, and Stephanie didn't press, less sure now that she wanted to hear this story. But after a heavily indrawn breath, Jeane went on. "The blow might not have done more than give Grace Ann a nasty bruise, but the porch rail behind her was as rotten as Jake's would be if Luke didn't keep everything up. She fell through, and . . . and there was an axe half-buried in a piece of kindling. . . ."

Stephanie shuddered as Jeane's voice trailed away. "You don't have to tell me any more," she said huskily.

"Yes." Jeane nodded, wiping at her tears. "Yes, I do, because Luke needs someone like you, and I can't let you go if you don't know what you're getting into." Her tone was fierce as she spoke, and she finished in a rush of words. "When Jake realized what he'd done, he walked straight out into the woods and shot himself. The worst part for Luke was what they were arguing about."

Stephanie waited in silence.

"Jake accused Grace Ann and Luke of—of—" She faltered momentarily. "Well, I wish that hadn't been repeated to Luke, but it was. And not just to him, the whole town heard about Jake's last words to his wife."

"Is—was it true?" Stephanie asked in a small voice.

Jeane didn't quite meet her eyes as she admitted, "That's something I'd never ask Luke. He gave up years of his life to keep our brother's family together. He doesn't deserve that kind of question from me."

But, Stephanie noted, Jeane didn't deny the possibility that Jake hadn't been too drunk to know what he was saying. She wanted to look on the tale as just that, a sad tale about people she'd never known and would never know, but sometime during its telling, she had become involved in a way that scared her. Her arms ached to hold the children who'd known such grief. The sorrow she felt for the broken lives of their parents was very real, and the curiosity she felt about Luke Tattersall was even more real. As real as the distaste she felt at the thought of Karl Hendricks' papery-dry skin.

By taking Jeane's good looks and giving them a masculine cast, she could even picture Luke. Always smiling, Jeane had said. Karl rarely smiled, afraid his half-rotted teeth would show.

"When . . . when would your brother want an answer?" Stephanie heard herself asking.

Jeane stared at Stephanie, and a slow smile started across her face.

Chapter Two

Luke, shirt sleeves rolled to the elbows and back muscles flexing with his efforts, stacked newly sawn board upon newly sawn board. The tangy scent of freshly planed lumber prevailed over the rival aromas drifting from old man Thornhill's smokehouse. Though Luke worked with brisk, efficient movements, his mind had strayed far from the job at hand.

"So, then, tomorrow's the day, eh?" Jason Weathersby propped one boot atop the board Luke was reaching for next, effectively drawing his attention.

The effort of straightening his back told Luke just how hard he'd been driving himself for the past few hours. He stretched tiredly and forced a smile as he nodded at the owner of the sawmill. He'd worked for Jason since he was little more than Kane's age. He had been there every afternoon after lessons, and since he'd completed his schooling, he'd worked at the sawmill every day except Sundays.

"Tomorrow's the day," he agreed, trying to sound like it was a day he'd been anticipating eagerly.

He'd missed only one day of work in five years. The day he'd buried Jake and Grace Ann. He'd miss another tomorrow.

The cool of early December brushed the bared flesh of Luke's arm, and he slowly rolled his shirt sleeves down and buttoned the cuffs. "I appreciate your doing without me tomorrow. We've been so busy, I hated asking."

A slow grin creased Jason's face. He'd passed his rugged good looks on to every one of his five sons and three daughters. Because he delighted in his marriage and his family, he thought everyone ought to be equally blessed. "Well, now, a man doesn't get married every day. We'll make do here." His smile faded just a little. "Sure wish you'd bring that gal back here so we could do right by the wedding."

Luke shook his head. "I appreciate the thought, but given the circumstances, I'd just as soon keep things quiet." Besides, he couldn't think of many besides John Marsh who shared Jason's desire to celebrate the wedding of Luke Tattersall to a girl this town had never heard of until recently.

Knowing how hard those circumstances had been on Luke, Jason could only nod in agreement. "Can't say as I blame you. I'm right anxious to meet the future Mrs. Tattersall, though. You plan on bringing her over for Sunday dinner real soon."

"I'll do that." Luke wondered how eagerly Jason's wife would look forward to that. It would at least give her an opportunity to be first with some gossip. Luke had had a bellyful of gossip lately; to call it idle talk was to be kind. He hoped his bride wasn't thin-skinned about that kind of thing.

"I'm really looking forward to meeting her," Jason said almost sorrowfully. He sure hated to miss a chance to kiss the bride. "You haven't said much about her, for a fact."

Luke didn't know much about her, for a fact. He wished Jason would find something else to talk about or someone else to talk to, but the other man showed no signs of leaving Luke to his work. "She's pretty," Luke finally offered. He hoped Jeane hadn't been fibbing about that.

Jason brightened. All brides should be pretty. "Pretty's fine," he said, poking Luke's ribs lightly, "but can she cook?"

"She can bake an apple pie better than half the state of Washington."

Now that Luke thought about it, Jeane had told him some fairly inane facts about his future bride. And she'd left some relatively important information out. Like why an attractive girl who could cook was so willing to travel ten days by train to marry a man with two half-grown kids that weren't even his. He worried about that, worried that Miss Stephanie Cotter bore some dreadful bane that prevented any eligible men in her hometown from wanting her for a wife.

Perhaps she was of an ill temper or unsound health. Luke didn't need a wife with either.

Thoughts like these sometimes brought him to the brink of calling off the whole thing, but then he'd see one of the older women look at him askance as he and the children walked into town or he'd recall the letter from Grace Ann's sister, a letter he'd grimly burned. Celeste Bigelow had expressed herself aware of the fact that her only sister's children were now virtually alone in the world. She and her husband were considering the trip to Mississippi in order to take Kane and Gracie into their Alabama home. She'd sounded hopeful that some good family had taken them in but, if such were not the case, Luke had only to let her know, and she would do her familial duty by them.

Luke had written back promptly that, while the offer was appreciated, he and his wife intended to raise Kane and Gracie as their own. He'd neglected to mention that his wife was still in Washington— and still unmarried at the time. He could only hope his bride's reasons for coming were no darker than his were for having her.

"Can't do much better than a pretty wife serving warm apple pie," Jason agreed, drawing Luke from his worries.

To Luke's relief, the other man lowered his boot to the ground and straightened his shoulders as if to leave.

"What time is that train due in to Evanston?"

"Noon." Luke had arranged with the Justice of the Peace for the ceremony to take place

347

just minutes afterward. When he arrived back in Merrill tomorrow about sundown, he'd be a married man, and Kane and Gracie would be orphans no more. The four of them would be a family. He hoped.

He waved as Jason sauntered off toward the sawmill office. He couldn't say that Weathersby's questions were any harder to answer than Kane's and Gracie's had been the past few weeks. Somehow a child's direct gaze didn't allow for much evasion.

Luke found the two weren't through with their questions when he returned home that afternoon.

They met him at the door.

"What time are we leaving in the morning, Uncle Luke?"

"What should I wear?"

Luke looked from one bright, expectant face to the other. That they might want to go with him was something he actually hadn't considered, and certainly hadn't planned on. "What about school?" he asked slowly.

Kane was the first to catch his uncle's underlying reluctance. He struggled manfully with his disappointment. "I expect we hadn't better miss lessons, huh, Uncle Luke?"

He looked so much like Jake that just looking at him made the pain grow in Luke all over again.

"But, Kane, I want to see my new Aunt Stephanie," Gracie wailed. The tiny pale freckles on her nose stood out a little brighter as tears welled in her eyes.

Luke had planned to see the kids safely off

to school before leaving. He'd arranged for a neighbor's eldest daughter to be waiting when they arrived home that afternoon and stay with them until Luke returned—with his wife.

Looking at them now, that didn't seem like the best arrangement. After all, this was their lives he was molding with his plans as well as his own. The girl he was marrying would be their new mama—though they might never call her that. Luke wasn't sure he'd ever want them to.

He took Gracie in his arms, but answered Kane first. "Well, son, now that I think on it, I might be needing your help. No telling how many bags Stephanie will be bringing with her." Luke still found it hard to say her name, though he had practiced enough while no one was around. "You know how women are," he added for good measure.

Relief lit the boy's eyes and creased his face in an ear-to-ear grin. He'd found it almighty hard to be grown-up these past weeks, but he'd known instinctively that that was what his Uncle Luke needed from him.

"And Gracie, I'm thinking a wedding calls for you to be wearing your best dress."

"My best Sunday-go-to-meeting dress, Uncle Luke?" Gracie breathed the question ecstatically.

"Well," he said as if deep in conjecture, "that's what I'm thinking. What do you think, Kane?"

Kane nodded gravely. "That's what I'm thinking, too, Uncle Luke." Then his solemnity gave way to another broad smile.

*   *   *

So it was that Luke and Kane and Gracie were waiting when their bride stepped down from the soot-darkened train steps in Evanston at noon the next day.

Luke didn't know what the children on either side of him were expecting, but Stephanie Cotter was about as far from his expectations as anyone could have been.

Pretty, Jeane had said. She was as beautiful as a rare porcelain doll. *Brown, curly hair.* The sun caught a dozen shades of gold and red and cast them back to anyone looking at her. *Grey eyes.* Dancing silver flecked with darker silver. *Small, but not skinny.* Petitely fragile. Curves, both slender and richly promising. *Well-dressed.* Elegant fabric of soft green touched with only a hint of lace at the collar and sleeves, a gown the likes of which Luke could never afford.

Luke stared grimly. Kane fell in love. Gracie burst into tears.

Stephanie's heart sank to the lowest point it had reached in the past week. Those long days on the train had proven far too long for her to be alone with her thoughts. By the time she'd crossed mountains and hills and eons of flat prairie grass, she'd had time to reconsider her decision a dozen times over from all angles. It seemed to her that she'd made that decision rather hastily, all things considered. If there had been any way to turn back, she likely would have somewhere around Iowa. She didn't even pretend, however, that her father would open his door to her after she chose to leave her home in the dead of night for a second time. The consequences of the first time had proven disastrous enough.

So she'd straightened her shoulders and obediently left the haven of the train when the conductor had announced the destination she had been both dreading and anticipating. She'd had no trouble recognizing the trio waiting for her. As a matter of fact, they were the only people on the platform. Despite that, she felt sure she would have known Luke Tattersall if he'd been surrounded by a crowd. She had memorized Jeane's description of her brother. But even if she hadn't caught sight of the strong line of his clean-shaven jaw, even if his broad shoulders hadn't begged for her attention, even if she hadn't been mesmerized by the dark blue eyes watching her so gravely, she would have known the children. They were both auburn-haired and beautiful. Jeane had described them well.

And the little girl was sobbing as if her heart would break. No, as if it had already been broken.

The man, Luke, turned from watching Stephanie to drop to his knees beside the child, and Stephanie rushed forward.

"Gracie, honey, what's wrong?"

Gracie sniffed, trying to catch her breath around the sobs. "S-She's n-not going t-to stay." Gracie cried harder.

Luke couldn't reassure her. That had been his first thought when he'd seen the toes of her soft kid slippers peeping from beneath the flounces that ruffled the hem of her fine gown. He wasn't sure what Gracie's reasons were for believing this girl wouldn't be settling long in Mississippi, but he knew what his were. When Miss Stephanie Cotter saw the weathered four-room house he was expecting her to make her home, she'd be back on the first train to Washington. By then, it would be too late. By then, she would be Mrs. Luke Tattersall.

Stephanie smiled tentatively at Luke as she dropped to her knees on the train station platform, heedless of the dirt and cinders smudging her gown. "I'm not going anywhere." She said the words with as much assurance as she could considering Luke Tattersall's less than welcoming expression as she'd stepped off the train.

Luke glanced at the gorgeously gowned creature from beneath his lashes, then asked his niece, "Why do you think she won't stay, Gracie?"

"She's t-too pretty for her own good," Gracie spoke the too grown-up phrase sadly, fresh tears scalding her face.

Despite the fact that Luke thought much the same, he hadn't the faintest notion of what Gracie was getting at. He knew she hadn't come up with that turn of words on her own. He turned to Kane a little helplessly and was surprised to see a flushed look of anger on the boy's face.

Slowly, he lifted Gracie in his arms, keeping his eyes on Kane. "What is it, son?"

Stephanie scrambled to her feet, dusting her skirt as best she could, doing more damage to her gloves than good to her gown.

"That's something she heard from Mrs. Banks."

"What is?" Luke fought to keep his temper in hand. The woman's very name had the ability to make him see red.

"Mrs. Banks said she always knew Mama wasn't long for these parts, because she was too pretty for her own good, and if Daddy hadn't . . . hadn't . . . if Mama hadn't died, she'd have run off with another man some day."

"Kane, I've told you kids not to stand and listen to other people gossiping." Despite his best efforts, even Luke heard the exasperation in his own voice.

Kane's few freckles stood out indignantly. "We weren't, Uncle Luke. Mrs. Banks was talking to us."

With a kind of fearful fascination, Stephanie watched the muscle jumping in Luke's clenched jaw. She caught her breath when he turned to look at her with anger blazing from eyes so dark with emotion they almost looked black.

"Welcome to Mississippi, Miss Cotter."

Stephanie refused to back away from the bitterness in the words. As far as she was concerned, she was home, no matter how rough the welcome.

"Thank you, Mr. Tattersall."

Luke tightened his hold on Gracie as he felt himself drowning in those silver eyes. Before the moment had any chance to stretch into something real and honest between them, it was broken by the sound of bags hitting the platform with astounding force.

"Hey," Kane yelled at the baggage handler,

"you be careful with those bags! Those are my mama's."

Luke stared at Kane in dismay, then turned to Stephanie in time to catch the startled expression on her face. Should he tell her that was something Kane had decided with no prompting from Luke? In fact, as Luke had suspected would be the case, he didn't particularly like hearing Kane call this woman Mama. It made Grace Ann's death seem that much worse, as if she'd lost not just her life, but her children as well.

Seeing Luke's dismay, Stephanie wondered just how much worse this introduction to her new life could get. Sighing, she stepped forward to tip the baggage handler, knowing it was expected even if it was undeserved. She took a coin from her handbag, but before she could extend it to the expectantly grinning young man before her, Luke called her name sharply.

She turned back to him. "Yes?"

Without bothering to answer, Luke walked past her, still holding Gracie and digging into his pocket for a hard-earned coin. Luke felt a sting of irritation. Did his future wife think he couldn't take care of his own? No doubt he didn't much look as if he could with his plain, boiled shirt and sturdy, mail-order jeans. Embarrassment overtook the irritation.

He handed the baggage handler the coin, then stood Gracie on her feet. Her tears were no longer flowing, but her face looked no happier, and Luke was no closer to knowing how to reassure her than he was before.

"Help me with these bags, Kane."

"Yes, sir!"

Kane stepped up smartly and began hefting two of the bags. He staggered under the weight of one and had to set it down promptly, his eyes wide.

"Those are my books," Stephanie told him apologetically, but the feeling of needing to apologize faded as the boy's eyes lit up.

"Books? To read?"

For the first time since setting foot in Mississippi, it seemed as if she'd done something right. "Books for reading," she agreed. With more confidence than she felt, she held out her hand for Gracie's as Luke obligingly lifted the bag Kane couldn't handle and left another for the boy.

Stephanie couldn't read Luke's expression, couldn't tell if he welcomed books—or any other thing about her—the way Kane did. To her relief, Gracie accepted her hand without demur, and they followed Luke and Kane to the wagon that waited beyond the railway office.

Kate and Gracie swiftly climbed up to the wagon seat, and when Stephanie would have done the same, a glance from Luke stopped her. His expression was similar to the one he'd worn when she stepped forward to tip the young man who had thrown her bags about with such reckless abandon, and she realized that she was on the verge of making another mistake. Evidently there were things Luke Tattersall did not allow a woman to do for herself.

Stephanie supposed that if she'd allowed young

men to come courting the past few years, waiting to be lifted to a wagon when she could climb up just as easily would have come quite naturally to her.

Luke was staring at her again, and she wished she might somehow have positioned the two youngsters between them.

"We need to talk." Realizing how abrupt he sounded, Luke cleared his throat and tried again. "I thought we might have some lunch before— well, before we do anything else." He tried not to think of the Justice of the Peace who would have heard the train's whistle and be waiting even now for their arrival.

He waited for Stephanie to respond. Those watchful grey eyes made him as uncomfortable as anything ever had in his life.

"I am a bit hungry," she finally lied. She didn't think she could force anything past the dry lump in her throat. She also didn't know that she wanted to hear what Luke Tattersall had to say. He looked alarmingly grim, and she wondered if her past had come back to haunt her. She'd heard many times that you reap what you sow, and she had brought a young man to the brink of the altar three years ago, only to refuse him at the eleventh hour. Was Luke Tattersall going to hand her a ticket back to Washington now that he'd laid eyes on her?

"Fine," Luke said and released the brake on the wagon, clucking to the neatly matched pair of bays at the same time.

The silence hung between them oppressively. Not even Kane or Gracie uttered a word.

"You have nice horses," Stephanie said when she could bear it no longer.

Luke opened his mouth to say they were Jake's animals, then closed it again. Everything that had been Jake's was his now. The house, the horses, the children. Which was why he was sitting on the seat of a buckboard just minutes away from marrying a complete stranger.

Stephanie very carefully swallowed a sigh. If they couldn't even exchange pleasantries, they were in a lot of trouble. *She* was in a lot of trouble.

Mercifully, the notion of eating in a real restaurant loosened both Kane's and Gracie's tongues immeasurably. They carried on sufficient conversation between them to smooth over the uneasy lack between Luke and Stephanie.

As soon as they were comfortably arranged around a linen-covered table—after Stephanie had carefully allowed Luke to seat her—and their orders had been taken, Stephanie took advantage of the children's willingness to talk.

"Your Aunt Jeane asked me to give both of you her love." She noticed that Kane smiled while Gracie simply looked at her rather blankly.

"Gracie was too young when Jeane and Henry moved away to remember much about them," Luke explained.

"Actually . . ." Stephanie tilted her head consideringly, looking first at Kane and then at Gracie. "You both look a good bit like your Aunt Jeane." And like their Uncle Luke. The resemblance was in the straight nose and strong line of jaw.

"I mostly look like my mama," Gracie said.

The little girl spoke with almost no inflection. Stephanie hoped she wouldn't say anything more than that, but the hope proved vain.

"Mrs. Banks says its a mercy I'm not really pretty like Mama, and maybe I won't come to a bad end."

"Da—" Luke caught Stephanie's quick look and bit back the curse. "Gracie, you are every bit as beautiful as your mama, and nothing bad is going to happen to you because of it. What happened to your mama was no fault of hers or her looks," he added emphatically.

Luke's words told Stephanie two things. Luke had found Grace Ann Tattersall more than pretty. And he was very defensive of his dead sister-in-law. Neither of which was a crime, she reminded herself.

"Miss Cotter."

Stephanie lifted her eyes from her lap.

"This kind of gossip is exactly what we need to talk about before—well, before you make up your mind."

For a long moment, Stephanie considered how to answer him. It was too late for second thoughts as far as she was concerned. She wouldn't be here if she hadn't already made up her mind. "Your sister is a good friend. She made sure I knew the facts, and I can imagine the gossip. Seattle has its share of gossipmongers." She hesitated only a fraction before adding, "I should know."

Luke frowned, wondering if she realized that hearing your friends and neighbors hashing and rehashing murder and suicide in your own family was far different from listening to the idle chatter of society matrons finding fault with each other's new gown or hairstyle.

She took a deep breath, "And I think you should begin calling me Stephanie."

Chapter Three

"We're getting married," Gracie announced with an air of satisfaction.

The Honorable Winston P. Manderly beamed at the little girl as he ushered the small group into the front room of his home. Of all his duties, he enjoyed performing marriage ceremonies the most, and fining rowdy drunks the least.

Stephanie paid little attention as Luke apologized for their being late, though she did notice he didn't give any excuses with his apology. Her interest was caught by the beauty of the room itself. Rich rose furniture gleamed of polish; not a speck of dust was to be seen. On every available surface, exquisitely crocheted doilies rested in starched perfection. She almost didn't see the tiny woman seated in a rocker, her fingers busily creating another lacelike web.

The woman rose gracefully as they entered, laying her work in the seat of the rocking chair she had just vacated. She smoothed her apron, smiled warmly at Stephanie, then moved to stand beside the man. The resemblance between the two of them was obvious in their light blue eyes, straight silver hair, and spare frames marked by a straight stature.

"Are we ready, Winston?" she asked in the softest of voices.

"Are we ready, folks?" he repeated the question, looking from Luke to Stephanie.

Stephanie nodded, and Luke cleared his throat as if to speak, then just nodded as well. Gracie slipped her hand into Luke's, and Kane moved closer to Stephanie.

"My sister, Amelia, will be your witness."

Amelia's face wrinkled in consternation. "Wait, Winston, I almost forgot." She bustled from the room.

Luke shifted restlessly, still not certain he was doing the right thing, but wanting to get it done as quickly as possible and be gone.

When Amelia returned, she carried a neat nosegay of vividly colored flowers, which she handed to Stephanie with a smile that was almost shy.

"How lovely! What kind of flowers bloom this time of year?" Of course, Jeane had warned her to expect a vast difference in climate, and she'd dressed accordingly. She'd shed her warm woolen coat two days ago. Now she wondered if even the flowers stayed in a state of confusion as to the season.

"Why, they're camellias, dear." Amelia's tone held a faintly questioning tone. "They only bloom in the winter."

Stephanie felt the warmth move to her face at her lack of knowledge. She supposed a great many things remained for her to learn about her new home.

"They're beautiful. Thank you."

She moved to stand beside Luke, and after a moment's hesitation, he took her hand, loosing Gracie's in the process. The hand he held was smooth, slender, and very cold. He gave Stephanie a sharp glance, but her expression revealed nothing as she looked at the man who was going to join their lives forever.

"I'm getting married, too," Gracie's voice piped up forlornly.

Stephanie turned toward her, and Luke tensed, uneasy that she might be less than patient with the child. But all Stephanie said was, "Of course you are, dear." And she pulled her hand from Luke's and gave it to Gracie. She then gave the little girl her bouquet of flowers to hold before reaching back to take Kane's hand as well.

She straightened and smiled at the justice of the peace. "*Now* we're ready."

Some of the tension left Luke's shoulders, and he took the hand Gracie held out to him.

The words Luke repeated after the justice were the same as those Stephanie had heard a dozen times as one by one her friends got married. She knew she would have no difficulty speaking her vows and scarcely noticed that she was wearing a serviceable shirtwaist gown with leg-of-mutton sleeves rather than a dressmaker's dream of satin and lace. What she *did* notice were the glances that Luke and Kane and Gracie kept casting her way. As if she were some odd creature just a little beyond their comprehension. And maybe she was.

"I, Stephanie, take thee, Luke," she repeated obediently when it was her turn, pulling her mind back from its wanderings.

Her accent intrigued Luke. Each word was clear and precise. She didn't talk like anyone he knew. For that matter, she didn't act like anyone he knew. Certainly not the giggling girls who had tried to catch his attention the past few years, despite their mamas' best efforts to curb them. Not like Grace Ann either, who had always been soft-spoken, as if the vitality had been sapped out of her from watching Jake drink and squander every dime.

Stephanie, though quiet and serene, almost seemed to vibrate with life, and Luke suspected she could be a joyous person were circumstances only a little bit encouraging. The way she had accepted and admired a last-minute handful of camellias as her wedding bouquet hinted at that trait. Luke guessed he should have thought to find flowers for her. Likely there were other things he had forgotten as well. Or didn't know about. He sure hadn't asked anyone's advice on the matter, though he suspected that John's wife would have helped willingly enough.

The truth of the matter was, Luke had spent the past two weeks avoiding discussion of his upcoming wedding as much as possible. Of course, Kane and Gracie had talked of little else.

Justice Manderly cleared his throat, and Luke jumped, realizing that he hadn't been paying attention and didn't know where in the ceremony they were.

"You may put the ring on her finger," Manderly repeated.

Stephanie had extricated both hands from the children's grasps and was extending her left one toward Luke. He removed the ring from the pocket of his waistcoat and took her fingers lightly in his. They were icy.

The ring slipped easily into place, a perfect fit, and Luke wondered if that could be construed as a good omen. He was ready for an encouraging sign that this wedding was meant to be and not some horrible mistake he was making.

Stephanie lifted her gaze from the gleaming band of gold and smiled shyly at Luke. She thought she could stare into those deep blue eyes for a lifetime and never tire of seeing them. And that, she realized, was just what her marriage vows had given her permission to do. That, and more.

Her blush nudged Luke, making him think that perhaps her thoughts had taken the same path as his. He leaned slowly forward, aware and heartened when she lifted her face slightly toward his. Their lips touched and lingered for no more than a heartbeat before parting.

Stephanie's pulse had taken on an erratic

rhythm, and her breath came a little faster than before. Her gaze clung to Luke's with the same intensity that her fingers held on to his.

"Uncle Luke." Gracie's tone grew more demanding. "Uncle Luke!"

Luke pulled his gaze from Stephanie's to take in the slightly anxious faces of his niece and nephew. He forced himself to smile as if his heart wasn't threatening to jump out of his chest. This was definitely not a reaction he had expected.

He extended his smile to Amelia and Winston Manderly. "I guess we're done here, then." He'd slipped the justice a silver dollar as they walked in the door earlier.

"Yes, son, I suppose we are." Justice Manderly was proud of his afternoon's work. Another couple joined in the eyes of God and the law. Indeed, in this instance, an entire family had been united.

When Luke turned back to Stephanie, he discovered Kane's and Gracie's hands firmly in hers once more. Somehow the sight warmed him. "Ready?"

Stephanie nodded. It was time to go home—whereever that proved to be now.

As Luke helped her into the buckboard, his glance fell on her baggage placed neatly in the back. This time, he didn't think of what kind of wealth they implied or held within. He considered, instead, the fact that they likely held all she owned in this world. They represented her life. A life now linked to his.

To marry him, this girl had left her family and home, all she had ever had or known. He was her only security in this new life. The thought gave him a protective feeling towards her, similar to what he felt for the children, but different at the same time.

He lifted the reins, aware of her beside him as she made sure the children were seated safely, hearing her ask Gracie if she was cold.

They were nearly out of town before Stephanie turned her attention to the well-traveled dirt road ahead of them. Luke felt her gaze touch his face, and he glanced at her.

"I'll try to make sure you're never sorry you left Washington." Once the words were out, Luke felt stupid. He could have said he'd try to make her happy or that he'd try to make her a good husband.

"I'm sure I never will be," Stephanie returned softly. She stared down at the flowers she held once more. Some were dark rose, some red, some white, all nestled in dark glossy green leaves. "Do we have camellias in our yard as well?"

Luke thought of the bare dirt that surrounded the house. "Not yet, but I was thinking of planting a bush or two."

Stephanie nodded. "That would be nice." She winced at the inane words and struggled for something more to say. Something witty or charming. The fact that they were complete strangers loomed greater and greater in her mind. There seemed no common ground for them to discuss. She felt as if she knew so little about him, despite the endless hours of questions she'd asked of Jeane. There was, she knew, no surer way of knowing another person than to live with him.

For example, she knew exactly the way her father preferred his tea, his dinner, and his laundry. She knew when to speak and when to remain quiet in his presence. These were, she supposed, all things she would soon come to know about Luke. But, what, in the meantime, would they converse about?

"Do you have a bicycle?"

She turned to find Kane staring at her bags with an expression full of hope. "I do—did. At home. In Washington, I mean." Mississippi was home now. She had to remember that.

Luke knew how much Kane wanted a bicycle, but he doubted he'd be able to afford one any time soon. Things were easier now that Jake wasn't drinking up any money not immediately put out for food and clothing, but Luke had no notion of how expensive a wife might prove to be. Especially one used to the things Stephanie Cotter was used to. Tattersall, he corrected himself. Stephanie Tattersall.

"I suppose we could have Jeane ship it to me," she was saying tentatively. She wondered if her father would refuse to let Jeane get it for her. The possibility was greater than she liked to admit, even to herself. But then she'd known she was burning her bridges when she stepped on board that train. She looked at Luke. "I don't have any idea how much it would cost to ship it such a great distance."

Probably as much as a new one, Luke thought, but he didn't say so. He couldn't, not with Kane looking almost prayerful. Besides, he didn't want to come across miserly from the very start. "I could ask," he said finally.

Stephanie leaned a little closer to him and lowered her voice. "If it proves affordable to have it sent, I suspect that would be a perfect Christmas surprise for Kane."

Luke jerked. "Christmas surprise?"

"Shhhh," Stephanie admonished, without considering how brave she was being. She sneaked a quick peak at Kane, who was pointing something out to Gracie. She turned back to Luke. "A Christmas present," she repeated. Maybe Luke thought she was being selfish in her giving. "From both of us, of course, with you paying the cost to have it here."

A long silence fell between them. Abram Tattersall hadn't been one to make much of holidays or birthdays. Jake and Luke and Jeane had never had Christmas treats of any kind. Consequently, neither had Kane or Gracie. Luke wondered how many times the two had admired the gifts other children in town received. The thought grieved him, and he regretted that he'd never considered the possibility before now.

Certain she had made a serious tactical error of some sort, Stephanie sat in silent misery. It was going to be difficult, then, this learning to be a wife to Luke Tattersall.

"That sounds like a fine idea," Luke said finally, hoping he could afford the expense even while disliking the thought that Stephanie would have to sacrifice something that belonged to her. "What about Gracie?" he asked diffidently.

Relief swept Stephanie. "Oh," she said quickly, "little girls are easy. I'll think of something—and then talk to you about it," she added, lest he find her intrusive.

But Luke wasn't thinking about Gracie by the time Stephanie finished. He was wondering what wealthy young women were accustomed to receiving as gifts. Jewels? Looking-glasses edged with gilt? Gowns trimmed in fine lace? His heart sank. He didn't have anywhere near that kind of money.

Stephanie leaned forward on the buckboard seat, sure Merrill was the prettiest place she had ever seen. In the days just past, as the train had rolled through little towns all along the way, she'd tried to imagine how her new home might appear. But the grandeur of mountains and the vast spaces of prairies could not compare to the pine-green woods surrounding the small Mississippi town.

The town itself comprised a number of well-tended buildings and bustled with a productive energy far different from the brash, bold zest of Seattle. Seattle had grown quickly—too quickly, as evidenced by raw board structures haphazardly thrown together. Merrill appeared to have developed with quiet, slow growth that allowed for forethought and planning.

As they rolled through the middle of town, Stephanie settled back with a sigh of contentment, feeling the warmth of the sun against her back. A warmth that would be unseasonal in Washington, but which appeared to be normal for Mississippi in early winter. She didn't think she would ever miss Seattle.

Luke's lips thinned slightly as he heard Stephanie's sigh and felt her slump at her first sight of Merrill. He suspected it looked nothing like what she was used to. Jeane's letters had described Seattle as a large town, growing larger every day, wealthy and busy and filled with entertainments. The highlight of Merrill was a church social.

He listened to Kane and Gracie eagerly pointing out what they deemed significant places of interest to Stephanie.

"There's the schoolhouse."

Luke noticed that it needed a new coat of whitewash.

"That's where we go to church."

Only the spire and bell marked it from the other plain board buildings.

"And the sawmill, where Uncle Luke works."

For wages that kept them warm and fed, but didn't allow for luxuries. Like a bicycle.

Beyond the sawmill, Stephanie could see the bends and turns of a river.

Stephanie laughed, then protested. "You two are making my head spin. I'll need you to guide me everywhere for a few days, so I won't get lost. You and Luke." She gave him another shy look, and found he wasn't smiling, not at the children's enthusiasm nor at her reaction.

Luke took a deep breath, aware he'd been holding it as he waited for her reaction. At least she wasn't taking the disappointment she must be feeling out on the children—or even letting them realize it.

He eased the buckboard to a stop in front of the house and waited for Stephanie's attention to turn in that direction.

For the first time, Stephanie felt honest dismay and knew she didn't hide her reaction as quickly as she should have. Everything about the place told of Luke's work and care, but nothing about it spoke of a real home. Instead of curtains at the windows, plain white cloth hung in a solid sheet. Fresh whitewash adorned the walls, but not one flower pot stood on one window sill or porch railing.

In silence, Luke climbed down and reached for Stephanie. Hell would freeze before he would apologize for a decent home. Though the children continued to chatter, the silence between Luke and Stephanie stretched as he took her arm and walked her up the steps of the porch and through the front door.

Stephanie barely had time to marvel at a place that allowed for homes to be left unsecured against thieves before her attention was fully caught by her new home. The unadorned appearance of the outside continued in the parlor, but Stephanie's mind was quick to see the possibilities. No lace doilies or bric-a-brac softened the look of the room, just as no brightly colored scatter rugs warmed the wide planks of the floor. Yet every piece of furniture had been crafted with great care, honed and planed and smoothed to show the beautiful grain of the wood. The cushions were well-worn, but immaculately clean.

If Luke had made the furniture, as Stephanie suspected was the case, then his had been the hand to make the house a home even when his sister-in-law had been alive. All too easily, Stephanie could picture a woman so beaten down by her husband's excessive drinking that she had given up her dreams for a home and merely existed in this house. Stephanie could just imagine what that had done to her children.

She noted the two doors that opened off one side of the parlor and suspected those were the bedrooms. The wall in front of her held a fireplace and an open archway. She glimpsed a cast-iron stove in the room beyond.

Totally unaware of Luke's presence now, Stephanie moved from the parlor to the kitchen and found that some thoughtful soul had left a covered dish on the iron stove. She touched a hand to the side of the dish to see if it was still warm, then realized by the heat emanating from the stove that a low fire must burn within. Behind the casserole stood a cloth-covered pan. Stephanie suspected it held warm bread.

She turned, almost bumping into a very broad chest. She blushed and stepped back, but Luke's gaze was not on her. He was staring at the letter lying in the center of the table.

Luke felt a definite chill as he recognized Celeste Bigelow's spidery writing. He didn't touch the letter and shifted his glance to Stephanie. "Kane and I will get your bags."

Stephanie had no need to hide disappointment

at Luke's lack of welcome, for she was too busy wondering about the look in Luke's eyes when he'd seen the letter. For a moment, she would have sworn she actually saw a hint of fear.

"Gracie and I will set the table," she said slowly. "You'll have to tell me who to thank for the meal."

Luke cast a quick glance toward the stove. "I'd suspect Willene Marsh. You'll meet her, soon enough."

Though his tone was innocuous, Stephanie thought the comment sounded almost ominous as she watched Luke turn and call for Kane to give him a hand.

Chapter Four

For the first time in many weeks, Luke woke to the aroma of breakfast cooking and to find the house already slowly warming. Usually, he had to drag his weary body out of the cocoon of coverlets to light the fire. The hearth stood between the kitchen and the parlor, opening onto both rooms at the same time, and he always made sure a blaze was going before he roused the children.

Stephanie. He knew he was alone in the bed, but he hadn't heard her get up. For a moment, he simply lay there, picturing her as she had looked the night before when he had finally come in from the barn. Evening chores had been his excuse for remaining outside far longer than need be.

He'd placed the kerosene lamp on the night table, careful not to look at her directly, but seeing so clearly the gleaming red-brown of her hair and the sweep of dark lashes against a creamy cheek. Shedding his clothes hastily while trying hard not to let his gaze stray in her direction, Luke acknowledged a disturbing thought. Though he hadn't the faintest idea what to do with a wife, his body seemed to know too well what to do with a woman.

He wished they'd discussed the situation earlier, that he'd told her he intended to give them both time to know each other before . . . well before they became intimate, but the perfect opportunity had never presented itself. And he'd let the less-than-perfect ones slip by.

He would have been snake-bit before he let himself begin that conversation when she was trying so desperately to pretend that she slept. Luke had known the pretense by the uneven rise and fall of her chest with every breath she drew. He'd slid into bed beside her without saying a word, then wondered if she could hear the pounding of his heart as he tried to keep his legs from bumping against hers while he tossed and turned for the next hour after that. Wondered, too, if she could somehow sense the very tangible evidence of his desire.

With a wry grin for his nocturnal suffering, Luke rose, automatically straightening the covers on the bed, though he could barely see in the faint grey light of dawn. He supposed straightening the bed was something Stephanie would expect to do during the day, but he'd made a habit after Grace Ann's death of seeing to whatever needed doing right away so he didn't have to come home to it later. Habits like that were hard to break.

When he stepped into the kitchen, Stephanie had her back to him, stirring a bowl of batter. Her slender shoulders moved with each stir of the large wooden spoon, and Luke found his gaze straying from there to the corresponding movement of her hips. "Find everything you need?" he asked, hearing the huskiness in his own voice that had only a little to do with the fact that he'd just awakened.

Stephanie nearly dropped the mixing bowl as she whirled to face Luke. "Yes-s-s," she stammered. "Everything. Thank you." What do you say to a husband of less than twenty-four hours? A husband you slept beside all night, but who never touched you? "Did I wake you?"

"No. I heard old man Hiram's rooster crowing." There were many mornings that Luke cursed that old rooster for waking him, but not this one. He wouldn't have missed the sight of Stephanie in her wrapper with one fat braid hanging over her shoulder for anything in the world. "I like your hair." He heard himself say the words, and still couldn't believe he'd said them when they were hanging in the air.

Stephanie blushed all the way to her toes. "Thank you." She turned her attention back to stirring the griddle-cake batter with great industry and concentration.

"I'll just bring in some more firewood," Luke said, as embarrassed as she appeared to be. Despite his words, he stood there a minute, just watching her. "What will you do all day?"

She didn't, he realized, know a soul in Merrill but him and the children. That wasn't anything he'd worried about before, but now he discovered that he disliked leaving her to find her way about on her own. Still, he couldn't miss another day of work.

Stephanie looked up from her stirring. Her brows drew together in faint surprise at the question. "Well . . . I suppose I'll help the children get ready and walk them to school. Then I'll come back here. I need some time to find my way around this house."

Luke considered that. Normally the children left as early as he did so that he could walk with them to the school before going to work. He supposed they'd be glad enough for a little extra time in the mornings. Then he frowned slightly. "Make sure you mark the path well in your mind so you don't have trouble finding your way back."

His concern warmed Stephanie's heart. "I will," she assured him.

That warmth stayed with her as she woke the children and put breakfast on the table. Not even Luke's seemingly indifferent good-bye as he headed out to work cooled it entirely. *What did you expect,* she chided herself as she filled the children's lunch pails, *a hug and a kiss on the cheek or maybe even a pat on the fanny like Henry gives Jeane?* She felt her cheeks grow warm at the mental image that thought produced!

Fortunately, Kane and Gracie couldn't read her mind as they finished their breakfast while she dressed. When she walked into the room, she noted with surprise that Luke had straightened the bedclothes. She felt as if she had made a discovery about her husband. The next thing she discovered was that there was no place to unpack her clothes. Grace Ann's dresses still occupied the armoire, but even if they had not, the space would not have been sufficient for Stephanie's multitude of gowns. Deciding that was something she could worry about later, she dressed quickly but carefully in a neat, modest navy-blue velvet. Her choice was facilitated by the fact that the gown fastened up the front of the bodice so that she could manage on her own.

Gracie's eyes grew round when Stephanie walked back into the room, while Kane just beamed. Stephanie had noted in her explorations that Grace Ann's gowns had been clean and in good repair, but of serviceable cloth and color. She suspected that Gracie's were all much the same, and an idea for Gracie's Christmas present began to grow in her mind.

Within moments, the children had joined her at the door. She gave a quick check of their clothing, decided they'd learned to do well on their own, then frowned. "Kane, where is your jacket? It's very chilly out." She'd stuck her head out a few moments earlier to check.

"Aw, Ma." Despite the protest, Kane grinned broadly at this evidence of her caring. He'd missed his mother's attentions more than he'd let anyone realize.

Ma? "Now." Stephanie forced herself to speak firmly though her heart was melting into a little puddle. Gracie seemed determined to remain a little distant, but Kane's acceptance of her in his life appeared complete.

Their early morning walk was pleasant and all too brief. Listening to their chatter, Stephanie realized that she would miss the presence of the children through the day. She had tried to catch a glimpse of Luke when they passed the sawmill, but it was too far from the road to see more than the tin roofs of several buildings. From inside she could hear the whine of the saws biting into lumber.

An older woman stood just outside the door of the one-room schoolhouse watching the dozen or so young people trooping her way. Stephanie introduced herself to Mamie Stringer, the school-mistress, who displayed equal amounts of welcome and curiosity upon meeting Luke's new bride.

Kane seemed a little reluctant to leave Stephanie's side even when Miss Mamie lifted the bell to signal the beginning of the school day. "Can you remember the way back home, Ma?"

Stephanie ruffled his hair, feeling a surge of affection. "Of course, I can, you silly," she chided softly. "I'll be fine." Hoping she wasn't passing Kane's boundaries or embarrassing him in front of his schoolmates, she bent down and kissed first his cheek and then Gracie's. "Should I meet you here after school to walk you back?"

"No, ma'am. Uncle Luke just doesn't like us to be in the house in the mornings after he leaves. Long as you're home when we get in, it'll be all right."

Kane grinned mischievously. "I think most likely Uncle Luke's afraid I'll play hooky if he leaves me there."

"I'll be there," she assured him.

She exchanged smiles with Miss Mamie, then turned to go. At the end of the little lane that led to the school, she made a quick decision and headed toward Merrill. The day was a crisp one with clear, blue skies and the nip of winter in the air. Stephanie imagined the dripping rain of Washington, constant and miserably cold against the skin, and smiled. She had a feeling she was going to like Mississippi weather.

Somehow, she wasn't surprised to find most of the shops open for business even at this early hour. She didn't go into any of them, just made a walking tour of the main street of town, looking about and smiling as folk studied her curiously. Every person she passed lifted a hand in greeting and returned her smile.

Feeling as if she'd taken the first step in making Merrill her town, Stephanie retraced her path back to Luke's house and began making that her home. By the time she had cleared the breakfast dishes, washed and dried and put them away, she at least knew where everything was in the kitchen.

She turned her attention to the parlor, walking around the fairly large, perfectly square room. Everything was pristinely clean, from the scrubbed planks of the floor to the heavy glass of the two deep windows. At least the windows had glass. She had noticed a house or two along the walk to school that had some kind of oiled cloth or hide stretched over the window openings.

With a brief sigh of regret, she thought of all the tatted doilies that had adorned her father's home. He would never have missed a half dozen or so, and they would have done so much to warm this room. She supposed that might be an art she could learn. If she could find someone to teach her.

After the parlor, she made an exploration of the children's room. Their beds were as neatly made as the one she shared with Luke. In the center of one bed lay a worn and faded rag doll. At the foot of the other was a trunk which she opened to find Kane's clothes in less than orderly fashion. Feeling very much like a mother, she took them all out, refolded them carefully and put them away again. Kane had two pair of school jeans such as the ones he'd worn this morning, one pair that looked as if they'd been dipped in every substance that could possibly stain, and a pair of trousers that Stephanie suspected were worn only to church. His shirts were much the same. Two of striped cotton, one of heavy chambray, and a white linen.

Gracie's clothes hung in a small armoire that appeared to have been built especially to be within a little girl's reach. Her dresses hung on knobs. All were of flower-sprigged cotton; only one with a ruffled hem and a touch of lace at the collar.

Stephanie noticed that the rag doll wore a dress which just matched the one with the ruffles and lace. The idea for Gracie's Christmas present grew, and Stephanie hurried to the room she'd shared with Luke, throwing open one bag after another until she found the one she sought. There, carefully nestled within, lay a fine porcelain doll. Stephanie had very nearly not brought it with her. There had been so much for her to manage as it was. Still, the doll was the last birthday gift her mother had given her, and she could not bear to leave it for her father to toss out with the rest of her things as if this treasure of her girlhood was just so much garbage. Now, thinking of Gracie's face on Christmas morning, she was glad that she had packed the doll.

At a solid rapping upon the front door, she replaced the doll carefully. Getting up off her knees, she dusted her skirt with painstaking thoroughness before hastening to answer the knock.

The small front porch seemed crowded with the number of women standing there. Several of them cradled infants or held the hands of very small children. All of them carried covered baskets, and all of them wore expressions of avid expectation. All, that is, except a tall, angular woman who waited a few steps behind the rest.

Stephanie knew a welcoming committee when she saw one and smiled graciously. "Come in, ladies, please." She opened the door and stepped back for them to enter.

One by one, they introduced themselves, and Stephanie prayed desperately that she would remember which name went with which face. Plump Suzanne Willis, the pharmacist's wife. Carrie McCutcheon, the postmaster's wife. Emily Lewis, the butcher's eldest daughter. Ruth Fulman, whose husband owned one of Merrill's several general stores. Rebecca Archard, the banker's beautiful wife. Red-headed Amelia, Jason Weathersby's wife. Elvira Banks, whose husband also worked at the sawmill and whose name Stephanie instantly recognized as the gossip who'd made Gracie cry. The sharp-faced woman who entered last was Willene Marsh. Her husband was the sheriff and Luke's best friend. She gave that information without a glimmer of a smile.

Stephanie closed the door against the cool breeze and turned to find the women had seated themselves all around her parlor. She noted that Elvira Banks had made sure she was in the center.

For a moment, recalling the spartan foodstuffs in her kitchen, Stephanie panicked. Then, instinctively, she looked at Willene. "I'm not very well prepared for guests, but I could make some tea."

In the same instant, Carrie and Ruth rose to their feet and lifted their baskets. "No need for that," Ruth said. "We've come to make you welcome. Not put you out." The two trooped off to the kitchen before Stephanie had a chance to respond. Moments later, she heard the clatter of crockery and the sounds of water being pumped for tea. At least the iron stove was still warm. She'd fed a little more wood into it, not knowing if Luke would return home for lunch and expect something prepared.

While that was going on, the remaining women began taking parcels wrapped in plain paper and stacking them on the low table that fronted the sofa. Willene stood up and pulled her chair to the table. "You sit here," she ordered Stephanie in a no-nonsense voice.

Feeling more flustered by the moment, Stephanie did as she was told. With the gifts came the comments and the questions. "Well, what do you think of Merrill?"

"Merrill is lovely," she answered honestly, unwrapping an embroidered tablecloth. "And so is this. What beautiful work!"

Emily Lewis preened while she jiggled the baby in her arms to quieten the whimpers that had started.

"I traveled here by train from Missouri," Rebecca said in a genteel voice. "I was heartily sick of it by the time I arrived. I can't imagine coming from twice that distance." She watched as Stephanie opened her offering.

"I love tea." Stephanie held the china teapot so that everyone could see. "And, yes, the journey did grow tedious."

"How is it that you and Luke came to know one another?" Elvira Banks leaned forward in her chair.

"Through his sister," Stephanie returned serenely. "Jeane and I are very close friends." She saw no need to mention what every one of these women surely already knew, that she and Luke had never met before their wedding day.

Next she opened hand-hemmed towels, which came from Amelia. "My husband is very fond of Luke. He's worked for him forever, you know."

"Luke seems very happy with his work," Stephanie said, as she admired the towels. She had no earthly idea if Luke liked being at the sawmill or not, but she'd swallow her tongue before she admitted it.

Suzanne, whose husband owned the pharmacy, had wrapped rose-scented water for Stephanie's gift. Carrie McCutcheon gave twelve envelopes already with stamps.

Stephanie smiled. "Jeane will be as grateful for this gift as I am." She wondered if her father would burn any letters from her.

"My Neda and Gracie are the same age," Carrie offered. She and Ruth had returned from the kitchen with laden trays of food and tea.

"Perhaps Neda could spend a Saturday with us, then."

Carrie beamed at the suggestion, and Stephanie began to wonder if Luke Tattersall's wife was enough of a novelty to be a social status symbol, at least for a while.

"I don't suppose you have much experience with children," Elvira said blandly. She had brought a chamber set, complete with basin, pitcher, cup, and chamber pot, which Stephanie duly admired.

"I don't think I'll need much with Kane and Gracie. I couldn't ask for two any sweeter."

There were two gifts left. The first was from Ruth, a Currier and Ives print. Stephanie could say honestly that it would hold a place of honor on the parlor wall. Ruth could see for herself that there was nothing there to vie for the position. The last gift was from Willene Marsh, a delicate hand-crocheted doily.

"You made this yourself?" Stephanie asked hopefully, with a gleam in her eye.

Willene looked surprised at her enthusiasm. "Why, yes, I did."

"Will you please teach me?"

Willene smiled for the first time. "I'd be delighted to."

Elvira sniffed. "Not much for homemade stuff myself, though that is quite pretty," she allowed.

Rather than appearing affronted, Willene merely rolled her eyes. "Ruthie, why don't you pour the tea now?"

Rebecca rose and walked from chair to chair with a tray of pastries while Amelia passed around the cups of tea that Ruth prepared according to each woman's instructions. The conversation turned harmlessly general until the group realized that it was nearly noon and time for them to be returning to their homes.

"You're a welcome addition to our community," Carrie said, wrapping her shawl around her thin shoulders.

"A lovely addition," Suzanne offered.

"Town, Carrie, dear," Rebecca corrected. "We're a town, now, not just a community."

"Yes, indeed, we are glad to have you here." Elvira picked up her empty basket. "I just hope you'll never be sorry you came."

With that comment, everyone in the room seemed to freeze in place.

"I'm sure I won't be." Stephanie was determined not to let the other woman dismay her.

"Well, I don't expect it'll be all that easy for you."

Elvira stepped a little closer. "You know, raising two children by another woman and living with the man who loved her."

Stephanie opened her mouth, then closed it again. What could she say to that, after all. For all she knew, every word of it was the truth.

"That's enough, Elvira." Willene stepped between Stephanie and the gossip. "We all loved Grace Ann. We all miss her, but Stephanie's here to take her own place in our town—not anyone else's."

With that, she stared the other woman down until Elvira muttered a hasty good-bye and was first to open the door.

Stephanie thanked each of the women as graciously as she could manage, more than a little shaken by Elvira's comment. Had Luke truly loved Grace Ann? In the way a man loves a woman he would take to be his wife?

Willene was last to leave, and she made sure she caught and held Stephanie's gaze as she said, "Elvira can't help what she is, but you can help listening to her."

Stephanie nodded and took a deep breath. "When can I start my lessons in crochet?"

Willene's hard-planed face softened. "Come to my house for a cup of tea in the morning. Luke can give you directions."

Stephanie had a feeling she'd just made her first real friend in Merrill.

Chapter Five

Luke and the children arrived home at very nearly the same hour. Stephanie heard the sounds of youthful exuberance and laughter just before Kane and Gracie burst through the back door. The smile that came to her face was as natural to her as breathing, and she knew in that moment that she could truly be a mother to these two.

Their faces lit up at the sight of the tray of warm cookies she placed on the table. She had brought milk from the spring house a few minutes earlier and poured them each a mugful as they shed their coats.

While Gracie bit daintily into the sweet warmth, Kane swallowed the first one whole, and Stephanie scolded him gently as she slid another cookie each onto the saucers in front of them. "You only get four, no matter how fast you eat them."

"That's right," Luke said from the back door. "The rest are mine." He spoke to Kane, but his attention centered on Stephanie, who had wheeled around to look at him with eyes as wide as the saucers on the table.

She was, he decided, the prettiest bride Merrill had ever seen. She'd pulled her hair up into some kind of a bun on top of her head, but the whole thing looked uncooperative by the tendrils that had escaped and curled around her face and neck. The style revealed her high cheekbones and straight nose to full advantage. An apron accentuated the narrowness of her waist and the fullness of her hips. Luke had an overwhelming urge to lean over and kiss her on lips that looked as if they'd been made just for his.

"Could I have another cookie?" Gracie asked, eyeing the one that sat precariously at the end of the spatula Stephanie held in mid-air.

Stephanie forced her gaze from Luke's. "Of course, sweetheart."

Luke grabbed a saucer and mug from the cupboard shelf and joined the children at the table. "Me too?" he asked innocently.

Stephanie knew she was blushing furiously, but there wasn't a thing she could do about it. "Of course." Her hand trembled the tiniest bit as she placed several cookies on the saucer he held.

Luke noticed she didn't call him sweetheart as she had Gracie. He marveled at the tiny bite of disappointment he felt. Maybe she was his wife, he reminded himself, but they'd only known each other twenty-four hours. He glanced her way and realized that she was watching Gracie rather intently.

"What is it, honey?" Stephanie asked the little girl gently.

The hesitant look on Gracie's face deepened. "Could I make cookies with you one day?"

"I'd like that," Stephanie said. "You're probably much better at it than I am."

Luke decided he could get very used to Stephanie's smile. "Are you finished, Kane? We've got chores to do."

"Can I have one more, Ma?"

"After dinner. You've had plenty now."

Kane thought about pleading, but a quick look at his uncle's face changed his mind for him. "Yes, ma'am. They were good."

"Very good," Luke echoed and was rewarded with another shy smile from his wife.

Deep blue eyes could be mesmerizing, Stephanie discovered. She pulled her gaze from Luke to Gracie. "Would you please help me finish getting dinner ready, Gracie?"

Although Luke had noticed Gracie's hesitance in accepting Stephanie, he didn't think it would be very long before her wall of reserve melted. Both kids had had a hard time of it, losing their parents like that. It surprised him a little that Kane had bounced back the quickest. He would have thought Gracie's young age would have helped her in that regard. Maybe it had something to do with her being a little girl. He just didn't know. Still, he felt things were going to be all right now that Stephanie was here.

He was halfway out the door before he even realized he'd had that thought—and what it meant. Was he really ready to give his trust? *Do you really have a choice?* he asked himself.

"I'd like an apron, too." Gracie eyed the pretty ruffles on the apron that did more to trim Stephanie's gown than protect it.

Stephanie agreed, relieved to recall that her aprons were not packed in the same bag as the doll. She held out her hand. "Come on. We'll go find one together."

It would be, she decided, the perfect time to discover Gracie's preferences in color and fabrics. Deliberately, she opened a bag she knew held many of her gowns, but not one apron.

She and Gracie knelt on the floor beside the bag and Stephanie lifted the dresses one by one and laid them aside. She watched carefully as Gracie touched each one reverently in turn. Lavender velvet. Pale rose damask. Silks. Muslins. Greens. Blues. Laces. Ruffles.

"Hmmm. No apron in that bag." She opened another and began the same process. Before long, she noticed that Gracie had turned her attention to two gowns in particular.

One was a pale yellow muslin. The other a velvet in soft green. That suited Stephanie. Both colors would enhance the little girl's golden coloring. She'd cut the muslin into a summer gown and put full sleeves in the velvet for winter weather.

If there was one thing Stephanie had faith in, it was her ability as a seamstress. The thought reminded her of some things she needed to ask Luke. Such as how the laundry was done. But then again . . . She looked at Gracie speculatively as she opened the bag she knew held her aprons.

"Will this one do?" She held up a blue apron with darker flowers imprinted upon the pocket.

Gracie's face lit up in the largest smile Stephanie had seen from her. "It's beautiful."

As Stephanie wrapped the sashes around the little girl's waist twice before tying it, she made up her mind to cut the apron down for the child the very next day.

"Gracie," she asked, "where did your mama wash your dresses?"

Wide brown eyes looked up at her curiously. "Outside. In the tub that hangs aside the house. There's a big, black kettle for heating the water out there, too."

"Did she build a fire outside to heat the water?"

Gracie shrugged. "Most times. In the summer, if it was real hot, she just washed them in water straight from the pump."

Stephanie thought about that. If the temperate winter was any indication of the summer to come, she could understand not choosing to plunge both arms into hot water up to her elbows.

As they left the bedroom, Gracie's glance fell on the gifts Stephanie had left on the table in the parlor. "What are those, Ma?" A distressed look came across her face.

Without thinking about it a moment, Stephanie dropped to her knees beside the little girl and caught her close. For just a moment, Gracie remained rigid against her, then she seemed to collapse into the warmth of Stephanie's embrace. She didn't speak or cry; she simply burrowed against Stephanie, who began to speak softly.

"Those are gifts from some of the women in town. They brought them as a sort of— well, a welcome for me and because I married your Uncle Luke. Wedding gifts, I guess you'd say. I'm your Aunt Stephanie now." Her voice softened into a croon. "Your Aunt Jeane calls me Steffie sometimes. You can call me aunt or just Stephanie or Steffie or something else if you choose." She hesitated. "I know Kane calls me Ma, and that's fine, too. If it hurts you to call me that, then don't."

Taking Gracie by the shoulders, she moved her gently back a step so that she could look into her face. Gracie's dry eyes looked back at her with the sorrow of a hundred years in their depths. "Whichever you prefer will sound wonderful to me. I promise."

"I like Steffie," Gracie said at last in a very small voice.

Stephanie smiled. "I like that, too. Would you like to see what the ladies brought me?"

Her reward was a smile and a nod.

"Well," Luke asked, leaning on his pitchfork for a moment. "What do you think of your—of Stephanie?"

Kane looked up from the harness he was oiling. "Ma's great! She's pretty and she talks soft and she's smart and she's—"

"Whoa!" Luke held up one hand and laughed, although he didn't disagree with anything Kane said. "I reckon you've answered my question."

Actually, Luke hadn't really needed to ask. Kane's opinion had been made pretty clear already. Luke had just wanted to be sure that Stephanie's manner when she was alone with the children hadn't contradicted the way she behaved with them when Luke was around.

"She bakes a pretty good cookie, too," Luke tossed in his own compliment.

Kane grinned. "The best."

After a moment, Luke's answering smile faded. "You know, son, I sure worried I might be making a mistake marrying someone I didn't know."

"But Aunt Jeane said she was all right," Kane reminded him.

"Yes, she did, but that didn't stop me from worrying." And worrying still. Luke didn't really want to find the snake in the garden, but so far, Stephanie Cotter Tattersall seemed too good to be true.

"Well, Uncle Luke," Kane said in a very mature tone, "I think you can quit worrying now."

Luke smiled silently and hoped he was right.

They finished the work that needed to be done and walked back to the house to find the welcome aroma of roast and vegetables and biscuits filling the kitchen. While they ate, Stephanie told Luke and Kane of the visit she'd had from the women of the community.

"Met Elvira, did you?" Luke glanced at her from under a lock of straight dark hair.

Stephanie had noticed one strand that had a tendency to fall forward across his brow and Luke's always impatient gesture in brushing it away again. She realized that Luke was still watching her, and she nodded. "She's no worse than others I've known."

"The woman has a viper's tongue." When Stephanie didn't respond, Luke probed harder. "What did she have to say?"

Stephanie glanced at the avidly listening children. Despite his persistence, she knew Luke wouldn't really want her to say anything that would be disturbing to them. She chose her words carefully. "Mrs. Banks expressed her concern that I would find I had married a man whose affections were already claimed by another."

To her surprise as well as Luke's, it was Kane who spoke up. "Well, you sure don't have to worry about that none—Uncle Luke never went courting at all."

For some reason, Stephanie found that not only *not* reassuring, but disturbing. Luke was too handsome a man not to have been chased after by every young female in town. She hated to think Kane's words were additional proof that Luke may have had eyes only for Grace Ann.

Luke read the doubt in Stephanie's eyes, but he didn't speak of it until the dishes were washed, homework done, and the children safely in bed. And even then, he didn't bring it up directly.

Instead, with the kerosene lamp flickering on the table between them, he opened Celeste's letter and read it aloud. If this became a fight, it was going to be Stephanie's fight as well.

When he was through, he found his wife watching him with indignation and a touch of apprehension. "What a cold woman! She's 'determined' to take on the 'burden' of Kane and Gracie? How charitable!" A frown creased her forehead as her apprehension overrode her indignation. "She can't take them from us, can she?"

Luke noticed she said 'from us' rather than 'from you'. He let his own anxiety show. "She's Grace Ann's sister. I'm Jake's brother. I reckon that makes us about equal where the law is concerned. If she'd tried before we . . . before you and I were married, I don't know that John Marsh could have backed her down."

"He's Willene's husband?"

"He's also the county sheriff."

"But now that you are married? I mean the children have a home, someone to be a father . . ." She hesitated. " . . . and me."

Luke surprised himself when he reached across the table and took Stephanie's hand. He'd made every effort not to touch her before she was ready, but the light from the kerosene lamp flickered across her face, highlighting the silver in her eyes and the gold in her hair, touching the scattering of freckles across her cheeks, freckles almost too pale to notice most of the time. He found he liked the feel of her hand in his, and she made no effort to pull away.

"Oh, I won't let Celeste have those kids. They need love and attention, and I don't know that Celeste has any to give. I remember her from before she left Merrill. I always thought how different she and Grace Ann were. Oh, they were both pretty enough, but it seemed as if Celeste got all the strength and Grace Ann had none."

Stephanie chose her response carefully. She wanted Luke to keep talking about Grace Ann, not shy away because she probed too deep. "Grace Ann wasn't a strong person, then?"

"Grace Ann? No, she was sweet and good-hearted, but she'd have been better off to take a frying pan to Jake's hard head. Maybe he would have straightened up."

"Maybe she should have taken the kids and left," Stephanie suggested tentatively.

"Left Jake?" Luke shook his head. "Jake and Grace Ann were as crazy about each other after twelve years of marriage as they were on the day they said 'I do'." He looked Stephanie straight in the eye. "No matter what the town gossip has to say on the subject."

Stephanie knew exactly what he was talking about, and a tiny coil of worry she hadn't known she carried slowly eased. Maybe someday they could talk about that gossip openly, but for now Luke's reassurance was enough. If he had cared more for Grace Ann than he should have, nothing had ever come of it. And if he still cared, Stephanie would make him forget. The determined thought came upon her so suddenly, she had no time to examine it before Luke was speaking again.

"I checked on shipping costs for a bicycle today. It wasn't as much as I was afraid it might be, so I went ahead and wired Jeane enough money to send the bike." His hand tightened slightly on hers. "But I want you to think about it, and if you'd rather, we can get Kane something else for his Christmas present."

"Oh, no. The bicycle will be perfect. It's in almost new shape. It was a Christmas present two years ago—I'd asked for a music box. Papa was fond of buying things for me I didn't want or need. That was one of them." Her voice grew wry. "Along with a hundred and one gowns."

Luke felt a lot was going unsaid, and he wondered how many other things Stephanie had wanted and never got. He was glad she'd told him what at least one of them was.

Chapter Six

Stephanie stepped back and admired her handi-work. A muslin gown she had always detested now graced the living room windows. The cream-colored fabric sprigged with pale green flowers that had always seemed insipid on her looked just right with the morning sun shining through it. Crisp ruffles edged the top and the bot-tom, and there were just enough gathers in the fabric to make the curtains look quite fash-ionable.

She wondered how Luke would like them.

For just a moment, she held the gathers of her new curtains aside to glance down the path leading to the house as if she might see him striding along, headed for home. Of course, the path was empty, as she had known it would be. Nevertheless, she acknowledged a tiny sting of disappointment that hours would pass before Luke was home for lunch.

For a moment more, she allowed herself to enjoy the beauty that lay outside her window. Sunlight sparkled on leaves still damp from the last of the melting frost. By noon, the temperatures would be spring-like, a fact that never failed to amaze Stephanie. In the two weeks since her arrival, Merrill had seen very few days of really cold, damp, blustery weather; the remainder had been sunny and almost warm. The speed with which the weather changed was almost as remarkable to her as the changes themselves.

She turned from the window to check the room carefully. Margaret, Reverend Samuel Hagan's wife, was coming to call. She had been out of town visiting her ailing parents when Stephanie first arrived. Stephanie had found her a warm and likeable person when they'd been introduced before church services began Sunday morning.

She checked the mantle clock and found the morning slipping quickly past. Within moments, she had water hot for tea and a pie she had baked earlier ready to serve. They would have to visit in the parlor. The delicate green gown Gracie had admired lay spread across the kitchen table. She had begun cutting the rich velvet into dress pieces for the little girl.

Right on time, Margaret Hagan knocked at the front door. Stephanie's ready welcome faded a little at the sight of Elvira Banks standing at her shoulder.

Margaret's brown eyes revealed more than her

smile. "Good morning, Stephanie. Elvira was on her way to visit you, too, and we crossed paths just in front of the sawmill."

Refusing to be daunted by the town gossip, Stephanie stepped back and welcomed them inside. They both accepted tea and pie in the parlor. Elvira's sharp eyes missed nothing, and while Margaret spoke of the church and community preparations for the Christmas festivities to come, Elvira studied the changes Stephanie had made.

"Store-bought curtains?"

Stephanie looked up in surprise. "Why, no. I made them."

"They're beautiful," Margaret said admiringly. "I would never undertake to make curtains, though Ruth Fulman has made several lovely sets for me."

Elvira's gaze sharpened. "I've never seen that particular fabric in Ruth's store."

"Two days ago they were a gown," she explained. Gesturing toward the kitchen, she added, "I'm cutting another down for Gracie, but please don't let that slip. It's a Christmas surprise for her. The curtains are a surprise for Luke." She found she liked saying his name, liked thinking of him, laying claim to him as her husband.

"Well," Elvira huffed, "I'm sure he *will* be surprised."

Stephanie looked at her quizzically, but Margaret merely shrugged her shoulders and moved the conversation back to what she hoped would become a Merrill Christmas tradition.

"Reverend Hagan plans to have a morning service that day, and ask each family to bring a covered dish. After service, we'll walk over to the schoolhouse and push the desks aside. Miss Mamie has several of the children practicing to sing or read essays and then we'll enjoy a fellowship lunch."

While Margaret spoke, Stephanie tried not to mind that Elvira wandered about the room and then actually walked into the kitchen to finger the green velvet that would be Gracie's gown.

"That sounds like a wonderful day. I do love Christmas."

Margaret seemed almost not to hear her. She was staring at Elvira's back with as much affront as if the woman had plundered her own home. After another word or two, she rose gracefully. "Well, Elvira and I must really be on our way. I believe I heard mention that Luke comes home for lunch these days instead of carrying it to the sawmill."

To Stephanie's own surprise, she blushed. She and Luke evidently remained a topic of discussion in Merrill. Still, Margaret said it so sweetly, as if Luke's coming home for lunch was a wonderful thing, that she could not be offended.

"Elvira," Margaret lifted her voice slightly, "you *are* ready to leave now, aren't you?"

The plump older woman must have sensed that any but an affirmative answer would earn her a frown from Margaret. Seeing her reluctant acquiescence, Stephanie gained an inkling of Margaret's standing in the community. She could actually bring Elvira Banks to heel.

On the way out, Margaret's glance fell upon a half-finished doily on a table by the window. "You crochet, too!"

"I'm learning," Stephanie said with a smile. "Willene Marsh is teaching me."

Margaret nodded. "Willene has a lot to share."

"Humph! If you can tolerate that prickly nature of hers!" Elvira clearly could not.

A twitch of Margaret's lips revealed her thoughts, but all she said was, "Come along, Elvira."

To Stephanie's faint disbelief, Elvira trotted off behind the far more graceful younger woman.

Luke started thinking about lunch mid-way through the morning. Or rather, he started thinking about going home for lunch and about Stephanie's warm presence in the small kitchen as she bustled about serving him. It had been her idea that he not lunch on cold meat and bread once she realized how quick the walk was from the sawmill to the house. Luke hadn't argued.

Some of the other men went home for lunch, and he'd always been a little envious, especially when they hiked back on a cold winter's day with grateful talk of hot stew and biscuits right out of the oven, or maybe a pie just baked that morning. Now he realized it wasn't so much the food as the love and the sense of family that went with it that he had envied. A kind of warmth he'd begun to allow himself to hope for in his own marriage.

The bonds between him and Stephanie were

growing day by day, so strong now that Luke thought maybe the time was right to move on to a new facet of married life. Lord knew he was sure ready for that. The children had proven to be a bond between them right from the start, but the things he was starting to feel for his wife—the things he was starting to think about her—had nothing to do with Kane and Gracie.

He and Carter Banks finished stacking the rough-cut boards that had just come from the blade. "Reckon I'll head on home for lunch, Carter." Even the words sounded good to his ears. *Head home* for lunch.

"See you later, then."

Carter's wife had brought his noonday meal by the mill earlier. Luke liked Carter, liked him a lot. He just couldn't bring himself to do more than tolerate the man's wife. In Luke's estimation, Elvira and Carter Banks were as different as a husband and wife could be.

He wasn't particularly pleased, therefore, to come face to face with the woman at the turnoff to the sawmill.

" 'Morning, Luke." Her gaze assessed him critically. "I've been to see that new wife of yours."

Poor Stephanie, Luke thought. "That's very neighborly of you, Mrs. Banks," he managed.

"She's got a lot to learn, but she'll do, I suppose." Elvira sniffed as if she doubted her own optimism. "I *am* surprised, though." She watched him expectantly.

Luke frowned. He had a feeling the woman was about to cast some aspersion, and he knew he wasn't going to like her making any criticism of Stephanie.

When he didn't oblige her with a question or comment, Elvira continued, "I don't know what you were thinking to let her cut up Grace Ann's gowns that way. Imagine how those poor children are going to feel to come in and see their mother's clothing used for window covering!"

Gritting his teeth, Luke counted to ten. "Thank you for your concern, Mrs. Banks. I'd best be getting on now." *Interfering old biddy.*

Elvira looked so disappointed that Luke made an extra effort to hide his reaction to her comments as she said good-bye and went on her way. Luke watched her for just a moment before he turned to look down the path that led home.

By the time Luke reached home, he'd lost his appetite. He couldn't believe that Stephanie could be so cold-hearted as to cut Grace Ann's dresses into curtain material without even considering the effect on the children. Sometimes Luke still had nightmares about the way Gracie had grasped the side of her mother's coffin, clinging with a frantic determination until Luke had been forced to pry her fingers away. Two weeks with Stephanie had made him disbelieve she could be so thoughtless, but surely even Elvira knew not to tell an outright lie, one that would be easily detected the moment he walked through his front door.

Instead of going in the back door, straight into the kitchen, Luke crossed the front porch and entered the parlor. His eyes were drawn unerringly to the now-bright windows. There were curtains there, sure enough, where there had been only squares of unbleached muslin stretched across when he'd left that morning. The curtains were of some fairly plain material, but Luke frowned, trying to recall ever seeing Grace Ann in something that light and airy. He suspected it had been years since he had.

Stephanie stepped into the room from the kitchen, stopping with a surprised look on her face at the sight of him. Surprise—or guilt? Luke wondered. Then his gaze dropped to what she held in her arms. They were full of material. Green and soft and rich looking. The fabric spoke of a luxury his brother's wife would not have had the money to purchase.

"That was never Grace Ann's gown," he said bluntly.

Stephanie's brows drew together in confusion. "Of course not," she said, studying his half-angry expression. She glanced down at the material in her arms, then back at him. "Luke? Why would you think it had been Grace Ann's?"

Instead of answering her question, Luke asked one. "And those?" he gestured towards the window. "Where did they come from?"

"Another one of my gowns," she said promptly. "Why?"

"I wanted curtains," Stephanie said, feeling her irritation grow. Irritation that Luke wouldn't tell her what this was all about, and irritation because she had begun to suspect for herself. She recalled Elvira's avid curiosity.

"You could have asked me for money." Luke felt

stung that she hadn't. Did she think them that poor or him that stingy of coin? He guessed he should have put curtains up before now, but they weren't something he'd thought of. Seeing how nice the room looked, he wished he had.

"I would have if I didn't have two dozen gowns in my bags that I'll never wear."

"Why did you bring them?"

The question was reasonable enough, but the answer brought a blush to Stephanie's cheeks. "Because," she admitted in a low voice, "I didn't want Augusta to have them."

"Augusta?" Luke repeated questioningly.

Her blush deepened. "Papa's . . . the housekeeper."

Luke understood. "What about that?" He gestured towards the green velvet she still held in her arms. "Is that one you'd never wear?"

"This?" Stephanie's hand caressed the plush softness. "No, this was one of my favorites."

Luke pictured that slim hand caressing his flesh with such pleasure that goosebumps rippled across his ribs at the thought. "Then why are you cutting it up?"

"It's for Gracie, for Christmas. She liked it."

"I thought you were giving her a doll you had."

"*We* are, a doll with a gown to match the one I'm going to make for Gracie as soon as I get some green thread." Stephanie frowned. "Now, are you going to tell me what this is all about?" She suspected it had something to do with her morning visitors.

There was a gleam in her silver eyes that made Luke's nerve fail. "I'd rather not," he admitted.

Carefully Stephanie laid the material on the sofa, then turned to face Luke, her arms crossed in front of her. She waited.

Luke sighed. "I met Elvira Banks as I was leaving the sawmill. She told me you were cutting up Grace Ann's gowns for window coverings."

With a sinking heart, Stephanie thought of all the times she had suffered because of gossip. The lies of one man combined with the malice of a dozen tongues had caused her many sleepless nights of tears. But no more. "I don't guess it ever crossed your mind to doubt her? Especially considering some of the things she's had to say about your family?" About Luke and Grace Ann.

"I'm sorry." That was all he could think of to say, and he could see the words weren't enough.

Stephanie glanced pointedly at the mantle clock. "You'd better eat so you won't be late. Your lunch is on the stove. All you have to do is dish it up."

"Aren't you going to eat with me?" She had been. Every day. And Luke looked forward all morning to the talks they shared.

"I think I'm going for a walk." Stephanie met his look squarely. "I have some things I need to think about."

Luke felt his heart sink. Watching her slip a

shawl around her shoulders and close the door behind her, he wondered if one of the things she was thinking about was leaving him.

When Luke left the sawmill that afternoon, he went into Merrill before heading for home. Carter Banks walked with him.

"You got business to take care of today?" Carter asked.

"I just need to pick up a couple things Stephanie needs from the mercantile."

They parted ways in front of the Fulman's General Store, but Luke stopped Carter just before he walked on. "Tell Mrs. Banks something for me if you would."

Carter frowned. What had Elvira been up to now?

"Just tell her that the gowns weren't Grace Ann's—but if they were, it would be all right with me."

"I reckon she'll understand that?" Carter asked a little grimly.

Luke nodded. "She will."

Carter was afraid of that. Not for the first time, he made up his mind to put a stop to his wife's meddling once and for all. He just wished he could find a way to do it.

Luke watched him for a moment before he went into the general store. He felt sorry for Carter Banks. He'd hate like blazes to have to go home to a woman like Elvira. Which made him worry all the more that maybe he wouldn't always be able to go home to Stephanie.

Ruth Fulman met him in the middle of the central aisle. "Well, Luke Tattersall, we don't often see you in here—especially not in the middle of the week."

Luke smiled at her. He'd always liked Mrs. Fulman. "Might happen more often now that I've got a wife needing things in the middle of the week." He hoped so anyway.

Ruth smiled back. "What does Stephanie need?"

Luke liked hearing the warmth in her voice. He'd hoped the women of Merrill would make his wife welcome. "She's making a dress for Gracie. For Christmas. She needs some green thread."

Ruth beamed. "She's going to do real well by those kids, Luke." Then she cleared her throat and became more businesslike. "Now, what color green?"

Luke looked confused. "There's more than one?"

Nonplussed, Ruth nodded and gestured for him to follow her to a basket which held dozens of shades of dozens of colors. Luke looked for a moment and finally picked one that he thought was close to the green of the velvet.

"Will that be all?" Ruth asked, moving toward the counter.

"Yes—no." Luke stopped.

Ruth turned to look at him, her head tilted questioningly. "Well?" Her voice held a smile. "Which is it? That's all or it isn't?"

Luke cleared his throat. "Christmas will be here in a couple of weeks."

This time Ruth nodded knowingly. "And you

don't know what to get for Stephanie."

"Actually, I do." He hesitated. "Do you have music boxes?"

Ruth smiled and stepped to a cupboard. "Come and see."

Chapter Seven

By the time Stephanie reached the river bank, the blood in her veins had cooled somewhat. She made her way to a fallen tree just at the edge of the water where she had spent a more peaceful hour earlier that week. In the time she had been in Mississippi, Stephanie had discovered a natural affinity for the river with its slow currents and whirling eddies. The river at her feet teemed with life, while above her, huge oaks dripped with grey moss that fluttered in an almost constant breeze.

She wasn't even sure which river it was. Luke had told her that Merrill had sprung up where the Leaf met the Chickasawhay River and combined to form the Pascagoula.

Checking first for ants or other creatures, Stephanie sat on the trunk of the tree, running her hand across the smooth surface. The bark had long since been worn away. Willing her angry heart to slow its pace, she strained to see the fish that rippled the surface of the water from time to time.

Hard as she tried to keep from dwelling on the incident just past, her recalcitrant thoughts teased her with comparisons between Elvira's gossip and that which had destroyed her hopes of marriage in Seattle. How naively she had trusted the first few young men to come calling after her disastrous elopement!

There's no need to hold back—not now, one had whispered as they sat together on the front porch swing. *Macon said you knew things Lily Mae's girls never learned,* said another as he tried to push her backward onto a picnic blanket. And in a buggy, grappling with a pair of hot, determined hands, *Come on, Stephanie, that's nothing that hasn't been touched before, now is it?*

And then there were the young ladies she'd thought were her friends. *Where there's smoke, there's bound to be fire.* When she walked into a room, conversation immediately lulled, then resumed, drawing her in. *Come on, Steffie, you can tell us. We won't breathe a word. Cross our hearts.*

Her pastor had called on her one Sunday afternoon, begging her to repent of her sins and come to the altar for cleansing.

Through it all, Stephanie had not cowered nor hidden herself away. She had continued about her life, though now her shoulders had a new stiffness as she walked to market, and the young men who came to call were turned away at the door. She spent her time with the few friends who stood staunchly by her and with the charitable activities of her new church.

If there was one thing Stephanie knew, it was that she was not going to let gossip destroy this new life of hers. With determined movements, she stood and brushed at the back of her skirts. Luke had a lot to learn about Stephanie Cotter . . . Tattersall!

On her way back, she passed the small Methodist church that overlooked the ebb and flow of the river. Like some of the houses that sat close to the water's edge, it was raised on posts high enough that Stephanie could have walked beneath without bumping her head.

Stephanie felt again the warmth of the congregation, embracing her, making her welcome. She recalled how Luke had hovered at her side, anxious that she find that welcome. She could feel Kane's hand holding possessively to hers, Gracie's fist tugging at the back of her skirt in sudden shyness. She thought of Seattle, where she'd been made to feel a pariah. Elvira Banks could not match those people for gossip. And Elvira Banks was no match for her!

She didn't really blame Luke for heeding the other woman's lie. Much. Still, she set her chin; the first thing she and Luke were going to have to do was to learn to trust each other.

By the time she was in sight of home, the last remnant of her anger had faded. All that remained in her was a determination to strengthen the bonds that already existed between her and

Luke. Jeane had told her that the way to do that lay within the marriage bed. "When someone or something threatens either marriage partner, the other doesn't consciously think of those times . . . in bed." Jeane had blushed then. "But it's . . . those times that make a marriage strong, make it close. You can bet that when a husband and a wife have trouble, it starts there and spreads outward."

Stephanie had not dwelt on Jeane's advice before now because she knew she hadn't been ready for any intimacy. But it was much on her mind as she walked toward home. She suspected Jeane was right; if she and Luke were ever going to be a family, they first had to be husband and wife. She knew Luke had had such thoughts for some time now. She wasn't completely ignorant of the signs of a man's interest in a woman. All she had to do now was let Luke know she was ready. But how? And was she really?

Stepping into the kitchen, she hung her shawl on a hook by the door. She felt a faint flash of relief that Luke had gone ahead and eaten lunch. At least she didn't have to worry about him finishing the day on an empty stomach. And she *would* worry, she realized. For some reason, the thought both warmed and amazed her. It made her feel like a wife. Luke's wife.

She picked his empty plate up from the table, revealing a scrap of paper beneath. Luke had scrawled two words. Just two, but they were enough to bring a smile to her lips and keep it there all afternoon. *I'm sorry.*

Just before the children were due home, Stephanie scooped up Gracie's dress material and hid it in the armoire in her bedroom. She paused before the mirror to check her appearance. Her hair was up in its usual chignon, but wisps had escaped to curl softly about her face. Instead of skimming them back in place, she lifted her hand and slowly pulled several more wisps free.

Her glance fell to the apron around her waist. It had protected her gown while she fixed their evening meal and held several stains to prove it. Hearing footsteps on the back porch, she yanked the sashes free and tossed the apron into a corner, tying a clean one in its place.

She hurried into the kitchen at almost the same moment Luke stepped in from outside. They each paused at the sight of the other, then Luke closed the door against the cold. Feeling suddenly nervous, Stephanie touched a tendril of hair that brushed her cheek.

"You look pretty." Luke felt stupid as soon as the words left his mouth, but Stephanie's shy smile eased that feeling and made him glad he'd said them.

"You're home early." Usually the children were several minutes ahead of him.

"We finished a little early. I had time to go into town." Luke took a step closer and held out his hand, palm up.

The green thread looked incongruous against his callouses. Slowly, Stephanie reached out and took the thread. In that moment, she knew she'd never get long and flowery speeches from Luke, not in apology or for any other reason. What she *would* get was sincerity and actions.

Her eyes met Luke's. "Thank you."

Before either could speak another word, the children bounded onto the porch, almost barreling into Luke as they pushed the door open. Hastily, Stephanie dropped the thread into her pocket, and she and Luke exchanged smiles of conspiracy.

Both Kane and Gracie came straight to Stephanie for the hugs they'd come to think of as their due. "I'm hungry." The words were said almost in unison. They'd come to think of an afternoon treat as their due also.

Stephanie feigned regret. "Well, all I have today is what's left of a . . . dried apple pie."

As Kane whooped, Luke chuckled wryly. "I didn't find that at lunch."

Stephanie's glance met his over the children's heads. "You didn't deserve it at lunch," she said with more than a hint of tartness.

Luke grinned, and Stephanie's heart gave a funny little tilt.

For Stephanie, that evening seemed a turning point in her relationship with Luke. Before, they'd been tentative with each other. Careful. Now, there was a new easiness, as if the incident had proven they could weather at least a small storm. For Stephanie, there was a new awareness, as well.

She wondered if it was just her. Maybe Luke had always watched her with that hint of desire—maybe she had just never noticed the heat in his dark eyes. She was noticing now. Those eyes seemed to watch her every move until it was almost a relief when Luke and Kane went out to take care of the evening chores.

After the farm animals were fed, homework done, and supper dishes washed and dried and put away, Luke helped tuck the children into bed, then followed Stephanie back to the kitchen. She was reaching to turn down the wick on the kerosene lamp, when Luke's hand stopped hers.

"Sit down a minute?" His voice sounded wary, even a little grim.

Stephanie looked at him uncertainly. His gaze almost seemed to caress her face, blending something that looked like anxiety with desire. She found it hard to breathe. "Of course."

She sank into a chair and watched as Luke took another. He laid a folded piece of paper on the table between them.

"The bicycle arrived today. Jason let me hide it at the sawmill so I could get to it on Christmas morning before Kane gets up." He gestured to the paper. "Jeane sent a letter with it."

Beneath her relief that the present had arrived with Christmas only a week away, Stephanie felt Luke's concern. She unfolded the paper and read. Then she began to chuckle. When she looked up, Luke was watching her, his look of worry replaced by one of amazement.

"I thought you'd be upset."

Stephanie thought about that. She might have been, once, but being here with Luke and Kane and Gracie, finding out what a real family felt like, had changed things for her. She might have wished for things to be different between her father and herself, but she was no longer going to mourn over the fact that theirs would never be a loving relationship.

"I rather suspected he would be difficult," she said finally. A gurgle of laughter escaped her, and she whispered so the children couldn't overhear. "But I can just see Jeane climbing over that fence to get the bicycle. Lord, can you imagine Henry's face if he ever found out she actually stole it?"

Slowly, Luke began to laugh as well. Henry could be a fanatic where Jeane's well-being was concerned. The fact had always given Luke assurance that his sister was all right, but he could just picture Henry's reaction over something like this.

Forgetting Jeane and her husband, Luke recalled the few pieces of her past that Stephanie had let slip. "You and your father weren't very close, were you?" He laid his arm across the table, holding out his hand to her.

Stephanie stared at that outstretched hand for a moment, before placing hers within it. Luke's fingers closed over hers, and she felt the warmth all the way to her heart. "No," she said at last. "We weren't close at all. I think Papa tried when I was younger, but without Mama there . . . Well, he just didn't know what to do with me, I guess. And then, after—" She stopped abruptly, looking at Luke.

Luke said nothing. It was up to Stephanie to decide what she would and would not share with him.

She took a deep breath. "When I was seventeen,

I fell in love with a young man by the name of Macon Tisdale. He came to Seattle from Boston that very year, and all the girls just swooned over him." She gave a self-deprecating little laugh. "Me worst of all. Macon was pretty enough to have been a girl, but not at all . . . feminine. Before too long, he'd convinced me to elope with him. I wasn't hard to convince," she admitted.

Stephanie fixed her gaze on her hand cradled in Luke's. "We sneaked off one night and made it as far as the next town. Macon whined every step of the way. The coach was too rough. The food we were served was disgusting. Nothing was right. Well, Macon found a justice of the peace, and we were standing in front of him when I—" She lifted her glance to Luke and shrugged. "I just couldn't marry him. I realized that he wasn't what I thought he was."

"What then? You went back to Seattle?"

Stephanie laughed, a brittle sound even to her own ears. "Back to Seattle. Back to the gossip. I found out more about Macon than I ever wanted to know. He couldn't bear that anyone might know he'd been thrown over. Before the week was out, he'd told half the town that he'd never intended to marry me. That once we . . . that once he had what he wanted, he jilted me."

Luke's eyes narrowed and his lips thinned. "People believed him?" He felt an overweening urge to take a buggy whip to pretty Macon Tisdale.

"Not everyone. But most."

"Your father?"

She nodded.

Luke thought of Elvira's lie and the fact that he'd been ready to believe the worst of Stephanie. He was in no position to criticize Stephanie's father. "Damn." He looked at her helplessly. "I'm sorry."

"I despise gossip." That was all she was going to say.

"You won't ever have to worry about it again," Luke promised. He intended to make good on that if he had to kill every gossip in Merrill. His fingers tightened on hers. "Come to bed?"

Stephanie's mouth felt suddenly dry. She knew what Luke was asking. Slowly, she nodded.

Luke stood, keeping her hand in his, drawing her with him. With his free hand, he extinguished the lamp, plunging them into complete darkness. With a slight tug, Luke pulled her close so that her breasts brushed the hard expanse of his chest. She felt his lips against her temple and wondered if he could feel the blood pounding in her veins there.

Then she wasn't thinking at all, as she lifted her lips to his, suddenly eager for his kiss.

Luke almost ceased to breathe as he lowered his mouth to hers. He was afraid the moment was a mirage that would slip away and leave him with the same longing that so many mornings had seemed to bring lately. But, no, the hand still nestled in his clung tightly. The lips beneath his parted on a sigh at the seeking pressure of his kiss. He burned everywhere they touched, chest to chest, thigh to thigh.

The blood rushed through his body, roaring and burning, hardening and lengthening. He forced his lips from Stephanie's and tugged at her hand.

She followed through the darkened parlor to their bedroom. Once there, Luke released her hand and carefully closed the door behind them. Then his hands were on her again, seeking the fastenings of her gown.

Stephanie stood trembling while he undressed her. When he drew the fabric from her shoulders, she half-laughed, half-sobbed, a funny little sound.

"Steph?" Luke hesitated with his hands at the waist of her gown.

Relieved that he wasn't any more self-assured than she, Stephanie stepped closer. The movement caused her gown to slide over her hips, leaving only her pantelets.

Luke stood motionless for a moment, his gaze fixed on the hint of white skin revealed in what little moonlight came through the window. Carefully, giving her every opportunity to stop him, Luke lifted his hands to cup the fullness of her breasts.

She shuddered with undefined need as the callouses on Luke's hands slid over her nipples. A soft moan escaped her, embarrassing her.

Encouraged, Luke skimmed her undergarments from her hips, allowing himself the pleasure of caressing her with every move that he made.

"Luke?" Stephanie couldn't believe the feelings that swept over her, the heat and the yearning. Unexpectedly, he scooped her up in his arms and carried her to the bed. The bare flesh of her legs against his arm sent her heart thudding against the wall of her chest until she thought it would escape her body. Even more heart-stopping was the feel of her nipple teased by the hair that curled tightly against his chest.

Luke placed her gently on the bed, and she lay without moving, almost without breathing, as he undressed. When he moved close to the edge of the bed, she lifted her arms to him, felt herself gathered up against him.

She felt little of the shyness she had expected to feel, experienced none of the sense of degradation she had feared as Luke brought her to a feverish need.

Warned by Jeane of what to expect, she held her breath through the sharp pain of Luke's entry, then gave herself over to the pleasure of her husband's touch.

Chapter Eight

Christmas Eve dawned with a sharp reminder that it was winter after all. Stephanie woke to find her face pressed to Luke's chest, his hand cupping her hip. He stirred, causing the cover to slip from Stephanie's shoulder. She gasped at the touch of cold air, and Luke opened one eye lazily.

"Good morning."

"No." Stephanie squeezed her eyes shut obstinately. "It's too cold to be morning. I'm not moving."

Luke chuckled. "You don't really want Willene to find us all still in bed, do you?"

The very idea sent Stephanie bolting upright, heedless of the chill in the bedroom. "I forgot." Willene had promised to be there bright and early to help Stephanie bake a sweet potato pie for Christmas dinner. She'd never heard of the dessert before coming to Mississippi and was thoroughly intrigued by the idea.

Besides, though lessons that day would be nominal, school *was* in session until noon. She had to get the children fed and off to practice their parts with Miss Mamie for the next day's Christmas program. The sawmill, too, would be operating for at least the early part of the day.

The next hour passed in a blur as Stephanie managed to get breakfast on the table and everyone out the door afterward. She then settled at the table with a cup of hot tea to wait for Willene. She had scarcely tasted it when the older woman's knock sounded at the front door. She smiled as she went to answer the summons. Willene was never late.

The older woman stepped into the parlor briskly. "Close the door quick, child. I swan that's a powerful cold wind!"

Stephanie smiled as she did just that and turned to look at her friend. As usual, Willene's grey hair was coiled tightly at the back of her head. Her spectacles were perched firmly on her nose.

She thrust a basket at Stephanie and removed her heavy woolen cloak with efficient movements before leading the way to the kitchen, leaving Stephanie to follow as she would. Stephanie had long since realized that Willene's brusqueness was superficial. The woman's heart was as tender as a child's, though her tongue could be as sharp as the blade of an axe.

Stephanie placed the basket on the table at

Willene's direction and Willene began withdrawing items in a haphazard fashion and scattering them about the table.

"You got that dough chilling like I said?" Willene asked sharply.

"It's as chill as that 'powerful cold wind' can get it," Stephanie retorted.

Willene looked up, and they exchanged a smile.

"Well, let's get started then!"

Three hours later, Stephanie proudly drew the second pie from the oven. Like the first, the bottom crust was perfectly browned. The uncrusted top of the pie was a rich pumpkin color. In fact, Stephanie wasn't sure she could have distinguished it from a pumpkin pie. Even the aroma was much the same, sweet and spicy. Willene assured her, however, that the difference in taste was distinct.

With the second pie safely out to cool, Willene began drawing on her cloak.

"Won't you stay for lunch?" Stephanie followed Willene through the parlor to the front door. "Luke won't be coming home today. They're going to work straight through and quit early."

"Like to, but I can't," Willene said. "Too much waiting for me to do at home."

"I really appreciate your help with these pies. Luke will be so proud."

Willene's eyes glinted with humor. "Boy's proud to bursting over you as it is. Don't know that he needs anything else."

Before Stephanie had time to blush, Willene

was halfway out of the door. "Now, let those set a spell before you cover them. If you don't let 'em cool first, they'll sweat and make the crust soggy underneath."

"I promise, and thanks again," Stephanie called. She started to close the door against the winter chill, but hesitated when she glimpsed a buggy turning down their lane.

She smiled at the way Willene's eyes narrowed in suspicion as the buggy passed her by. Then Stephanie's attention was caught by the occupants of the buggy itself as it pulled to a stop just at the porch. A very tall, strongly built man set the brake and leapt down. He assisted the woman, who paused to settle her skirts about her before she turned toward the house.

By this time, Stephanie had stepped out onto the porch, closing the door behind her. She watched the woman approach, feeling more anxious by the moment without really understanding why she should. When the woman spoke, she knew why.

"I'm Grace Ann's sister. I guess you're that foreigner the Tattersall boy married."

Celeste Bigelow was not an unattractive woman if one could overlook the sharp creases of a permanent frown etched into the sides of her mouth and eyes. She had golden-brown hair that gleamed in the midday sun and large, dark eyes. Eyes that watched Stephanie narrowly.

"Foreigner?" Stephanie said faintly.

"Northerner," Celeste added as if that clarified the matter.

Perhaps for her, it did, Stephanie thought.

"Won't you come in?" she asked without commenting on the woman's rudeness. This was Kane and Gracie's aunt. She had to remember that.

"James Edwin," she called to the man behind her. "Come along inside."

As he strode toward the porch, Stephanie wondered if he'd actually been waiting for his wife's permission to approach the porch. She smiled at him, trying to find some Christmas warmth to go with it. He bared his teeth in a semblance of a smile that left as quickly as it had been summoned.

She led the couple into the parlor and took the cloak Celeste handed to her for all the world as if she were some servant. Stephanie hung it on the rack by the door. "Would you care for some tea?"

"No, thank you," Celeste said crisply, answering for both of them as she perched on the sofa and patted the spot beside her. Her husband sat obediently. "I have some questions about the children."

Stephanie seated herself in a wing chair. "Of course." Stephanie wasn't averse to answering questions if all the woman wanted was to ascertain their well-being, but she prepared herself for battle should the visit prove to be something more ominous.

"Kane is eleven now, isn't he? Or is it twelve?"

Stephanie lifted one brow. Didn't she even know? "Kane won't be eleven until June."

Celeste frowned and glanced at her husband. "A little younger than we thought."

James Edwin shrugged and said nothing.

"Is he a strong boy?"

Stephanie began to think she didn't like these questions or anything they implied. "Both of the children are very strong and healthy," she said stiffly.

Celeste waved one hand in the air. "I'm sure, I'm sure. But is the boy strong enough for a day's work on a farm?"

Stephanie had to unclench her teeth to answer. "That scarcely matters, since it will be several years before Kane is through with his schooling. When it's time for him to do a man's work, he'll be plenty strong enough."

Hearing the challenge, Celeste leaned back and lifted her chin. She abandoned the subject of Kane. "Does the girl whine much?"

"Gracie never whines, but if she did, I would certainly find the reason for it and hold her until she was comfortable again." Stephanie looked at James Edwin, certain she had heard something like a snort of laughter emanate from him. But no, he sat watching the exchange calmly.

"I can't abide a whining child," Celeste said flatly.

"Do you have children?" Stephanie asked.

Celeste shuddered. "We've never been blessed." She made the last word sound more like a curse.

"God certainly chooses best, doesn't he?"

James Edwin coughed. Hard.

"Are you certain you wouldn't like some tea?" Stephanie asked sweetly.

He shook his head, managing to avoid his wife's glare.

"Where are the children?" Celeste asked.

"They had classes this morning. They should be home very soon." Stephanie recalled that Celeste was a grieving sister and felt an unwilling sting of sympathy. "Would you like to visit Grace Ann's . . . grave while you wait?"

Celeste's lips pressed together. "We've been there. I'm appalled that Luke saw fit to bury her next to her murderer." Her eyes snapped. "I'm equally appalled that the church allowed him to be buried on hallowed ground. The man not only killed my only sister, he killed himself, after all!"

Stephanie opened her mouth to argue Jake's case, then closed it again. She would do no one any good by reminding this woman that it was his love for Grace Ann that caused Jake to take his own life. Luke's brother would never willingly have hurt his wife. Though she'd never met the man, Stephanie was sure of that.

She tensed as she heard the children at the back door. Celeste turned toward the sounds coming from the kitchen, her mouth pursed as if she'd tasted something bad.

"Ma, whose buggy is that?" Kane was first through the door, with Gracie just after. Both skidded to a stop at the sight of the guests. Stephanie could tell by their expressions that neither of them recalled or, perhaps ever even knew, their aunt and uncle.

Celeste rose gracefully, her well-made skirts

settling neatly about her as if they dared do nothing else. "Come closer," she commanded.

Kane looked at Stephanie. "It's all right, children. This is your Aunt Celeste. Your mother's sister."

Kane took a step toward his aunt, while Gracie darted behind the sofa to fling herself at Stephanie. Stephanie lifted the little girl onto her lap.

Celeste circled Kane carefully, actually reaching out to touch the hard muscle along his shoulder. "Look, James Edwin, he's very big for his age."

Her husband nodded, eyeing the boy the way he might a draft mule he was considering purchasing. "Very big."

Affronted, Stephanie watched the woman turn her attention to Gracie. "Come here, child."

Gracie snuggled harder against Stephanie. Celeste's face took on a more pinched look than it already had. "Not very obedient, is she?"

"Gracie is extremely obedient." Stephanie's glare defied the woman to argue the point.

"I suppose six isn't too very young," Celeste murmured. "She'll learn soon enough, I'm sure."

"Learn what?" Stephanie asked ominously.

"Well, to help with the housework, of course. Dust, sweep. Lord knows, there's always enough work for a dozen women on a farm."

"Gracie isn't a woman. She's a child." Stephanie eased out from under the little girl in question and got to her feet, placing herself between Gracie and Celeste's piercing stare. "Come here, Kane."

Kane hurried to her side.

"I don't like anything you're implying. It doesn't

matter how strong these children are or how much work you think they can do."

"That's not for you to worry about."

"I'm their mother," Stephanie said without hesitating.

"You are not! My poor sister was their mother, and she's dead. I'm all they've got in this world! They belong with me."

"They have me and they have Luke. Their uncle. And they aren't going anywhere!" Stephanie was furious. This woman actually thought she could take these children and turn them into servants for her and her husband!

"We have a legal right to these children!" Celeste said triumphantly. "James Edwin, show her that piece of paper."

The man carefully withdrew an impressive-looking document from his coat pocket. Stephanie ignored it, turning Kane to look at her. "Go to the sawmill and get your Uncle Luke. Hurry."

Frightened by Stephanie's obvious fear, Kane turned in a burst of energy and headed for the door.

"James Edwin, stop him!" Celeste had every intention of being gone before Luke Tattersall arrived.

Her husband started after the boy, but Stephanie stepped into his path, her eyes daring him to put a hand out to push her aside. He didn't.

"James Edwin!"

"It doesn't matter none, Celeste. We've got the law on our side. We'll just show the man the paper and take the kids and leave."

Kane had been gone only a moment when Stephanie heard voices nearing the house. Taking Gracie up in her arms, she stepped to the window and drew the curtain aside. The sight that greeted her caused her mouth to drop open. A full dozen women and a half-dozen men led by Willene Marsh had gathered in her front yard.

Ignoring Celeste and James Edwin, Stephanie wrapped a cloak around herself and Gracie and stepped out onto the porch.

Willene eyed her. "Are you all right, Stephanie?"

"I've sent Kane to get Luke." Despite the relief she felt at seeing Willene, she could hear the tension in her voice, feel it in her spine. She wouldn't feel the children were safe until Luke arrived.

The door opened behind Stephanie, and Celeste and her husband stepped out onto the porch. Celeste made a soft sound of dismay at the crowd milling in front of the house. This wasn't going to be as easy as she'd thought.

Willene looked her up and down. "I thought that was your pinched-up mouth I saw in that buggy, Celeste."

"We've come to take the children to give them a Christian upbringing," Celeste said.

Stephanie hugged Gracie tighter.

"They're in church every Sunday morning," Willene retorted.

"I'm their aunt. Grace Ann would have wanted me to have them."

"In a pig's eye!" Luke made his way through the crowd. Kane was close at his heels.

"What?" Celeste fairly hissed the word as Luke strode up to stand beside his wife.

Stephanie leaned against him gratefully. Luke put his arm around her shoulder and squeezed his reassurance.

"I said, Grace Ann would want you to have these kids in a pig's eye," Luke repeated in a hard voice.

"My own sister!" Celeste looked properly shocked at the notion.

"Your own sister, who wrote to you for help five years ago when she barely had enough money to feed the kids."

Dark color marred Celeste's cheeks at the words. She smoothed the fine fabric of her gown. "We're scarcely rich people. We do well to pay our own bills, much less those of a ne'er-do-well like Jake Tattersall!"

"Well, then," Luke said laconically, "why are you wanting to take on two more mouths to feed?"

"It's our Christian responsibility," Celeste answered in dramatic tones.

"She wants two free servants," Stephanie said, making sure every person there heard her words.

The murmurs that followed proved that they had.

"You'll not have them," Luke said flatly.

James Edwin waved his official-looking paper. "We've the law on our side."

"The law of this county isn't here yet," Willene put in, "but I've sent for him." She winked at Luke.

"Well, there's really no reason for us to wait for

the law of *this* county," Celeste retorted. "James Edwin, get the children."

James Edwin looked at the muscles bulging against Luke's shirt sleeves, then looked at his wife uncertainly. It was almost a relief to him when some activity beyond her caught his attention. "Here now, what are you people doing!" He started down from the porch.

Luke eyed his friends and neighbors in disbelief. Two women led the buggy horses in opposite directions while two men busily removed the wheels, tossing them to the other four men as they passed on their way into town.

"Don't reckon you'll be needing us any more today, will you, Luke?" Carter called as he straightened up with his hand on the last buggy wheel.

"Reckon not." Luke grinned. "Thanks."

John Marsh rode slowly past the buggy as it sat ignominiously in pieces on the ground, glanced idly at James Edwin, who shook his fists at the retreating men, then dismounted. He looked at his wife. "Woman, is my supper going to be late?"

Willene smiled slyly. "Not at all, John. I'll be waiting for you at the hotel restaurant. Miss Cherry is having a very festive holiday meal served tonight."

John watched his wife march down the lane toward town, and he shook his head in defeat before turning his attention to the problem at hand. "Well, Luke, what's the ruckus?"

"Celeste and her husband have some kind of paper giving them legal rights to our kids."

Stephanie's gaze locked on the sheriff's face as

435

he solemnly accepted the paper James Edwin thrust at him with a grand gesture. Her heart thumped loudly within her breast. Surely he wouldn't let these people take Gracie and Kane?

John handed the paper back. "Not in this county."

"What!" Celeste looked livid as she stepped up to the sheriff's chest. "I know what that paper says! The judge made us guardians over my niece and nephew!"

John pushed his hat back on his head and eyed her with something less than civility. He remembered Celeste from when they were just kids. He hadn't much liked her then, either. "I know what it says, too. But it doesn't give you squat in this county. Not even in this state."

"Well," Celeste said, leaning into his face, "I'll find a *Mississippi* judge, then!"

John sighed and nodded, not meeting Luke's eyes as he answered. "I'm sure any judge will be glad to give you guardianship, with you being willing to take on Kane's medical bills and all. That says a lot for a couple's good intentions."

"Medical bills?" Celeste's voice rose rather dramatically. "What medical bills?"

That's what Stephanie wanted to know. She looked at Luke, who shook his head with an almost imperceptible movement.

The sheriff stepped closer so that neither of the children could hear his words. "Well, with Kane being consumptive, you know they're going to get bad. Doc's already wanting to put him in a sanatorium."

Celeste eyed the ten-year-old askance. "He looks healthy to me."

"They do at the beginning, you know." John sighed. "It sure is a sad thing."

"Yes, well . . ." Celeste almost grabbed her husband's arm. "We've got to be leaving, now. We'll be back to fight another day, you can be sure."

"Oh, I'm sure," John said to her retreating back.

James Edwin stopped short, forcing his wife to stop with him. John looked beyond them to the hapless buggy. "Tell you folks what. It's too late to start for home tonight. Tell Miss Cherry at the hotel your room is on the town. Your buggy will be ready for you at first light."

"You expect us to walk into town!" Two spots of color blazed on Celeste's cheeks.

"My wife just did."

"Come along, dear." James Edwin pulled her with him. He'd known this trip was a mistake from the very beginning, and as soon as they were alone, he was going to tell his wife so. He glanced down at her outraged expression. *Maybe.*

"Consumptive?" Luke almost choked on his laughter. "What if they decide to talk to doc?"

"What if they do?" John retorted. "He was the one who reminded me how horrified Celeste was of germs as a little girl. It was his idea."

John mounted his horse and turned back to tell the young family good night, but when he caught Luke and Stephanie wrapped in each other's arms, Gracie and Kane nearly smothered between them, he just smiled and let the words die in his throat.

Chapter Nine

A low, sweet tinkling of music lured Stephanie from her dreams. Her mind insisted that she identify the source, and her eyes opened slowly to the insistence. The first thing she saw was Luke's muscular arm just inches from her nose. The tinkling sounds continued, a slow, dreamy melody.

Stephanie lifted her head, and unexpected tears burned her eyes. Perched on Luke's broad chest was a music box, atop which a beautifully gowned woman and a handsome man revolved gracefully in time with the music.

"Oh, Luke," she said huskily.

"Merry Christmas," he returned. He shifted slightly in order to press a kiss to the tip of her nose.

He was just about to take advantage of the

tender lips so close to his when Kane's whoop from the parlor opened both their eyes. "Ma! Pa! Come quick and see!"

"I don't suppose it's dawned on him that we've already seen," Stephanie said with a smile.

When Luke didn't answer, she turned to him curiously. He had the funniest, proudest kind of look upon his face. "Luke, what is it?"

"It's Kane." Luke cleared his throat. "He called me Pa." Through the pride, a flash of pain caught him low in the gut. "I don't want him to forget Jake. Jake wasn't a bad man, and he loved his kids."

"He won't forget," Stephanie promised. "We'll make sure they both remember Jake and Grace Ann." But Stephanie knew it was time for a new beginning for all of them. "We'd better 'come see' now," she said softly.

Gracie emerged from her room just as they made it to the parlor, where Kane sat on the floor running his hands over every gleaming inch of the bicycle. The little girl never looked at her brother or his proud new possession. Her eyes were fixed wonderingly on the porcelain-skinned doll, beautiful in green velvet, that sat carefully upon the sofa. Right next to her was another green velvet gown just Gracie's size.

"Now for you," Stephanie murmured, leaning into Luke's side as they watched the faces of the children. She slipped her hand into the pocket of her dressing gown and drew out a handsome pocket watch.

Luke's expression told her that Ruth Fulman

hadn't steered her wrong. He'd been eyeing the timepiece for a long while.

Luke kissed her hard, then lifted his head just enough to whisper, "Let's go back to bed for a few minutes."

Stephanie's eyes widened until she realized that he was teasing. She blushed and retorted, "And you can explain to Reverend Hagan why we were late for the Christmas service."

Luke grinned without any sign of remorse.

"Mama." Gracie tugged at Stephanie's gown. "Can I wear my new dress to church?"

Stephanie blinked back the tears burning her eyes. They were a real family now. A Christmas family.

Author's Note

Merrill, Mississippi, is a beautiful, once bustling, now sleepy little community. The Leaf and Chickasawhay Rivers still merge into the Pascagoula and flow to the nearby Gulf of Mexico. Moss-covered oaks still grace the river banks.

Though the place is real, the characters I have depicted in my story are not. They live only in my imagination and, I hope, in yours.

For those of you who would like to try your culinary talents with a real Southern treat, I've included a recipe for Sweet Potato Pie.

Sweet Potato Pie
1 ½ cups mashed, cooked sweet potatoes
½ stick butter, melted
2 eggs
½ cup milk

Susan Tanner

¾ cup sugar
¼ cup brown sugar
½ teaspoon salt
1 teaspoon each nutmeg, allspice, cinnamon
1 teaspoon vanilla extract
1 unbaked 9-inch pie shell

Combine ingredients. Beat well. Pour into pie shell. Bake at 425 degrees for 45 minutes to 1 hour (or until set).

MOONSPELL

TIMESWEPT

NELLE McFATHER

Bestselling Author of *Tears of Fire*

Legend says that the moonstone will bring love and good fortune to whoever possesses it. Just one touch of the magic stone sweeps Annabel Poe back through the years to an ancient English castle. Caught in a world of poets and highwaymen, lovers and thieves, Annabel is drawn relentlessly to a virile nobleman whose secrets threaten untold peril—while his touch promises undreamed ecstasy.

_51964-X $4.99 US/$5.99 CAN

LEIGH GREENWOOD'S
SEVEN BRIDES
Laurel

Although Hen Randolph is the perfect choice for a sheriff in the Arizona Territory, he is no one's idea of a model husband. After the trail-weary cowboy breaks free from his six rough-and-ready brothers, he isn't about to start a family of his own. Then a beauty with a tarnished reputation catches his eye and the thought of taking a wife arouses him as never before.

But Laurel Blackthorne has been hurt too often to trust any man—least of all one she considers a ruthless, coldhearted gunslinger. Not until Hen proves that drawing quickly and shooting true aren't his only assets will she give him her heart and take her place as the newest bride to tame a Randolph's heart.

_3744-0 $5.99 US/$6.99 CAN

Dorchester Publishing Co., Inc.
65 Commerce Road
Stamford, CT 06902

Please add $1.75 for shipping and handling for the first book and $.50 for each book thereafter. NY, NYC, PA and CT residents, please add appropriate sales tax. No cash, stamps, or C.O.D.s. All orders shipped within 6 weeks via postal service book rate. Canadian orders require $2.00 extra postage and must be paid in U.S. dollars through a U.S. banking facility.

Name _____

Address _____

City _____ State _____ Zip _____

I have enclosed $_____in payment for the checked book(s).

Payment <u>must</u> accompany all orders.☐ Please send a free catalog.

WINTER LOVE
NORAH HESS

"Norah Hess overwhelms you with characters who seem to be breathing right next to you!"
—*Romantic Times*

Winter Love. As fresh and enchanting as a new snowfall, Laura has always adored Fletcher Thomas. Yet she fears she will never win the trapper's heart—until one passion-filled night in his father's barn. Lost in his heated caresses, the innocent beauty succumbs to a desire as strong and unpredictable as a Michigan blizzard. But Laura barely clears her head of Fletch's musky scent and the sweet smell of hay before circumstances separate them and threaten to end their winter love.

_3864-1 $5.99 US/$7.99 CAN